ACCOUNTING LEGAL IMPLICATIONS

A GUIDE FOR MANAGERS, BUSINESS OWNERS, AND ENTREPRENEURS

David W. Tate, CPA, Esq.

A concise, understandable guide covering:

- Management's legal accounting standards.
- Developing internal control.
- Fraud—detection and prevention.
- How to deal with financial disclosures.
- The audit committee.
- Review of auditing services/reports.
- Review of accounting principles.

LIMITATION OF SCOPE, CONTENTS, AND REPRESENTATIONS

This guide is a summary of significant legal/accounting issues that any manager may be required
to address. Accordingly, this guide does not contain all accounting and legal pronouncements or
authorities that may apply in a particular circumstance, nor does it contain complete details or
discussions of the topics and issues addressed. Information about the topics and issues discussed
has been condensed and generalized to fit within the scope of this guide. This guide does not
address or apply to any particular actual or hypothetical individual, entity, factual situation, or
circumstance, nor does it contain, represent, or constitute legal, accounting, or other professional
opinions, representations, or advice. You should consult with an appropriate attorney,
accountant, or other professional for advice. Although the information contained in this guide is
believed to be accurate at the time of its production, the author assumes no responsibility for
damages that arise from any action that is based on information contained in this guide.

From a Declaration of Principles jointly adopted by a Committee
of the American Bar Association and a Committee of Publishers.

Sponsoring editor: Michael E. Desposito
Project editor: Denise Santor-Mitzit
Production manager: Jon Christopher
Interior designer: Jeanne M. Rivera
Cover designer: Tim Kaage
Compositor: Precision Typographers
Typeface: 11/13 Times Roman
Printer: R. R. Donnelley & Sons Company

Library of Congress Cataloging-in-Publication Data

Tate, David W.
    Accounting and its legal implications : a guide for managers,
business owners, and entrepreneurs / by David W. Tate.
        p.   cm.
    Includes index.
    ISBN 1-55623-761-8
    1. Corporations—Accounting.   2. Corporations—Accounting—Law and
legislation.   I. Title.
    HF5686.C7T37   1994
    657—dc20   93-39278

Printed in the United States of America
1 2 3 4 5 6 7 8 9 0   DO   10 9 8 7 6 5 4

ABOUT THE AUTHOR

David W. Tate is an attorney in San Francisco and specializes in accountant and accounting related matters and business litigation, including CPA and director/officer liability. Mr. Tate also is a CPA, a member of the Government Relations, Amicus, and Professional Conduct Committees of the California Society of CPAs. Mr. Tate acquired auditing and tax experience with Deloitte, Haskins & Sells, predecessor to the "Big Six" accounting firm Deloitte & Touche, and national law firm experience with Pillsbury Madison & Sutro. Mr. Tate holds a Bachelor of Science Degree in Finance and a Masters Degree in Taxation and is a member of the State Bar of California and the American Institute of CPAs. Mr. Tate has written and lectured on various topics relating to professional malpractice, accounting, tax, and directors' and officers' duties.

PREFACE

The corporate accounting function and the activities of senior managers with respect to that function are receiving ever greater attention from stockholders, investors, legislators, regulators, creditors, and other members of corporate management. That increased attention is further magnified by the substantially increasing number of laws, regulations, legal decisions, and accounting guidelines that relate to the corporate accounting function. Given this environment, it is imperative that senior managers understand the scope of their accounting duties, duties involving legal and accounting disciplines and much judgmental interpretation, and implement a methodology or system to satisfy those duties. This guide necessarily covers topics commonly associated with diverse and separate disciplines, including accounting, law, and management. Although it is possible to obtain the information in this guide by analyzing many lengthy professional sources of information, to my knowledge no other single source currently exists that combines these topics, let alone presents them in a concise source written primarily for the nonprofessional reader. This guide will assist senior managers, working with other directors, officers and managers, internal auditors, certified public accountants (CPAs), and attorneys, attain accountability within the business and assurance that the business is disclosing proper and requisite accounting and financial information. It will also help the senior manager obtain reasonable comfort that his or her legal accounting responsibilities have been satisfied.

This guide can be used not only by executive officers and directors but also by management personnel responsible for the operations of departments, divisions, groups, or units within the business structure and by persons who need to understand the importance and function of the accounting system to the executive officers, directors, and the overall business's product. Thus, although some of the cases and statutes discussed specifically refer only to directors or officers, within the scope of this guide and for simplicity the terms *senior manager* and *management* generally refer to directors, officers, and other managers who have decision-making authority or are involved in financial or accounting matters.

A business's financial information and financial/accounting internal structure and function tell a story about that business—how the business has performed and, possibly, how that business may perform in the future. The financial function of a business is part science and part art, involving not only recording and presentational rules and regulations but also the use of significant interpretation and estimations. It is unfortunate that many people, often lacking basic accounting education, first greet a discussion about accounting or finance with apprehension, because almost no significant portion of business or society is unaffected by financial information. Positive financial information can create tremendous opportunity and wealth. Unfortunately, the opportunities to misrepresent financial information are numerous, and for some people the reasons to do so may seem compelling. This guide does not needlessly sensationalize past cases of fraud or mismanagement, but it does present relevant case studies and information necessary to analyze and understand both proper and improper presentation of financial information. The information in this guide is useful not only to analyze extremely complex financial scenarios but also to understand financially related information and misrepresentations reported by the news services.

This is a time of tremendous challenge and potential for change in the areas of internal control, financial recording, and financial reporting. Financial statement users are demanding greater accountability, nonfinancial information disclosure, and explanation of the financial information provided. Businesses should take steps to better educate senior managers about the importance of the topics covered in this guide and how to understand and implement the topics for the benefit of the business.

This concise and to-the-point guide reduces the extremely large volume of pertinent and necessary information covered to a manageable form and size. For ease of reference, each of the guide's six main topic areas (management's standard of accounting care, accountability-internal control/fraud, financial disclosures, the audit committee, review of auditing services/reports, and review of accounting principles) can be read independent from the other portions of the guide. I anticipate this guide will be read by people with widely divergent business, educational, and accounting backgrounds. Thus, I have attempted to present the material in an easy-to-understand manner while including in scope relatively basic concepts through sophisticated and up-to-date concepts and legal holdings.

David W. Tate

CONTENTS

CHAPTER 1

MANAGEMENT'S LEGAL ACCOUNTING STANDARDS

CHAPTER OBJECTIVE: To describe and explain the minimum course of action that a senior manager must take to fulfill the legal standard of care pertaining to his or her accounting function duties.

The stories and tales are endless of the actions senior managers took or should have taken to fulfill their duties in various situations. Unfortunately, whether actions taken or not taken were appropriate under the circumstances often can only be determined after the occurrence, when it is too late to take a different course of action. In fact, there are numerous statutory and case law standards that may apply to the senior manager, depending on the business's legal jurisdiction (i.e., where the business is located or transacts its business and the type of transaction or activity involved). Those standards, or duties, may be considered general because they apply to all senior management–related activities (e.g., fiduciary duty); however, they may also be considered specific because they apply to individually identifiable matters that the senior manager may be required to address. This chapter describes the range of commonly applied standards that may apply to the senior manager with respect to the organization's accounting function, and suggests a model for management's accounting conduct by integrating the various standards to provide the senior manager with reasonable comfort that his or her legal accounting responsibilities have been satisfied.

BUSINESS JUDGMENT RULE

The business judgment rule holds that management, not a court of law, is better charged with the management of the business of the corporation. The courts have recognized that generally they are ill-equipped to second-guess the validity of complex business decisions, management needs latitude in decision making, and undue liability exposure is a deterrent to service as a senior manager, particularly with respect to outside directors. The business judgment rule is applied when the senior manager acts in good faith, does not have a direct or an indirect interest in the transaction or the transaction is approved by a majority of the disinterested directors, has in fact exercised his or her judgment through reasonable diligence (e.g., has not unreasonably delegated or abandoned his or her management and decision responsibilities or failed to act with conscious decision), and has acted with the standard of care required by governing state law.

It was once widely believed that as a practical matter, the business judgment rule shielded the senior manager from liability except in cases of self-dealing, bad faith, or fraud. That belief was rebutted by several cases that held otherwise in the mid-1980s.[1] Case law now holds that the senior manager should proceed with a critical eye in an informed and deliberate manner, exercise reasonable care gathering and considering relevant material information prior to decision making, and act independently, with his or her best judgment and without regard to influence or pressures exerted by others, including other directors, officers, managers, or controlling stockholders. Similarly, if the senior manager decides not to take action, his or her inaction, lack of attention, or decision to delegate should be supportable under the business judgment rule; that is, made with the standard of care required by governing state law.

The senior manager may rely on the reports of others, including other directors, officers, managers, experts, or agents, if proper care is exercised in the selection of the report preparer and reliance is reasonable under the circumstances. The report preparer must be qualified and sufficiently informed—reliance on the reports of others may not be given blindly. A court of law will look to determine whether there is basis or support for believing that the senior manager acted in the best interests of the business. Reliance on a report prepared by another person is warranted when the senior manager acts in good faith, has knowledge of the contents of the report, and has had opportunity to consider, question, and receive responses regarding the contents of the report.

The sufficiency of care taken with respect to matters considered should be evidenced in some manner—the senior manager should consider the extent to which business meeting minutes or other written documents should reflect discussions and deliberations to provide after-the-fact proof of appropriate and reasonable investigation and deliberation.

GOVERNING STATE LAW[2]

The Revised Model Business Corporation Act and the majority of state statutes require the senior manager to discharge his or her duties, including his or her duty as a member of a committee, in good faith; with the care that an ordinary prudent person in a like position would exercise under similar circumstances; and in a manner he or she reasonably believes to be in the best interest of the corporation. Many statutes only address director conduct. However, as mentioned above, for the purpose of this guide it is appropriate to discuss those statutes in conjunction with the duties of the senior manager. The Model Act and most state statutes require the senior manager to act as an ordinary person would if that person were a senior manager under similar circumstances. The "similar circumstances" provision has been interpreted to mean that the measure of responsibility may vary depending on the senior manager's qualifications, his or her position within the management of the business, and the nature and structure of the business entity. Skill, or technical competence, is not mandated by the Model Act, but the senior manager may be held to a higher standard of care if he or she has a higher skill level. He or she must also perform his or her duties in good faith; that is, with honesty and without partaking in actions designed for personal benefit to the detriment of the business.

Alternatives to the Model Act standard of care generally vary in form between the Delaware and California standards. There is no specific Delaware statute defining the senior manager's required standard of care. However, Delaware courts have held that the senior manager is bound to use that amount of care that ordinary careful and prudent persons would use under similar circumstances. California provides a statutory standard of conduct requiring the performance of senior manager duties with "such care, including reasonable inquiry, as an ordinary prudent person in a like position would use under similar circumstances." "Reasonable inquiry" requires inquiry as ordinary prudence would warrant under the circumstances, after being put on notice by suspicious circumstances.

SECURITIES REGULATION

Depending on his or her decision-making authority and activities, the senior manager may also be subject to numerous other statutes imposing duty or conduct requirements. Because of the great variety of management activities, it is not possible to identify or generalize all of the senior manager activities that are statutorily regulated or governed. However, it is possible to summarize some of the numerous federal securities statutes and rules that specifically relate to the senior management accounting function. Below is a summary of some of the more commonly encountered federal securities statutes and rules: Sections 11 and 12(2) of the Securities Act of 1933 (Securities Act), Section 14(e) of the Securities Exchange Act of 1934 (Exchange Act), and Rules 14a-9 and 10b-5, enacted under the Exchange Act. Chapters 2 and 3, in part covering the Foreign Corrupt Practices Act and financial disclosure requirements, respectively, discuss additional statutory requirements and the meanings of significant terms relating to those requirements.

Section 11 generally provides for liability arising from a securities registration statement that contains an untrue statement of a material fact or omits to state a material fact required to be stated or necessary to make the statement not misleading. Section 12(2) generally provides for liability arising from the offer or sale of a security by means of a prospectus or oral communication that includes an untrue statement of material fact or omits to state a material fact. The senior manager generally can present a defense to Section 11 liability by establishing that, after reasonable investigation, he or she reasonably did believe that the statement made was materially complete and true, or that with respect to any statement made based on the authority of an expert, the senior manager had no reasonable ground to believe that the statement was materially untrue or incomplete. Section 12(2) also allows for a similar reasonable care or due diligence defense. However, in practice, courts generally have held under Section 12(2) that, with respect to financial or management issues or decisions, it may be difficult for the senior manager to sustain his or her burden of proof that he or she did not know, and in the exercise of reasonable care could not have known, of the untruth or omission.

Section 14(e) of the Exchange Act generally provides for liability arising from an untrue statement of material fact or omission of material fact necessary in order to make the statement made, in the light of the circumstances under which it was made, not misleading, or to engage in fraudulent, deceptive, or manipulative acts in connection with a tender offer or request or invitation for tenders.

Rule 14a-9, supplementing Section 14(a) of the Exchange Act, generally provides that no proxy or notice of meeting shall contain any material, false, or misleading statement, or omit to state any material fact necessary to make the statement made not false or misleading or necessary to correct any earlier proxy or notice of meeting that has become false or misleading.

Rule 10b-5 generally provides for liability arising from the purchase or sale of a security by means of an untrue statement of a material fact or omitted statement of material fact necessary in order to make the statement made, in light of the circumstances under which it was made, not misleading.

The culpability standard for liability under Sections 11 and 12(2) and Rule 14a-9 generally is one of negligence. Section 14(e) and Rule 10b-5 require a showing of intent or recklessness. However, as viewed by a jury, recklessness simply may be a higher showing of negligence based on the circumstance of the case as presented.

A MODEL FOR MANAGEMENT'S ACCOUNTING CONDUCT

After reviewing the preceding standards, it is generally possible to develop a single suggested omnibus model of conduct. Although some of the above-mentioned authorities do not require that informed decisions be made only after personal investigation of the facts or review of reports prepared by qualified and knowledgeable agents, various court decisions have held otherwise, and it is likely future decisions also will hold otherwise given appropriate circumstances. Accordingly, the senior manager generally should consider acting at least in accordance with the following standards.

He or she should perform his or her duties, including his or her duty as a member of a committee:

1. With honesty and without personal benefit.
2. As an ordinary and prudent person would if that person was in the position of the senior manager, in a similar posture within the business, and with the qualifications, skills, and knowledge of that senior manager.
3. By critically gathering, considering, inquiring about, analyzing, and at least attempting to comprehend most, if not all, of the reasonably available information that is relevant and material to the decision at hand.

Generally observe three additional practices or caveats:

1. It is common practice that the senior manager must necessarily rely on other people in the performance of his or her accounting function. This obviously is so because in most circumstances the senior manager, as a decision maker, gathers and analyzes information. The senior manager generally does not personally complete transactions or maintain accounting records but rather receives requested reports and information. However, reliance on a report or other information provided by another person only is warranted if that other person is sufficiently informed and qualified to provide the report or information.

2. Although the senior manager generally is not required to have any particular accounting skills, in the absence of adequate accounting knowledge, it may be questionable whether the senior manager sufficiently comprehends the material information that he or she should consider and analyze when making informed decisions. Thus, the senior manager is well advised to obtain accounting knowledge sufficient to enable him or her to make informed decisions.

3. The senior manager often attains that position because of friendships and business associations. Those relationships cannot be allowed to interfere with the senior manager's decision-making process, nor can the threat of disagreement, ridicule, or loss of status or position. The senior manager should make decisions based on the betterment of the business and its investors.

The above-described statutory and judicial standards of care in fact merely require the performance of those actions that generally would be required before making an informed business decision. Of course, a court of law can always second-guess the actions of the senior manager after the fact by determining that his or her actions, although taken in good faith and thought by the senior manager to be sufficient under the circumstance, should have been more extensive. Thus, unfortunately the senior manager generally cannot be completely certain in most circumstances that his or her consideration or analysis of a particular matter is sufficient.

Understanding the reasoning and scope of the various standards of care is the first step towards obtaining reasonable comfort that the senior manager's accounting function duties have been satisfied; the second step, discussed in Chapter 2, is to develop and implement an accounting methodology or system to assist in satisfying the various standards.

CHAPTER 2

DESIGNING A SYSTEM OF FINANCIAL ACCOUNTABILITY

CHAPTER OBJECTIVE 1: To identify, design, and implement key elements of an accounting and asset control system to ensure timely, accurate, and complete accounting information and asset safety.

CHAPTER OBJECTIVE 2: To identify means of perpetrating financial statement and accounting fraud, and to design and implement procedures to prevent and/or detect fraud.

This chapter and Chapter 3 (relating to financial disclosures) discuss some of the more interesting accounting-related topics. Internal control and fraud relate to the same topic, but internal control tends to be identified more closely with prevention and detection, whereas fraud more typically is identified with wrongful means of violating the business's accounting and disclosure functions. As indicated in the preface to this guide, it is not my objective to unnecessarily fill written space by sensationalizing discussions about fraudulent or misleading accounting or disclosure activities. However, with the information in this chapter and in Chapter 3 at hand, you should be able not only to understand and design an internal accounting control system but also to analyze news accounts pertaining to financial fraud and misstatement and to identify how a wrongful act was perpetrated, the weakness in the accounting system, and the means of correcting that weakness. For example, time and again, relevant material in this guide can be directly applied to analyze management liability and professional malpractice issues in the savings and loan, banking, and corporate investor areas. Although governmental and pension accounting rules and principles tend to be somewhat different and specialized, most of the discussions in this chapter can also be applied to those areas.

Management is responsible for the development and operation of the business's accounting system and for the presentation and disclosure of accounting information and reports. However, senior management, or more particularly, the board of directors, as overseer of management, arguably has ultimate responsibility for the actions of management. This is not to say that management and other persons or entities (e.g., CPAs expressing an opinion on the financial statements) may not also be responsible, perhaps primarily or completely responsible, for erroneous or misleading accounting information. However, within the organization's hierarchy, senior management, or more particularly, the board of directors, may have ultimate responsibility. Although the possible accounting system design variations are almost endless, each accounting system must in some fashion be comprised of at least the following three primary components: (1) the business's internal control, (2) senior manager accounting knowledge, and (3) the audit committee. Due to its importance and specific scope, the audit committee is discussed separately in Chapter 4.

INTERNAL CONTROL

The accounting function significantly depends on the senior manager's ability to receive timely, competent, and complete accounting information. For this reason, internal control is the first and primary element of the accounting methodology or system. The importance of internal control cannot be overemphasized. An analysis of internal control helps quantify the extent to which the accounting records of the business can be relied on. Internal control is one of the first areas that a CPA evaluates before beginning what is generally considered the substantive portion of the audit process.

Internal control is designed to provide reasonable, cost-effective safeguards against unauthorized access to or use of the business's assets and reasonable assurance that the financial records and accounts are sufficiently reliable for reporting and management purposes. Internal control can be breached by unintentional noncompliance or neglect, management override, intentional noncompliance, or collusion. The American Institute of Certified Public Accountants (AICPA) Statements on Auditing Standards (SAS) describe internal control as being composed of three primary components: control environment, accounting system, and control procedures.

Control Environment

Control environment primarily relates to the business's politics, management philosophy, structure, method of assigning authority and responsibility, and operating style. From an accounting viewpoint, the optimum business environment is one in which management and employees exhibit honesty and integrity; there is a regular flow of information both up and down the corporate structure; teamwork is emphasized at all levels; employees receive regular evaluation and training, are properly supervised, complimented, or rewarded when appropriate and warranted and commensurately compensated; voluntary recognition of mistakes is encouraged and considered part of the solution process; and employees are fairly reprimanded in confidence. Those policies will substantially increase the integrity of the accounting system. In the alternative atmosphere, the likelihood of error, misinformation, and cover-up in the accounting system is substantially increased. Of course, it is possible, given a particular circumstance, that any one of the above-listed policies may not be the best course of action from a business viewpoint and should not be followed at a particular time; nevertheless, those policies should remain in overall practice to maintain the integrity of the accounting system.

Accounting System

The accounting system refers to the nuts and bolts of the organization's methods and records established to timely identify, classify, value and revalue, record, and report transactions and maintain accountability over the transactions, assets, and liabilities. In this regard, the senior manager wants assurance that the accounting employees and management are honest, knowledgable, receive necessary training and education, have access to and consult with necessary resources, act with good judgment, and are well supervised. The accounting system should be organized, up-to-date in the recording of transactions, and provide the senior manager with timely, accurate, and complete information and reports.

Control Procedures

Control procedures refer to the actual policies and procedures established to ensure proper implementation, operation, and integrity of the control environment and accounting system. For example, broad policies and procedures may include:

1. Adoption of a documented hierarchical structure of authority and responsibility within the business and accounting/financial function.

2. Required receipt of informed authorization for specific transactions and activities.
3. Segregation of duties and responsibilities within the transactional process.
4. Design and use of adequate transaction documents and records.
5. Maintenance of secured and limited access facilities.
6. Periodic independent verification, testing, or investigation of the operations of the accounting records and internal control systems.

Foreign Corrupt Practices Act

The title of the Foreign Corrupt Practices Act (FCPA) is misleading. This federal act not only contains provisions prohibiting foreign bribery but also requires domestic corporations to maintain appropriate accounting records and internal control safeguards. Penalties for violation of the FCPA can be extremely onerous.

The bribery provisions of the act generally make it unlawful for any person, business, or other entity to pay (including by money, gift, transfer of an item of value, or otherwise) a foreign official for the purpose of obtaining business if the person making or associated with making the payment is aware or substantially certain that it is an unlawful payment; for example, a bribe or what ultimately will become an unlawful payment at a later time (i.e., if the payment initially is legal but subsequently will be used for an unlawful purpose). A payment is not considered a bribe if it is lawfully made under the laws of the foreign country or if it is made to secure the performance of a routine governmental action such as the processing of documents, also referred to as "grease" payments.

It is not within the scope of this guide to discuss in detail the intricacies of the FCPA bribery provisions. However, the bribery provisions, decisions thereunder, and related "red flag" areas must be considered and understood to design and implement systems that comply with the accounting and internal control provisions of the act. Some red flag areas that may be considered are the manner (e.g., cash, check, or property and named payee), place (e.g., to the country in question or to an unrelated country), and amount (e.g., within the normal range for similar transactions) of payment; past experiences with and reputations of the country and agent in question; and the type of product involved. Accounting records and internal control systems, including the use of protective contractual terms and pretransactional due diligence, should be designed to prevent illegal payments, or at least to establish the senior manager's reasonable lack of substantial knowledge of illegal payments, primarily by the implementation of prepayment safeguards but also by postpayment detection methods.

The accounting records and internal control provisions of the FCPA generally apply to publicly held corporations and require that a business:

1. Keep books, records, and accounts that, in reasonable detail, accurately and fairly reflect the business's transactions.
2. Devise and maintain a system of internal controls sufficient to provide reasonable assurances that:

   a. Transactions are authorized by management.
   b. Transactions are recorded to permit preparation of financial statements in conformity with Generally Accepted Accounting Principles (GAAP) and other applicable standards, and to maintain accountability over assets.
   c. Access to assets is permitted only with management authorization.
   d. Recorded accountability for assets periodically is reconciled with existing assets.

Similarly, the FCPA also requires a corporation holding voting power over another corporation, including a foreign corporation, to comply with the provisions of the FCPA with respect to that other corporation. The Securities and Exchange Commission (SEC) has indicated that when a corporation controls more than 50 percent of the voting securities of a subsidiary, compliance with the FCPA is expected with respect to the subsidiary. Similar compliance is expected when a corporation controls 20 to 50 percent of a subsidiary, subject to contrary proof by the corporation that its ownership does not amount to control. When a corporation owns less than 20 percent of a subsidiary, the burden is on the SEC to demonstrate the corporation's control, if any, over the subsidiary.

The accounting provisions of the FCPA primarily are intended to address three areas of concern: (1) situations where transactions are not recorded, (2) situations where transactions are falsely recorded (e.g., when an amount is recorded in an incorrect account), and (3) situations where transactions are recorded correctly but are also misrepresented in substance (e.g., when a payment is correctly recorded as being made to the appropriate person but with substantial certainty that person then will transfer the payment to another person for an unlawful purpose). The FCPA does not mandate a specific internal control system, standard, or form. The act requires reasonable detail and assurances. However, with respect to the accounting and internal control provisions, "materiality" is *not* a minimum threshold safe harbor, nor are lack of knowledge or substantial certainty. The SEC has stated that, although the act does not require the board of directors or most senior management to become involved in the "minutia" of recording and accounting, management and the board play important roles in monitoring and evaluating the adequacy of the business's records and controls. Management cannot make nominal gestures of compliance while delegating or abandoning its responsibilities to others.

No single system of accounting records and internal control can be designed for use by all businesses. Since the FCPA does not mandate a specific type of accounting system, the management of each business must decide what system design will satisfy the needs and concerns of that business. Most likely any accounting system design used by a business will evolve and change over time and may include experimental phases. For all systems, education of and communication between the participants will substantially increase the potential for reasonable success. Depending on the needs of the business, a system of accounting records and internal control may require various levels of participation not only by the board and the audit committee but also by internal and outside auditors, attorneys, management, and other accounting personnel, including data processing. In addition to other policies and procedures, the business may consider adopting some of the policies and procedures listed in this chapter.

Violation of the FCPA accounting provisions is generally punishable by civil liability and injunctive relief, but it may also be punishable by criminal liability if a person knowingly circumvents or fails to implement a system of internal accounting controls or knowingly falsifies any book, record, or account. The SEC has stated that upon the occurrence of a violation of the act, the SEC will evaluate the adequacy of the internal control system, the involvement of top management in the violation, and corrective actions taken once the violation is discovered.

Many FCPA cases involve internal control violations that are so egregious they are not worthy of discussion. In fact, most cases involving violations of the FCPA accounting provisions also involve other wrongful acts (e.g., securities laws violations relating to material misstatements of financial information). But the act remains a substantial additional deterrent in light of its bribery prohibitions, broad internal control requirements that can be invoked in most situations of wrongdoing, and penalty provisions. The two case summaries that follow are useful illustrations because they involve fact situations that are not particularly unusual. For most cases cited and discussed in this guide, case citations, but not the names of the parties, are provided. The names of the parties have been omitted because they do not significantly add to the value of the information provided by the case material and for various reasons some parties may prefer that names be omitted.

1. In one case[3] involving a violation of the FCPA accounting provisions, the chief executive officer (CEO) was authorized by his employment contract to use for his personal benefit certain secretarial, other staff, and office facilities. In that case, the CEO controlled the granting and receipt of the benefits, and there was no independent review by the directors, the audit committee, or disinterested management. Additionally, the corporate books and records did not with reasonable detail accurately reflect the nature, business purpose, or valuation of the transactions and benefits accruing to the CEO. The company stipulated to an order by the SEC that its books and internal controls were inadequate to identify benefits granted to and related-party transactions involving the CEO.

2. In another case,[4] a corporate investment adviser and manager of an investment fund discovered, but not until preparation of the fund's monthly general ledger trial balance, that a clerk in the fund's shareholder accounting department had embezzled $1.55 million. The corporation failed to maintain adequate internal accounting controls in that wire transfer instructions were transmitted without required signatures; wire transfer instructions were not routinely reviewed by supervisory personnel; blank wire transfer instruction sheets were not safeguarded after they were prepared and made available for delivery; and assigned duties were not properly segregated between employees in the fund's shareholder accounting department. The corporation consented to sanctions arising from its failure to maintain adequate internal accounting controls.

Audit/Evaluation of Internal Control

An audit of the financial statements is not an audit of internal control. However, the independent auditor may give a report to management or the board of directors evaluating internal control within the limitations of the audit procedures performed on internal control during the business's financial audit; that is, during the audit, the internal control system, although not specifically audited, is evaluated to determine the extent to which it may be relied on by the auditors. The independent auditor can also specifically be engaged to perform an audit of internal control. However, AICPA AU Section 642.12 and recently issued AICPA Statement on Standards for Attestation Engagements No. 2 provide that an auditor's opinion on management's compliance with laws, regulations, rules, contracts, or grants does not provide a legal determination of that business's compliance. That same proposition may be extended to hold that an audit of internal control does not provide assurance of a business's compliance with any legal standard or requirement relating to internal control. Chapter 6 contains additional discussion of management and other reports, and the new internal control requirements of the Federal Deposit Insurance Corporation Act of 1991 are generally discussed in endnote 72.

Selected Internal Control Safeguards

Many accounting resources provide extensive lists or charts of possible internal control safeguards. Those resources are helpful and may be consulted for suggestions and to save time when developing or reviewing a business's internal control system. However, it is more beneficial to understand the basic concept of internal control: to have different employees perform different key duties or activities in the transactional process to prevent mistakes and intentional breaches. The following is an example of an internal control safeguard breakdown allowing employee embezzlement to go undetected at least initially: The company bookkeeper is given responsibility for recording transactions in the bookkeeping records, has access to company checks, and has bank statement reconciliation duties, thus allowing the bookkeeper to forge checks without detection. As discussed further below, in this example the bookkeeper was illadvisedly given control or custody over the accounting records, checks, and reconciliation of the bank statement. In this example, proper internal controls would have at least required that the bank statement reconciliation be performed by a person other than the bookkeeper and that a person other than the bookkeeper routinely justify a sampling of the checks written by reviewing supporting documentation such as bills and expense vouchers.

The transactional process generally can be divided into five broad functional areas, each of which should, if possible, be staffed by employees who are independent of the other functional areas:

1. The transaction; for example, the sale of merchandise by a clerk.
2. Authorization: for example, credit department or other approval when required by the business's policies.
3. Accounting recordation.
4. Asset custody; for example, cash, checks, or inventory custody.
5. Verification/reconciliation; for example, intradepartmental account reconciliation and/or verification by independent personnel such as internal auditors.

Some businesses may not have sufficient personnel to permit different employees to perform each of the five functional areas. In that circumstance, the business should attempt to achieve maximum employee independence within the functional areas and depend more heavily on the fifth function, verification/reconciliation.

Most of the specific personnel duties within the transactional process generally can be classified into the following activity areas:

General ledger	Accounts receivable
Cash receipts	Accounts payable
Cash disbursements	Mail
Sales	Banking deposits
Purchasing	Banking reconciliation
Credit	Payroll delivery
Billing	Petty cash
Payroll	Personnel asset/
Shipping	cash custodian/inventory
Internal control/internal auditors	Management authority
Receiving	

Rather than completely relying on lists or charts of possible internal control safeguards, for any given transaction it is possible to trace the transactional process and staff personnel so that broad functional areas and key personnel duties or activities are performed by independent/different personnel.

A typical sales transaction may involve the following personnel activities in chronological order.

Credit	Mail
Sales	Collections/cash receipts
Accounts receivable	Bank deposit
Inventory/shipping	Bank reconciliation
Billing	

A typical purchase transaction may involve the following personnel activities in chronological order:

Purchasing	Inventory
Accounts payable	Cash disbursements
Receiving	Bank reconciliation

A typical payroll transaction may involve the following personnel activities in chronological order:

Personnel	Payroll delivery
Payroll	Bank reconciliation
Cash disbursements/check preparation	

For the sales, purchase, and payroll transactional processes just described, each personnel activity should, if possible, be performed by a different employee. Cash custody personnel should be independent of general ledger, accounts receivable, accounts payable, cash disbursements, cash receipts, and banking personnel. General ledger personnel should at least be independent of cash custody, cash receipts, and cash disbursements personnel and as many other employees performing activities in the transactional process as possible. Employees responsible for making bank deposits should be independent of cash custody, cash receipts, cash disbursements, and bank reconciliation personnel.

Similar to the previous discussion relating to the five broad functional transaction areas, in some businesses—for example, small- and medium-sized businesses—it is more likely there will be insufficient personnel to allow all of the above-described activities to be performed by independent personnel. The business should attempt to achieve maximum separation of activities with the employees available and may consider hiring additional personnel if it is deemed necessary. As maximum separation of activities becomes less possible, more emphasis must be placed on documentation, limiting unnecessary personnel access to facilities/assets, transactional and asset custody authorization, intradepartmental reconciliations, and independent verifications by internal auditors or other sources.

Additional selected internal control safeguards may be considered for adoption. However, each business must analyze its particular internal control needs and requirements. Although the following list does not include all possible safeguards, and in fact the number of possible safeguards is endless, the list includes many of the important safeguards and, more importantly, in conjunction with the previous discussion, provides a reference that you can apply to most any internal control situation. The list also should be considered in conjunction with the fraud discussion that follows later in this chapter. For readers with limited or only vaguely remembered accounting knowledge, it may be useful to review the accounting conventions described in Chapter 6 before continuing with the remainder of this chapter.

1. General safeguards
    a. The business maintains an organizational chart of personnel and a chart of accounts.
    b. The business has adopted and documented its business ethics policies and the responsibility and authority of each significant participant or group of participants in the accounting and internal control system.
    c. Procedures have been adopted and documented safeguarding access to and storage of the accounting records, including computerized records.
    d. The business has adopted procedures for testing and investigating the integrity and reliability of its accounting and internal control systems (including the use of individuals outside the business when necessary for independence or confidentiality purposes with respect to discovery by outside third-party persons, entities, or agencies, or people inside the business).
    e. The business requires preventative pretransactional due diligence in all appropriate situations to help avoid later disputes or unexpectancies.
    f. Transactions between the business and related parties (e.g., management, owners, the immediate families of management and owners, and other persons or entities that can signif-

icantly influence the management or policies of the business) receive appropriate authorization and are conducted at arm's length similar to transactions between the business and unrelated parties.

g. Employees who handle cash, checks, securities, and other valuables are bonded.

h. Employee functions and duties are regularly rotated; vacations are enforced.

i. Budgets are used, and at least significant deviations from those budgets are investigated.

j. Special accounting journal entries require approval or at least are routinely reviewed by independent personnel.

k. To the extent possible, management has knowledge of the employees who participate in the various accounting functions and their relationships to other employees in those functions.

l. When a corporation owns or controls 20 percent or more of another corporation, including a foreign corporation, and also perhaps in some circumstances when the corporation owns or controls less than 20 percent of another corporation, the owning or controlling corporation investigates the internal control of the owned or controlled corporation to ensure that the internal control satisfies the provisions of the Foreign Corrupt Practices Act, discussed previously in this chapter.

m. The business employs an in-house public relations person who is the only designate responsible for public disclosures, except in special or limited circumstances. Further, each time the business makes a statement of opinion interpreting or estimating its existing or expected future financial situation, that statement first must be evaluated and approved by designated, competent, and knowledgeable personnel or professional advisors.

n. Accounting estimates, contingencies, allowances, expense deferrals and revenue accruals in unusual situations (e.g., revenue accruals when there is a right of return or it is not clear the earnings process is complete) are evaluated and approved by designated, competent, and knowledgeable personnel.

2. Cash receipts and disbursements safeguards
   a. Personnel who open the mail place restrictive endorsements on checks and make a list of cash, checks, and any other payments received.
   b. The list referred to in Item (2a) is verified against daily deposit slips and the cash receipts journal.
   c. Prenumbered receipts or other transactional documentation records are prepared for cash sales, and cash sales are reconciled daily with cash collections and receipts records.
   d. Personnel independent of the sales, accounts receivable, and cash functions review customer discounts and allowances.
   e. Expense and other payments (other than payments from petty cash) are made by prenumbered check.
   f. Checks are signed by an appropriately authorized person who is independent of the employee(s) who prepares the checks.
   g. Payments are made only if a check or a request for payment from petty cash is accompanied by supporting documentation and the documentation then is marked as paid.
   h. Petty cash and check disbursements above specified amounts require approval.
   i. Payments from petty cash, as all other payments, are, in some manner, recorded on prenumbered slips.
   j. Petty cash fund balances are small, requiring frequent reimbursement.
   k. Access to and authority over company credit card use is strictly controlled. Credit card bills are routinely reconciled with supporting vouchers and bills.
3. Receivables: Notes and accounts safeguards
   a. Notes require proper authorization.
   b. The notes custodian is independent of the cashier and other accounts receivable personnel.
   c. An aging of accounts is maintained and reviewed by an employee who is independent of credit and accounts receivable personnel.
   d. Write-offs and prenumbered credit memoranda require approval by a designated employee who is independent of the credit manager and accounts receivable personnel.
   e. Employee advances require authorization.

4. Inventory safeguards
   a. Inventory access is limited to authorized personnel and, when necessary, is controlled by a documented log.
   b. Inventory receiving, issuance, and shipping reports are maintained.
   c. Inventory records are maintained by personnel who do not have access to the inventory.
   d. Physical inventories with the use of prenumbered tags are taken by personnel who are independent of inventory personnel.
5. Securities/investments safeguards
   a. Securities are stored in a vault that requires at least two authorized persons for access.
   b. A log is maintained of all persons visiting the vault.
   c. A log of securities placed in and taken out of the vault is maintained by personnel who are independent of personnel who have access to the vault.
   d. Prenumbered vault deposit and withdrawal vouchers are required.
   e. Physical securities inventories are taken periodically by personnel who do not have access to the vault or vault records.
   f. The securities custodian is independent of the securities records, general ledger, and cash receipts and disbursements functions.
6. Property, plant, and equipment safeguards
   a. Purchases, retirements, and dispositions of property or equipment require authorization, and a work order or voucher system is maintained for such.
   b. A record is kept of assets assigned for use by employees, and that record is periodically verified by physical confirmation.
   c. Property and equipment inventories are taken periodically by employees who do not have access to inventory records.
7. Payables: Notes and accounts safeguards
   a. Significant borrowing is approved by management and requires at least two signatures.
   b. An employee who does not have authority to sign checks or notes keeps the payables register.
   c. Paid notes, interest coupons, bonds, and other documents indicating a liability are marked as canceled or paid.

    d. Account payable adjustments or corrections require approval.

  8. Capital securities safeguards

    a. A registrar and a transfer agent, both of whom are independent of the business, are employed to control capital stock custody, transfers, and dividend payments, or those duties are assigned to a designated officer.

    b. Surrendered or retired certificates are canceled.

    c. Corporate stamps and seals are controlled by a designated officer.

  9. Sales, shipping, and receiving safeguards

    a. Sales orders, sales invoices, and shipping memoranda are prenumbered.

    b. All sales orders, or those above a specified amount, are approved by designated personnel.

    c. The receiving department prepares prenumbered receiving reports.

    d. Prenumbered credit memoranda are prepared for returns and require appropriate approval.

    e. Sales to employees are handled in the same manner as sales to customers (e.g., they receive no special treatment, unless appropriately authorized).

  10. Purchases safeguards

    a. Purchase orders and invoices are prenumbered.

    b. Purchase orders and invoices, or those above a specified amount, require approval.

  11. Payroll safeguards

    a. Payroll is periodically verified with personnel records by employees who are independent of payroll.

    b. Payroll is signed by the payroll employee preparing it and authorized or approved by a designated officer, or it is prepared by the payroll department and signed by a designated officer.

    c. Employees are paid by check.

Fraud

The following discussion primarily pertains to the incurrence of fraud in financial statements (i.e., financial statements that are intentionally or recklessly made to falsely enhance the financial picture of a business). For the purpose of this discussion, financial statement fraud refers to false statements intended to deceive persons outside the company, not to an action of taking from within the company, such as embezzlement. The internal control guidelines previously discussed are also useful to prevent fraud. However, internal control safeguards may not always prevent fraud. Thus, it is useful to separately discuss some of the means of perpetrating and detecting financial statement fraud.

Means of Perpetrating Fraud

In the broad sense, financial statements can be fraudulently enhanced by one or a combination of the following five means: (1) reduce liabilities, (2) increase assets, (3) increase revenues, (4) reduce expenses, or (5) reclassify assets or liabilities as being long term or short term. The following discussion assumes that the person perpetrating a fraud will be attempting to enhance the financial statements. However, in some circumstances, the objective of the perpetrator may be to degrade the financial statements (e.g., when the amount of a payment or liability due is based on the financial status of the business and will be favorably reduced when that status is diminished). Many of the items listed in this discussion are also useful for detecting fraud when the objective is to degrade the financial statements. In that circumstance, you often need merely reverse the emphasis of the method of detection. For example, one means of enhancing financial statements is to reduce cost of goods sold by increasing ending inventory. The reverse would be a means of degrading the financial statements; that is, an increase in the cost of goods sold would degrade the financial statements. Such an increase could be accomplished by reducing ending inventory, possibly by consignments.

There are also means of enhancing financial statements that arguably may not constitute fraud. Examples may include smoothing (i.e., manipulating the financial numbers to obtain a steady rate of growth); grouping accounts, transactions, or financial amounts so as to hide or disguise the individual components of the group; or recording transactions or amounts in the wrong account for a similar concealment purpose. Fraud is a legal definition generally requiring (1) a misrepresentation, concealment, or nondisclosure, (2) knowledge of or reckless disregard for the fraudulent conduct, (3) intent to induce reliance on the conduct, (4) justifiable reliance on the fraud by the defrauded person, and (5) damages. Thus, it is possible that in appropriate circumstances (e.g., when knowledge or reckless disregard of the fraudulent conduct is present), conduct such as smoothing could also be determined to be fraudulent.

Every financial statement account is susceptible to fraudulent enhancement. However, in practice, a perpetrator probably would attempt to enhance financial statements by the following means in order of priority: (1) by affecting income statement revenue or expense accounts to increase net income; (2) by increasing assets or reducing liabilities to enhance the overall balance sheet picture; and (3) by reclassifying long- or short-term assets or liabilities to enhance the current asset or net current asset portion of the balance sheet.

The following is a representative, but not conclusive, list of the balance sheet and income statement accounts and related possible means of fraudulent enhancement. Similar to the previous discussion pertaining to internal control, the number of possible means of fraudulently enhancing financial statements is endless. Thus, the following list should not be considered conclusive. However, the list includes many of the common means of fraudulently enhancing financial statements and, in conjunction with the previous internal control discussion, provides a reference that you can apply to analyze most any financial statement fraud issue. In the majority of the financial statement fraud cases that I encounter, the means of fraud employed is generally at least closely related to one or more of the means listed below. Some of the means are listed under several different accounts because their effects are broad and not limited to just one account.

1. Cash
   a. Delaying until the next accounting period the recording of disbursements made near but before the balance sheet date.
   b. Recording amounts received in the next accounting period as being received in the current period.
   c. Fabricating fictitious cash items, such as bank accounts, transactions, or entries.
   d. Not disclosing that certain cash accounts are in some manner restricted.
   e. Classifying long-term cash accounts as current assets.
2. Accounts receivable
   a. Fabricating fictitious sales invoices.
   b. Reporting goods on consignment as sales.
   c. Overbilling for merchandise sold.

  d. Invoicing/shipping merchandise that was not purchased.

  e. Failing to recognize or disclose the value of return rights or contingent liabilities on sales that contain those rights.

  f. Underestimating the allowance for bad accounts or returns.

  g. Unreasonably lowering required credit qualifications to increase sales. This action would also affect the allowance for bad accounts or returns.

  h. Factoring receivables with recourse, but not recognizing an appropriate contingent liability for the recourse.

  i. Overreporting receivables arising from sales to affiliates. For consolidated financial statements, intercompany receivables should be eliminated. Even if the elimination of affiliate or intercompany receivables is not required, those receivables may not have arisen from actual sales or arm's-length transactions; that is, valuations of those transactions may be suspect.

  j. Extending or modifying receivable due dates or terms without making necessary disclosures or recognizing an appropriate valuation loss.

  k. Reclassifying long-term receivables as current receivables.

  l. Recognizing revenue when the revenue-generating process is not yet complete (e.g., the collection of the sales price is not reasonably assured).

  m. Recognizing revenue from ''sales'' of merchandise to customers but holding or warehousing the merchandise for later use by the customer and delaying billing—essentially, pre-selling merchandise.

  n. Carrying as receivables amounts due from related parties (e.g., subsidiaries) when there is no expectation of payment or delay in payment is expected.

  o. Recognizing revenue from installment sales prior to the appropriate period.

3. Inventory

  a. Overvaluing existing inventory.

  b. Counting nonexistent inventory or sold merchandise that is being warehoused for customers.

  c. Not reducing the value of obsolete, damaged, or slow-moving inventory.

  d. Improperly changing or disclosing a change in inventory accounting methods.

    e. Failing to disclose pledged inventory when required.

    f. Reclassifying old and new inventory to alter valuation under the inventory accounting conventions (e.g., under the LIFO and FIFO inventory methods). (See Chapter 6 for additional discussion regarding inventories.)

    g. Counting inventory sold and warehoused under a repurchase agreement.

4. Property, plant, and equipment

    a. Recording expenses as acquisitions of property, plant, and equipment to delay recognizing the entire immediate expense.

    b. Reducing or delaying depreciation.

    c. Recording inflated property, plant, and equipment values (e.g., recording those assets at fictitious values or at appraised value instead of cost).

    d. In a purchase of multiple assets, allocating the purchase price to property, plant, and equipment as opposed to short-term assets such as inventory so as to write off expenses over a longer period of time.

    e. In a purchase of multiple assets, reducing values allocated to tangible assets so as to increase goodwill, which can be amortized over a longer period of time.

5. Investments/securities

    a. Overvaluing investments or securities—assigning an excessive value when no readily available market determines the value or, in the case of transactions with related parties (e.g., in an asset for stock transaction), overvaluing the asset to allow overvaluation of the stock.

    b. Reclassifying a long-term investment/security as a current asset to increase liquidity.

    c. Pledging investments as security without appropriate financial statement disclosure.

    d. Classifying current marketable securities as noncurrent assets to allow an unrealized loss of value to be recorded as a reduction of equity instead of as a reduction of net income. Similarly, for noncurrent marketable securities, improperly classifying an unrealized loss in value as temporary instead of as other than temporary to allow the loss to be recorded as a reduction in equity instead of as a reduction in net income.

6. Taxes
    a. Recording an excessive or insupportable income tax receivable as a liability under new Statement of Financial Accounting Standards 109. (See Chapter 6 for additional discussion regarding income taxes.)
7. Leases
    a. Improperly treating a lease as an operating lease (e.g., instead of as a sales lease) in an attempt to avoid recording or disclosing lease payment liabilities.
8. Goodwill
    a. Reducing current expenses by allocating purchase costs to goodwill, which is amortized over a longer period of time.
    b. Paying too much for goodwill to increase assets. Although not necessarily fraudulent, as with all assets carried at historic cost, the current fair value of goodwill may be less than indicated on the balance sheet because the goodwill may have lost value (e.g., due to changes in the market, product, or the business subsequent to the initial valuation and recording of the goodwill).
9. Intangibles
    a. Overvaluing an intangible (e.g., the allowable value of a patent) to increase total assets.
    b. Similar to goodwill, although not necessarily fraudulent, the current fair value of an intangible may be less than indicated on the balance sheet because the intangible may have lost value (e.g., the market, product, or the business may have changed or become obsolete).
    c. Similar to goodwill, reducing current expenses by allocating costs to an intangible asset, which is amortized over a longer period of time.
10. Liabilities
    a. Not recognizing or disclosing contingent liabilities.
    b. Improperly treating a sales lease as an operating lease.
    c. Not recognizing or disclosing the value of a right of return with respect to a sale.
    d. Improperly recognizing a sale when the earnings process is not yet complete.
    e. Restructuring or modifying loans or receivables when they become uncollectible without recognizing or disclosing,

when required, a corresponding loss in value, contingent liability, or change in terms.

f. Factoring an asset such as a receivable with recourse but failing to record or disclose the contingent recourse liability.

g. Recording a loan as receipt of cash and an increase in equity instead of as a liability increase. The business makes the monthly payment by crediting cash and debiting owner's equity, thereby making the monthly payment look like owner drawing and allowing the business not to record the liability.

h. Improperly classifying a current liability as long term to improve net current asset value.

11. Equity

a. Recording a loan from the owners as equity and payments on the loan as owner withdrawals.

Note: The list of possible abuses of the equity account is almost endless. Thus, all significant changes in the equity account should be reconciled to determine that they are in fact not more appropriately classified as entries affecting other balance sheet or income statement accounts. See also item (5), Investments/securities, with respect to recording unrealized losses as reductions in equity instead of reductions in net income.

12. Revenues/gains

a. Recognizing revenues from sales for which the earning process is not yet complete (e.g., collection of the sales price is not reasonably assured).

b. Recognizing unearned revenues before appropriate.

c. Recognizing revenues in the current period for sales that will occur in the following period.

d. Failing to recognize the value of a right of return or repurchase obligation with respect to sales that contain those terms.

e. Classifyiing nonoperating or extraordinary revenues or gains as operating.

f. Inflating revenues from sales to related parties, affiliates, or subsidiaries (e.g., by reporting fictitious sales, overvaluing sales amounts, or not eliminating intercompany transactions in consolidated financial statements).

g. Deferring until the following period credit memoranda, sales returns, and allowances that are attributable to the current period.

   h. Recording consignments as sales.

   i. Increasing sales through unusual circumstances by the use of adjusting or general journal entries.

   j. Fabricating fictitious sales invoices.

   k. Overbilling for merchandise sold.

   l. Invoicing/shipping merchandise not purchased.

   m. Underestimating the allowance for bad accounts or returns.

   n. Increasing sales by unreasonably lowering required credit qualifications and not evaluating the adequacy of the allowance for returns.

   o. Recognizing revenue from installment sales prior to the appropriate period.

   p. Recognizing revenue from ''sales'' to customers, but holding or warehousing the merchandise for later use with a corresponding delayed billing.

   q. Recognizing currency translation gains from foreign operations as income instead of as a separate component of equity.

   r. Failing to properly disclose or account for a change in accounting method, change to an improper accounting method, or improperly changing to an accounting method that is otherwise acceptable but that is not a preferred method when compared to the method currently in use.

13. Cost of goods sold

   a. Overvaluing ending inventory to reduce cost of goods sold, resulting in higher net income.

   b. Counting nonexistent inventory.

   c. Not reducing the value of obsolete, damaged, or slow-moving inventory.

   d. Counting inventory sold but warehoused for customers.

   e. Reclassifying old and new inventory to alter valuation under the inventory accounting conventions (e.g., under the LIFO and FIFO inventory methods). (See Chapter 6 for additional discussion regarding inventories.)

   f. Counting inventory sold and warehoused under a repurchase agreement.

   g. Counting inventory consigned to the business, or inventory received from an affiliate but not owned by the business.

14. Expenses
    a. Recording an expense as a prepaid expense, an asset with a usefulness extending beyond the end of the current fiscal year, thereby reducing or delaying current period charge-off to future periods.
    b. Delaying until the next accounting period the recording of disbursements made near but before the balance sheet date.
    c. Recording current expenses as acquisitions of property, plant, and equipment, thereby deferring or eliminating the expense.
    d. Reducing or delaying depreciation.
    e. In a purchase of multiple assets, allocating the purchase price to property, plant, and equipment as opposed to short-term assets such as inventory so as to write off expenses over a longer period of time.
    f. In a purchase of multiple assets, reducing values allocated to tangible assets so as to increase goodwill, which can be amortized over a longer period of time.
    g. Not recognizing or disclosing liability contingencies.
    h. Not recognizing or disclosing the value of a right of return with respect to a sale.
    i. Recording a loan as a receipt of cash and an increase in equity instead of as a liability increase. The business makes the monthly payment by crediting cash and debiting owner's equity, thereby making the monthly payment look like owner drawing and allowing the company not to record the liability.
15. Pension plans
    a. Pension plans are accounted for as independent entities separate from the general business accounting records and financial statements. It is not within the scope of this guide to discuss accounting principles for pension plans. However, although not necessarily related to fraudulent practices, analysis of the financial statement of a business may also include analysis of the financial statement disclosure notes pertaining to the business's pension plan liabilities, including various past and current costs or liabilities, unrealized gains and losses, types of investments, and asset fair valuation.

Detecting Fraud

Internal control safeguards are the primary means of detecting and preventing fraud. Of course, it becomes more difficult to detect or prevent fraud when two or more employees become joint perpetrators or when a lower-level employee such as a middle manager allows improprieties by senior persons out of fear of reprisal. Fraudulent conduct is not limited to senior personnel—it is not unusual for mid- or lower-level personnel to perpetrate fraud to achieve business growth objectives, advancement, or recognition or to conceal failures or mistakes.

The following is a listing of some of the means of detecting fraud, including potential warning signals.

1. Analyze the integrity of management. Is management honest, cooperative, not overly egotistic, and willing to work with others? Does management set reasonable objectives? Is there a propensity to obtain desired results at all costs? Is undue pressure placed on personnel to achieve management's goals? Does the business have a mechanism for allowing employees to report improprieties or to make suggestions of improvement, in confidence if necessary? Is compensation unreasonably tied to the performance results of the business?

2. Does the business have a reliable accounting department and internal control system and an appropriately trained and staffed internal audit department that has sufficient authority to perform its function? Does the audit department work with senior management, and also independently report to the directors? The audit committee may consider reviewing all audit department employment hiring and terminations. Do the internal auditors approach their duties and investigations with skepticism?

3. Does the audit committee seek to obtain independent auditors (including the lower-level staff accountants of the independent auditors) who are knowledgeable about the business and who understand the business's desire not just to obtain a "clean" audit opinion but also to constantly improve the internal control system, keeping in mind cost-benefit considerations? The audit committee may consider obtaining comments from the lower-level auditors about the conduct of the business's employees during the course of the audit.

4. Analyze the practices and trends in the industry as compared to

the practices and trends of the company. Is the business highly visible? Is there an impression that the business is a high flyer such that less than extraordinary results would be considered disappointing? Is the business experiencing unusual profits, growth, or losses? Are the company and its primary areas of business on solid financial and business grounds?

5. Material fraud often is exposed by analytic analysis of changes in financial information, account balances, and significant financial ratios between different accounting periods. Significant changes should be investigated in detail. Analytic analysis should be performed on a business comparison basis; that is, by comparing current business financial information with similar prior financial information of that same business, and by comparing the business to industry averages and trends and other similarly situated businesses. Although cost benefit should be kept in mind, such an analysis can also be done at the department level on smaller accounts. The following are some of the key ratios that may be considered for fraud analysis. Most of the ratios are also useful for general financial analysis and budgeting.

   a. Sales or revenues compared to cost of goods sold.
   b. Sales or revenues compared to assets or investments.
   c. Gross sales or revenues compared to returns and credits.
   d. Sales or revenues compared to average inventory.
   e. Sales or revenues compared to average receivables.
   f. Average receivables compared to sales per day.
   g. Current assets compared to current liabilities.
   h. Reserve for uncollectible receivables compared to receivables.
   i. Cash plus cash equivalent current assets compared to current liabilities.
   j. Total debt compared to total assets.
   k. Profit or income compared to net worth, assets, sales, or revenues.
   l. Earnings compared to interest expense.

   Statement of cash flows ratio analysis should also be considered, but this topic is not often discussed. The statement of cash flows, also discussed in Chapter 6, presents changes in actual cash accounts during a period of time, as opposed to the income statement, which accrues income and expenses although actual cash may not have been received or disbursed. Thus, the statement of cash flows is useful to managers and analysts as an indicator of a business's ability to generate actual cash to pay debts and dividends or meet operations' cash needs. With respect to financial statement fraud, the statement of cash flows may be useful as an indicator of the business's going concern status—that is, an indicator of the likelihood of bankruptcy—and to detect unusual changes in sales or inventory. The following may be useful ratios for statement of cash flows analysis:

a. Cash from operations compared to sales.

b. Cash from operations compared to accounts receivable.

c. Cash from operations compared to income from operations.

d. Cash from operations compared to inventory.

e. Total debt compared to cash from operations.

f. Cash from operations compared to debt payments (long and short term), operations asset purchases plus dividends paid, and individually, debt payments, asset purchases, and dividends paid compared to cash from operations.

6. Compare the financial statements or other pertinent information to another source that is comparable and more likely to be reliable. For example, tax return information, if available, may be a more reliable indication of sales and expenses than the financial statements because the business would be interested in keeping taxable income low.

7. Determine whether accounts receivable turnover is slowing down or whether accounts receivable is growing faster than sales.

8. Determine whether inventory turnover is slowing down or whether inventories are growing faster than sales.

9. Investigate whether employee turnover is unusually high in any particular department or within any broad authority level, such as mid- or upper-management.

10. Investigate whether the business has a history of changing audit firms, has recently changed audit firms, or has had disputes with its auditors.

11. Investigate transactions with related parties, subsidiaries, or affiliates.

12. Determine whether the business engages in transactions that require appraisals or valuations for reporting purposes.
13. Investigate whether insider purchases or sales of the corporation's securities are unusually high or low.
14. Determine whether the business has adequate working capital.
15. Determine whether the quality of receivables is deteriorating based on an aging of receivables.
16. Determine whether inventories are increasing in comparison to normal cost of goods sold ratios.
17. Have sales incentive programs become unreasonably liberal?
18. Have sales returns or credits increased, especially after the end of the accounting period?
19. Investigate the business's off-balance-sheet financing.
20. Determine whether the business is engaged in industry or business areas or has assets that are highly susceptible to contingent liabilities.

SENIOR MANAGER ACCOUNTING KNOWLEDGE

The provisions of the Federal Deposit Insurance Corporation Improvement Act of 1991 require, with respect to depository institutions, that the audit committee include members with banking or related financial management expertise. Other than that, no statute or case specifically holds that a senior manager is required to have particular accounting knowledge; that is, specific skills is not a legal requirement for being a director, officer, or other senior manager. However, a reasonable level of accounting knowledge will help the senior manager evaluate accounting and financial information. As a guide, but not based on any particular authority, it may be useful for nonaudit committee directors and other nondirector senior managers involved in the accounting function to obtain at least a background accounting knowledge that is commensurate with beginning college-level accounting material. It would be more useful if those persons obtained background accounting knowledge commensurate with college-level intermediate accounting, and college-level managerial accounting or beginning finance. It also would be useful if nonaudit committee directors and other nondirector senior managers involved in the accounting functions obtained background accounting knowledge of the specific accounting pronouncements and practices that are peculiar to the specific industry in which their business operates. A director on the audit committee should have an adequate understanding of both accounting and auditing; that is, GAAP, Generally Accepted Auditing Standards (GAAS), and specific industry standards.

CHAPTER 3

FINANCIAL DISCLOSURES, MISREPRESENTATIONS, AND OMISSIONS

CHAPTER OBJECTIVE: To explain financial disclosure requirements, including when disclosures must or may be made; what to disclose; manner or method of disclosure; and when and how the withholding of information is permissible.

Many financial statement disclosures are specifically required by accounting and securities rules and pronouncements that explain in detail and specificity what information must be disclosed. Those disclosures are relatively easy to comply with. This chapter discusses the more difficult determination of whether information must be disclosed because it is material to the financial statements or financial presentation of the business, although disclosure of that information is not specifically addressed by rules or pronouncements. The disclosure of information discussed in this chapter requires a greater amount of subjective analysis in conjunction with knowledge of SEC pronouncements and judicial holdings. Unfortunately for the senior manager, whether or not disclosure is required and the proper manner and amount of disclosure are often only finally decided by the SEC or a court of law subsequent to an after-the-fact investigation or complaint. Nevertheless, the SEC and courts have made it clear that businesses will be required to give greater attention to the disclosure of "material" information as this interesting area of law and accounting continues to develop.

Significant portions of the information businesses disclose relate to financial or accounting matters. This chapter outlines principles relating to financial and accounting information disclosures, with emphasis on federal securities laws requirements. In general, management should consider (1) whether the information is material, other than of preliminary negotiations, or "soft" in nature; (2) whether there is a duty to disclose; (3) the means of disclosure if disclosure is required or is voluntarily or mistakenly made; (4) what information to disclose; (5) how to respond to rumors; and (6) how to respond to inquiries. The outline provided at the end of the following securities law disclosure section illustrates a suggested decision process that may be useful when determining what information to disclose and when and how to disclose it.

SECURITIES LAW DISCLOSURE REQUIREMENTS

Securities transactions, disclosures, and reporting requirements are regulated under both federal and state law. This chapter emphasizes federal regulation. The SEC is primarily responsible for enforcement and administration of federal securities laws. The discussion in this chapter covers relevant portions of the federal Securities Act of 1933 and the Securities Exchange Act of 1934. The two acts generally regulate public offerings of securities and trading in securities that are already issued and outstanding.

Federal securities laws generally prohibit the making of an untrue statement of a material fact, or the omitting of a statement of a material fact that causes other statements or the circumstances to be misleading. For example, it has been held that Rule 10b-5 prohibits statements that convey false impressions; half truths that misleadingly describe some facts but fail to disclose other necessary facts; statements that are not understandable; and statements that are unclear and hence are interpreted incorrectly. However, even if it is justified that information not be released, insiders, aiders, abettors, tippers, and tippees with knowledge of inside—that is, material and nonpublic—information may be liable if they are connected or associated with securities that are traded prior to adequate disclosure of that information.[5] A person receiving inside information in the course of business is an insider. Disclosure of inside information in the course of the company's business generally does not constitute tipping and is permissible. However, liability may be found if the person transmitting the inside information knows or should know, at the time he or she passes the inside information to the recipient, that the recipient probably will tip or trade on the basis of that information.

While certain of the authorities discussed in this chapter appear to state explicitly which financial information must be disclosed and which information need not be disclosed, the senior manager should always be aware that generally in all circumstances federal securities laws require, in addition to that information explicitly specified, disclosure of all additional *material* information that may be necessary to make the required statements not misleading. Information about which disclosure is required generally need be given only insofar as it is known or is reasonably available and can be obtained or developed without unreasonable effort or expense. However, if the required information is not known and cannot be obtained or developed, the business may also be required to so state in appropriate circumstances.

Regulation S-K

Regulation S-K generally governs nonfinancial statement information required to be included in securities registration statements, annual reports, and proxy and information statements. Selected provisions of Regulation S-K are discussed below. A copy of the current text of Regulation S-K is attached as Appendix A. A copy of the current text of Regulation S-B is attached as Appendix B. For the purpose of this guide, the pertinent provisions of Regulations S-K and S-B contain similar reporting requirements, but Regulation S-B applies to "small business issues" that are generally defined as United States or Canadian companies with revenue less than $25,000,000 and whose outstanding securities have a total market value less than $25,000,000. There are many other federal securities forms the senior manager may decide to review to obtain an overview of federal securities reporting requirements. Those forms include, but are not limited to, Form S-1, federal registration of securities under the 1933 Securities Act; Form 10-K, pertaining to federal submission of an annual report; Form 10-Q, pertaining to the federal submission of a quarterly report; Form SB-2, federal registration of securities under the 1933 Securities Act for small-business issuers; Form 10-KSB, pertaining to the federal submission of an annual report for small-business issuers; Form 10-QSB, pertaining to the federal submission of a quarterly report for small-business issuers; Form 10-SB, federal registration of securities under the 1934 Securities Exchange Act for small business; federal Schedule 13E-3, pertaining to certain transactions such as 1933 Act securities registrations and tender offers (see Item 9 in Schedule 13E-3, pertaining to opinions and appraisals); federal Schedule 13E-4, pertaining to issue tender offers; and federal Schedule 14A, pertaining to proxies.

Item 101—General Business Development
Item 101 variously requires description of (1) the general business development of the company during the past five years, and for earlier periods if material to an understanding of the general development of the business,

and (2) industry segments and foreign and domestic operations of the business during the past three years. Areas of description may include at least the following:

1. Revenues, expenses, operating losses, and profits.
2. Acquisitions and dispositions.
3. Mergers, consolidations, and reclassifications.
4. The near-term plan of operation, including anticipated material acquisition or budget requirements and dispositions.
5. Principal products and services, including for those products and services the status of development, markets, orders and customers, inventory and sources of materials, and competitive business conditions.

Item 103—Legal Proceedings
Item 103 requires description of any material pending legal proceedings, other than routine litigation incident to the business. A proceeding generally is material if the amounts involved (plus the amounts in related proceedings involving the same legal and factual issues) exceed 10 percent of the value of the current assets of the business. However, the business should also evaluate whether a proceeding involving an amount equal to less than 10 percent of the value of its current assets may be material in light of the circumstances, and, thus, may require disclosure. See the discussion later in this chapter pertaining to facts that are material.

Item 301—Selected Financial Data
Item 301 requires disclosure of selected financial data in comparative columnar form for at least the past five years, and additional years when necessary to keep the information from being misleading. The purpose of the data is to highlight significant trends in financial condition and results of operations. Areas in which disclosure of financial information is required generally include, but in circumstances are more extensive than, those areas mentioned above relating to Items 101 and 103. Disclosure generally should also be made of material uncertainties that might cause the data reflected not to be indicative of the future financial condition or results of operations.

Item 303—MD&A
Item 303, Management's Discussion and Analysis of Financial Condition and Results of Operations (MD&A), requires discussion of the business's

financial condition, changes in financial condition, and results of operations primarily with respect to liquidity, capital resources, and results of operations, but also including other information that management believes to be necessary to an understanding of the financial condition and results of operations. The SEC has determined that this narrative explanation is needed because numerical presentations may not be sufficient for an investor to judge the quality of earnings and the likelihood that past performance is indicative of future performance. MD&A is intended to give the investor an opportunity to look at the business through the eyes of management by providing short- and long-term analysis of the business.

Discussion and analysis is required of the financial statements and other statistical data that the business believes will enhance a reader's understanding of the business's financial condition. Such information should focus specifically on material events and uncertainties known to management that would cause reported financial information not to be indicative of future operations (e.g., past events that are not expected to have an impact on future operations, and expected future events that have not had an impact on past operations).

With respect to liquidity—that is, the ability of the business to raise cash—the business is generally required to identify any known trends, demands, commitments, events, or uncertainties that will result in or that are reasonably likely to result in liquidity materially increasing or decreasing, and, if a decrease is identified, the action the business has taken or proposes to take to remedy the deficiency. Those discussions essentially relate to amounts and certainty of cash flows. They should consider short- and long-term sources of, and needs for, capital, which may include, but are not limited to, significant balloon payments, payments due on long-term obligations, demands and commitments (including off-balance-sheet financing), and material payments to be incurred beyond the next 12 months, as well as proposed resources of funding required to satisfy those obligations.

With respect to capital resources, the business is generally required to disclose material commitments for capital expenditures and anticipated sources of funds needed to satisfy those expenditures, and to describe any known material trends in the business's capital resources. Those discussions should generally include expected material changes in the mix and relative cost of resources, and changes between equity, debt, and any off-balance-sheet financing arrangements (e.g., certain leases).

With respect to results of operations, the business is generally required to describe unusual or infrequent events or transactions or significant economic changes that materially affected the amount of reported income from continuing operations, any other significant components of revenues or expenses that the business believes should be described in order to understand the business's results of operations, and any known trends or uncertainties, including competitive business trends, that have had or that the business reasonably expects will have favorable or unfavorable material impact on net sales, revenues, costs, or income from continuing operations. The business may also be required to discuss the impact of inflation and changing prices on net sales, revenues, and income from operations.

Disclosure is required of currently known trends, events and uncertainties that are reasonably expected to have material effects—a disclosure duty generally exists when a trend, demand, commitment, event, or uncertainty is presently known to management and reasonably likely to have material effects on the business's financial condition or results of operation. In contrast, *optional* forward-looking disclosures (projections or forecasts) involve anticipating future trends or events or anticipating less predictable impacts of known events, trends, or uncertainties. The projection safe harbor rule, discussed later in this chapter, applies to required statements concerning the future effect of known trends, demands, commitments, events, or uncertainties, as well as to optional forward-looking statements.

When a trend, demand, commitment, event, or uncertainty is known, management should assess whether the trend, demand, commitment, event, or uncertainty is reasonably likely to occur. If not, disclosure generally is not required. Alternatively, disclosure is generally required if the occurrence is reasonably likely, unless management determines that a material effect on the business's financial condition or results of operations is not reasonably likely to occur. The SEC has indicated that when it investigates a material change in financial condition or results of operations, it will review the matter to determine whether the business failed to discuss a known trend, demand, commitment, event, or uncertainty in a prior period.

In a significant March 1992 ruling,[6] the SEC sent a message that MD&As will be carefully analyzed and that the SEC may bring an action even when there is no evidence of an attempt to deceive or misguide the public. In the March ruling, the SEC determined that a parent corporation (corporation) should have disclosed future uncertainties regarding the operations of its Brazilian subsidiary and the risk that the corporation could have materially lower earning as a result of that uncertainty. More noteworthy, the SEC also held that there was insufficient disclosure of the impact of the subsidiary on the corporation's overall operations. The corporation disclosed combined Latin American sales growth and noted uncertainty regarding the Brazilian economy due to potential postelection policies and inflation. The SEC held that accounting standards did not require separate disclosure of the subsidiary's financial information as an industry segment but, nevertheless, the magnitude of the subsidiary's contribution to the corporation's overall earnings (approximately 23 percent of consolidated net profits but only 5 percent of consolidated revenues) should have been disclosed because the subsidiary's earnings materially affected the corporation's income from operations. The SEC also held that the corporation should have discussed significant components of the subsidiary's revenues, including currency translation gains, export subsidies, interest income, and Brazilian tax loss carryforwards.

In a recent SEC Accounting and Auditing Enforcement Release relating in part to an MD&A section disclosure that the business's investments in high-yield/high-risk obligations would have no material adverse effects, the SEC held that such a disclosure was improper and failed to take into account the charges to income that the business should have accrued for other than temporary declines in value incurred by securities held by the business.[7] (See also discussion of investments—debt and equity securities—in Chapter 6.)

Regulation S-X

Whereas Regulation S-K governs nonfinancial information, Regulation S-X generally governs financial information required to be included in securities registration statements, annual reports, and proxy and information statements. Although Regulation S-X is extensive, for the purpose of this guide only the provisions relating to pro forma financial information are discussed. Section 210.11-01 of Regulation S-X requires that pro forma, or projected, financial information be furnished in certain situations. Those situations generally include significant real estate or business combinations, purchases, distributions, or reclassifications, and consummation of other events or transactions that have occurred or become probable and for which information would be material to investors. The pro forma information should also include a description of the transaction and an explanation of what the pro forma presentation shows. Generally, for the period covered by the financial statements, pro forma financial statements do not report the operations of a segment that has been discontinued, extraordinary items, or the cumulative effects of accounting changes. For purchase transactions, pro forma adjustments include financial information as if the transaction had occurred at the beginning of the financial reporting period. On occasion, it may be necessary to disclose pro forma information for multiple years.

Rules 11-01 and 11-03 allow the filing of a financial forecast in lieu of required pro forma information, except when GAAP requires the filing of a pro forma statement. The forecast should be prepared with the same degree of detail that would have been required if pro forma statements had been prepared, and assumptions used in the forecast should generally be disclosed.

Environmental Disclosures

Accounting for liabilities, contingent liabilities, and expenditures relating to environmental laws is receiving specific and increasing attention because of the potentially large dollar amounts involved and the difficulty of estimating possible damages. There is indication that environmental disclosures, or the lack of those disclosures or adequate valuation, will be receiving increased SEC scrutiny and investigation.[8] Items 101 and 103 require description of contingent liabilities that may arise from environmental laws. Item 303 MD&A also may require disclosure in circumstances in which disclosure is not required under Items 101 or 103.

Item 101 requires discussion of the material effects that compliance with federal, state, and local provisions that have been enacted or adopted regulating the discharge of materials into the environment, or otherwise relating to the protection of the environment, may have on capital expenditures, earnings, and the competitive position of the business for the remainder of the business's current fiscal year, its succeeding fiscal year, and for further periods as the business may deem material. Thus, in addition to recording current and next succeeding fiscal year contingent environmental liabilities, if management has estimates suggesting that after the two-year period there will remain material capital expenditures necessary to comply with environmental requirements, disclosure of those estimates may be required. Further, if management has reason to believe that material expenditures will be necessary after the two-year period, but does not have estimates of those expenditures, management may be required to develop and disclose expenditure estimates. Those estimates may involve contingencies to which AICPA Statement of Financial Accounting Standards 5, Accounting for Contingencies, would apply (see also the discussion in Chapter 6 relating to contingencies), and also may require management to disclose the sources of its estimates, the assumptions and methods used in reaching the estimates, and the extent of uncertainty that projected future costs may occur.

It appears that a material contingent environmental liability should be recorded regardless of whether it is possible to estimate an insurance recovery. Thereafter, any contingent insurance recovery should be separately evaluated as probable, in which case the estimated recovery will be accrued separate from the liability; as reasonably possible, in which case the estimated recovery will be disclosed but not accrued; or as remote, in which case the estimated recovery will not be accrued or disclosed.

Item 103, relating to legal proceedings, requires disclosure of all legal proceedings, whether administrative or judicial, arising under federal, state, or local provisions that have been enacted or adopted regulating the discharge of materials into the environment or primarily for the purpose of protecting the environment if (1) the proceeding is material to the business or financial condition of the business; (2) the potential damages, costs, or liabilities involved exceed 10 percent of the current assets of the business; or (3) a governmental authority is a party to the proceeding (whether the proceeding is initiated by the government or not), which involves potential monetary sanctions, unless the business reasonably believes possible aggregate sanctions arising from all related matters will total less than $100,000. The definition of an administrative proceeding is construed by the SEC very broadly, and may include administrative orders, whether or not there has been a "proceeding," and pending proceedings contemplated by a governmental authority. With respect to government proceedings, management may also be required to disclose the relief sought by the government, and, when applicable, to estimate the expenditure amount of pollution control equipment that is required by a governmental entity to be installed.

There is no specific requirement that a business disclose its environmental policy, but disclosure may be required if its policy approach towards compliance with environmental regulations is reasonably likely to result in substantial fines, penalties, or other material effects on the business. In that circumstance, it may be necessary for the business to disclose the likelihood and magnitude of those fines, penalties, and other material effects in order to prevent the business's disclosures relating to its business, financial statements, capital expenditures, and legal proceedings from being misleading.

SEC Financial Reporting Release No. 36 contains an example where potential environmental liability disclosure is required under Item 303 MD&A but not under Item 103. In that example, a business had been designated a potentially responsible party (PRP) by the Environmental Protection Agency. It appears that designation as a PRP will not in and of itself trigger disclosure under Item 103, but the example states that if management has knowledge of the designation, disclosure nevertheless is required when management is unable to determine that a material effect on future financial conditions or results of operations is not reasonably likely to occur. The Comprehensive Environmental Response Compensation and Liability Act of 1980 generally defines the term *PRP* as a current owner or operator of a hazardous site or facility, anyone who was previously an owner or operator of a site or facility at the time hazardous substances were disposed of thereon, and anyone who generates or transports hazardous substances disposed of on the site or facility.

Recently issued SEC Staff Accounting Bulletin (*SAB*) No. 92 (June 8, 1993) discusses several matters pertaining to accounting and disclosures relating to loss contingencies and environmental liability. Staff Accounting Bulletins are not "official" rules or interpretations of the SEC, but they are the SEC's staff's interpretations and practices used in administering securities laws disclosure requirements. In summary, SAB 92 discusses the following matters: (1) contingent liabilities and related contingent recoveries are not normally reported at net amount but shall be reported separately; (2) it may not be necessary to report the full amount of contingent joint and several liability depending on the likelihood that other joint and several parties will pay liabilities apportioned to them; (3) guidance regarding estimation of the amount of a contingent liability; (4) in limited circumstances, it may be permissible to recognize future contingent liability on a discounted present value basis if the total amount of obligation and the amount and timing of cash payments are fixed and determinable; (5) guidance regarding environmental liability disclosure requirements, both inside and outside the financial statements; and (6) treatment of site restoration, exit, and postclosure environmental liability costs. SAB 92 also refers to pertinent accounting pronouncements: AICPA Statement of Financial Accounting Standards 5; Financial Accounting Standards Board Interpretation 14; and Financial

Accounting Standards Board Emerging Issues Task Force Issue 93-5, Accounting for Environmental Liabilities.

Facts versus Conclusory Information

Disclosure of facts is required, but generally not explanations of those facts, possible conclusions or future events arising therefrom, social effects, motives, or alternative courses of action.[9] However, disclosure of bare facts alone is not sufficient when atypical facts, significant issues, or reasonably probable consequences that are not obvious to the reasonable investor are also not disclosed (e.g., when the information provided is misleading to the reasonable investor).

Facts that Are Material

The courts have attempted to develop tests and criteria as indicators of materiality. The reasonable investor or stockholder test is the test of materiality that has been applied most often. That test of materiality may generally be described as requiring disclosure of those facts where there is a substantial likelihood that a reasonable investor would consider the facts important in deciding whether to buy, sell, or trade a security, how to vote, whether to accept a tender offer, or whether to grant a proxy.[10] Issues of materiality apply to representations and misrepresentations and to the omission of disclosures. Another test of materiality that has been applied, but perhaps less often, attempts to quantify materiality by balancing the magnitude of an event against the probability that the event will occur.[11] A 1992 article cites a speech by a former SEC commissioner for the assertion that a 40 percent probability may be considered "reasonably likely."[12]

In addition to Regulation S-K, Item 103, which generally provides that at least a claim or contingency exceeding 10 percent of current assets will be considered material, the following cases provide some illustrations of what information may be considered numerically material. Any consideration of materiality requires detailed analysis.

1. An October 9 proxy statement, including interim financial statements for the three months ending June 30, was materially misleading because it did not disclose a material (25 percent) increase in inventory and a material increase in short-term debt during the quarter ending September 30.[13]

2. Tender offer material was materially misleading for failure to adequately disclose the amount of a judgment the offeror obtained against the target corporation when the amount of the judgment was equal to 10 percent of the offeror's equity.[14]

3. Failures to disclose anticipated changes in accounting method and fiscal year were material because they would result in 4 percent and 18 percent decreases in revenue and net income, respectively.[15]

4. A 5 percent reported total revenue error was not material.[16]

5. A corporation's failure to discuss in MD&A that a major customer had shut down operations was material when purchases from the customer accounted for 15 percent of the corporation's revenues and 33 percent of its income and because after the customer's purchases resumed, they were expected to be reduced by 30 to 50 percent of normal for an indefinite period.[17]

6. A company materially overstated income before taxes for various quarters and years by as little as 3 percent and as much as 61 percent in its Form 10-Q and Form 10-K reports by failing to reduce obsolete inventory to the lower of cost or market. The company's MD&A also failed to disclose material information by describing the situation as only a general reduction in inventories.[18]

7. Form 10-K and proxy materials were materially misleading when they failed to disclose that shares were repurchased by the corporation in a greenmail transaction at a 25 percent premium over market from a seller who threatened control of the company.[19]

As a general guideline, in the case of a misstatement the SEC at least will investigate the effect of that misstatement on gross profit, net income, shareholder's equity, and the specified item misstated. A misstatement of less than 5 percent of each of those criteria (e.g., a misstatement amounting to less than 5 percent of gross profit, net income, shareholder's equity and the specific item misstated) generally is not material; a misstatement of 5 percent to 10 percent may be material; and a misstatement greater than 10 percent generally is material.

For the purpose of this guide, it is relevant to briefly discuss the materiality of illegal acts or statutory violations because they are matters that may directly or indirectly relate to a business's financial/accounting posture and directly relate to the independent audit of the business (see also Chapter 4 for additional discussion). This is an unsettled area of continuing development. In keeping with the general definitions of materiality described above, illegal acts or statutory violations may be material if a material amount of business is dependent on the wrongful conduct or, although the act itself may not be material, business/economic ramifications arising from the conduct are material.[20] However, cases also have held or at least implied that, regardless of economic materiality, illegal conduct or even allegations of illegal conduct prior to indictment may be material if a reasonable investor might have considered the information important in making an investment decision.[21] One court held that information about bribery is relevant to management's competency—management's willingness to engage in activities that are probably illegal and may put the business at risk may be important factors to investors.[22] Other courts have held that in the absence of material economic impact, self-dealing, breach of fiduciary duty to the business, or specific disclosure requirements (e.g., proxy disclosure requirements relating to criminal convictions or pending criminal proceedings), information relating to management, integrity and ability need not be disclosed.[23] However, a business may open the door to liability exposure and place management practice, quality, competency, or integrity at issue when the business makes an affirmative representation about management (e.g., by making representations characterizing management as cautious, conservative, experienced, qualified, adequate or honest). Any disclosure relating to potentially illegal conduct requires careful analysis and research of the recent decisions in the relevant legal jurisdiction. Regardless of materiality, in appropriate circumstances disclosure may also be specifically required (e.g., in proxy material or with respect to information relating to management's self-dealing or breach of fiduciary duty or trust to the business).[24]

Buried Facts

The buried fact and similar emphasis doctrines apply to long or complex documents such as registration statements, tender offers, merger agreements, and some proxy statements. Pursuant to the buried fact doctrine, facts that have greater materiality shall receive greater attention, may not be located in the document where they are less likely to be noticed or to receive appropriate notice, and may not be fragmented throughout the document such that it is more difficult to assimilate or gleam the totality or importance of the information. The similar emphasis doctrine holds that a fact that is necessary to make a statement not misleading shall receive emphasis or prominence equal to the statement that it augments.

Changes in Earnings or Sales Trends

There is no set rule for determining when a sales or earning trend becomes material. For example, depending on the facts and circumstances, a one-month change in earnings may or may not be material. The determination of materiality is made by evaluating several criteria, which may include the nature of the event or events from which the earnings or sales arise, the length of the trend, outside events that may influence the earnings or sales, and the nature of the security to which the trend relates (e.g., a trend may have varying materiality to holders of corporate debt or quasi-corporate debt as compared to holders of equity securities).

Projections/Forecasts/Safe Harbor Rule

Projections and forecasts, even those that include disclaimers or warnings, are statements subject to disclosure rules. Projections and forecasts should be soundly based, qualified as necessary, conservative, and factual, and may require updating if subsequent developments are other than as originally represented. The business should believe there is a reasonable basis for a projection or forecast when it is made. Statements of subjective analysis or extrapolation are considered soft information. Examples of such soft information include opinions, motives, and intentions, or forward-looking statements like projections, estimates, and forecasts.[25] Soft information may be material—as a matter of law, it is not considered immaterial. A court will make a determination whether disclosure of soft information is required or sufficient on a case-by-case basis, weighing the potential benefit of the information to investors against potential harm such as undue reliance.[26]

   The general provisions of Regulation S-K and Item 303 specifically encourage businesses to supply forward-looking information. Forward-looking information is distinguished from presently known material information that will impact future operations, which must be disclosed. The Securities Act of 1933 Rule 175 safe harbor generally provides that a projection of revenues, income or loss, earnings per share, capital expenditures, dividends, capital structure or other financial items, a statement of management's plans and objectives for future operations, a statement of future economic performance contained in MD&A pursuant to Item 303, and disclosed statements of the assumptions relating to any of the above will not be deemed fraudulent unless shown to have been made or reaffirmed without reasonable basis or disclosed other than in good faith. Regulation S-K provides that management must have a reasonable basis for a projection. A history of operations or experience in projecting may be valid factors to consider when making a projection, but a business need not always have a history to formulate projections with a reasonable basis. Review/analysis of the basis for a projection by an outside expert may lend additional support for its reasonableness.[27] Management should take care to ascertain that the items projected are not susceptible to misleading inference through selective projection only of favorable items. Projections have traditionally been prepared for three different primary financial presentations: revenue, net income or loss, and earnings per share. Generally, it may be misleading not to include projections for at least those three items. Management should select the most appropriate period to be covered by the projection, but that period will vary depending on the circumstances. Management should also disclose when possible what, in its opinion and based on the assumptions made, is the most probable specific amount or the most reasonable range for each financial item projected.

Management should disclose the basis for and limitations of a projection. Management should generally caution investors against attributing undue certainty to a projection,[28] and disclose management's intention regarding the furnishing of updated projections and which, in management's opinion, are the assumptions most significant to the projections or are the key factors on which the financial results of the enterprise depend, especially those assumptions that may be different from what a reasonable investor would expect. Management should also consider in appropriate circumstances disclosing the accuracy or inaccuracy of previous projections made to further emphasize the limitations of the projection.

With respect to previously issued projections, management should be mindful of the responsibility to make full and prompt disclosure of material facts, both favorable and unfavorable, regarding the financial condition of the business. This responsibility may extend to situations when management knows or has reason to know that a previously disclosed projection no longer has a reasonable basis (see the discussion later in this chapter regarding corrective information). Businesses are also encouraged by the SEC not to discontinue or resume making projections in filings without a reasonable basis.

Not surprisingly, it may be argued that businesses in general do a better job of predicting favorable future developments than unfavorable ones. But realistically, and keeping in mind that predictions do not raise to the level of material known events or actions that must be disclosed, the natural tendency of almost any senior manager would be not to create concern or uncertainty that may ultimately prove to be unfounded or that may become a self-fulfilling prophecy. On the other hand, as management integrity appears to become of greater importance to shareholders, at some point that integrity must be subject to question if predictions are ultimately shown to be skewed towards the positive. It would seem reasonable for shareholders to monitor the business's forecast batting average for those forecasts both made and not made. Further, disseminating material and presumed reasonably probable unfavorable forecasts allows the business the advantage of avoiding undue shock should the unfavorable event actually occur, flexibility in selecting the manner and terminology used to disclose the forecast, and may lessen the threat of future litigation for nondisclosure or insider trading.

The following cases illustrate holdings in projection/forecast actions:

1. A forecast was materially misleading, and in light of the information available to management when the forecast was made, at least for the following reasons, management should have known it was highly improbable that the forecast would be satisfied and that substantial losses would be avoided:

  a. All prior forecasts made in that year had been materially incorrect.
  b. The unexpectedly large losses in prior quarters should have put management on notice that forecasts were risky.
  c. Conditions in the industry (e.g., availability of supplies) were uncertain and difficult to predict.
  d. Substantial and sustainable improvements in the performance of at least some of the company's divisions were required to avoid substantial losses, and the prospects of making those improvements were too uncertain to warrant the forecast.
  e. Many factors contributing to the prior quarterly losses were beyond the control of management. The court also held that the company was required to disclose the basis for the forecast and that previous earnings forecasts for the company as a whole had been incorrect.

The prospectus contained the following statement:

While it is not possible to determine when these factors will be corrected, it is expected that they will continue to affect the results of operations for the balance of the fiscal 1966. Therefore, it is very likely that net income, if any, for fiscal 1966 will be nominal.

The company argued this statement was intended to be a warning that profits, if any, would be nominal. The court held that, considering the company's positive prior year net income, the reasonable investor could interpret the statement to mean that the company thought substantial losses were improbable, and that, therefore, the statement was materially misleading.[29]

2. A second case held that a forecast was materially misleading at least because it contained earnings projections that were entirely insupportable, and failed to disclose previous losses and a change in accounting that resulted in increased earnings.[30]

3. Recently, the Ninth Circuit held that a business was not required to publicly disclose in its initial public offering prospectus negative projections that were provided at about the same time to a lender, although the prospectus contained representations that the business would generate results and earnings at least at the same levels that had been generated in the prior year.[31] In rejecting a requirement that a business publicly disclose the "whole truth," based in part on the SEC's position that forecasts (i.e., forward-looking information) need not be disclosed, the court specifically recognized a situation where business "may be called upon to make confidential projections for a variety of sound purposes where public disclosure would be harmful." The court indicated, however, that its holding would have been different if the nondisclosed projections were based on existing actual facts known by the business at the time the projections were made. However, the holding of the court is arguably contradictory in that the business was allowed to include a positive forecast in its prospectus notwithstanding the negative projection provided to the lender at the same time.

Curing/Correcting Information

Any curing/correcting information discussion really must address three different possible situations: (1) when a business discloses information that is incorrect when it is disclosed; (2) when a business discloses information that is correct at the time of disclosure but later becomes incorrect; and (3) when a third-party independent of the business discloses incorrect information about the business. The third situation is discussed later in this chapter in the section on negotiations, rumors, and inquiries.

In the first situation, when a business discloses information that is incorrect at the time of disclosure, subsequent disclosure of material information correcting the incorrect or omitted information is advisable to limit damages accruing after the correcting release, and generally is required by federal securities laws and/or stock exchange rules. For example, one court held that material misrepresentations were made when a business did not take steps to counter the effects of an erroneous press release that materially inflated earnings.[32] The wording of a correcting release should be considered in light of the totality of information contained in related prior releases, and the manner, including the method of disclosure, in which prior information was released. Care should be taken that facts stated in the correcting release that are contrary to facts stated in the original release or releases do not merely add confusion as contradictory facts. When evaluating whether information was properly disclosed, the courts will evaluate the total mix of information contained in all of the releases taken as a whole.

In the second situation, when a business discloses information that is correct at the time of disclosure but later becomes incorrect, subsequent disclosure of material new information may be required when the original information is forward looking or remains active; that is, when the original information remains relevant to investors and those investors could reasonably rely on that information. For example, one court held that a corporation was required to disclose subsequent new information contradicting prior correct information regarding its product's safety, operation, market success, and implied future market success prospects.[33]

Appraisals

Whether management is or is not prohibited from or permitted or required to disclose the results of an asset appraisal is a topic of continuing development, ambiguity, and inconsistency. The answer is often not clear and at least appears to depend on the reliability or certainty of the appraisal, the law or regulation governing the document in which disclosure is proposed, the nature of the activity, event, or transaction about which disclosure of information is proposed, and the legal jurisdiction that will govern any dispute that may arise from the disclosure or nondisclosure of the appraisal. (See also federal securities Schedule 13E-3, Item 9 pertaining to opinions and appraisals in certain transactions such as 1933 act securities registrations and tender offers.)

Appraisals are considered soft information; that is, "statements of subjective analysis or extrapolation, such as opinions, motives, and intentions, or forward looking statements like projections, estimates, and forecasts."[34] The general rule that disclosure of appraisals is discouraged, if not actually prohibited, has been modified by regulatory authority at least with respect to tender offers and proxy statements in circumstances involving issues relating to partial or entire asset or business liquidation,[35] and in certain circumstances when an issuer takes action to purchase its own securities.[36] More noteworthy, and perhaps more difficult to analyze, are the recent cases in which some circuits have held fast to the general rule that the disclosure of appraisals is at least discouraged, while other circuits have moved towards a more general test of materiality. A sampling of those cases is discussed below.

With respect to a tender offer not involving a going concern issue, the Third Circuit has held:

> Henceforth, the law is not that asset appraisals are, as a matter of law, immaterial. Rather, in appropriate cases, such information must be disclosed. Courts should ascertain the duty to disclose asset valuations and other soft information on a case by case basis, by weighing the potential aid such information will give a shareholder against the potential harm, such as undue reliance, if the information is released with a proper cautionary note.
>
> The factors a court must consider in making such a determination are: the facts upon which the information is based; the qualifications of those who prepared or compiled it; the purpose for which the information was originally intended; its relevance to the stockholders' impending decision; the degree of subjectivity or bias reflected in its preparation; the degree that the information is unique; and the availability to the investor of other more reliable sources of information.[37]

The first circuit, in a 1984 case,[38] held, at a time when the SEC policy was to discourage disclosures, that management was not required "to include speculations about future profitability in proxy statements" (i.e., projection of future income). A more recent 1990 district court case from Rhode Island followed the Third Circuit reasoning discussed above."[39]

With respect to a tender offer bid, the Sixth Circuit has held that:

1. A cause of action under Rule 10b-5 first requires the establishment of a duty to speak.
2. The duty is imposed only with respect to material facts.

The court held that "soft information such as asset appraisals and projections must be disclosed only if the reported values are virtually as certain as hard facts''; that is, ''[a]n example is when the predictions in fact state a fixed plan of corporate activity.''[40] The court also held that a duty to disclose the possible terms of any transaction arises only after an agreement in principal, regarding the fundamental terms as price and structure, has been reached.[41]

The Second Circuit has held, in a case that was determined in part based on the position of the SEC prior to its mid-1970s reversal of the policy discouraging forecasts, that a corporation was not liable for failing to disclose market value appraisals in a proxy statement relating to the approval of a merger.[42] However, a more recent district court decision from the Southern District of New York held on a motion to dismiss that:

1. The court could not hold that as a matter of law the failure to disclose an appraisal is immaterial.
2. In general, reliable information going to the financial conditions of a business must be disclosed, especially if the same material or equally available material is not otherwise available.[43]

A recent decision of the Tenth Circuit,[44] following a decision of the Fifth Circuit,[45] held that disclosure of soft information such as appraisals may be required on a case-by-case basis, depending on the nature of the predicative information and its importance, reliability, and investor impact.

Ninth circuit decisions from the early 1980s hold that there is no requirement that financial projections be disclosed, at least when there is no evidence that the estimates at issue were made with reasonable certainty,[46] and that there is no requirement that appraisals be disclosed, at least when the appraisals are ''neither based on objective, reasonable certain data nor prepared by a qualified expert.''[47] However, more recent cases clearly appear to leave the question open as to whether material, reliable appraisals need to be disclosed in light of the SEC's forecast policy reversal.[48] Thus, the Ninth Circuit arguably appears undecided whether disclosure of at least certain appraisals may be required in specific circumstances.

Negotiations/Rumors/Inquiries

Issues relating to the disclosure of negotiations and responding to rumors or inquiries require knowledge and analysis of most or all of the primary disclosure issues discussed above. For that reason, the following discussion serves as a review of many of the other disclosure-related discussions in this guide. Analysis of these issues often requires greater subjective reasoning because (1) the opinions or holdings of the three primary rule-making entities—the courts, the SEC, and the exchanges—conflict regarding allowable disclosure or nondisclosure; and (2) often, it is not clear whether information is material, has been leaked by the business, or is merely preliminary in nature.

The general view is that the federal securities laws impose no requirement that a corporation continuously disclose information—a duty to speak must exist or a corporation must voluntarily or mistakenly disclose information before there is a requirement that the corporation disclose all material information necessary to make the statements made not misleading.[49] The exchanges generally require prompt disclosure of material information,[50] but an individual has no private cause of action based on violation of exchange rules.[51] Disclosure generally is necessary as specified by required filings and reports, in the circumstance of a special relationship, such as company or insider trading, and when there is a partial leak of material nonpublic information by the business.[52]

If the disclosure of information is required, the business must determine the appropriate means and place of disclosure (e.g., required disclosure in a filing does not necessarily require similar disclosure to the press).[53] If the disclosure of information is required or is voluntarily or mistakenly made, the information disclosed must be materially complete and accurate.[54] Facts that are not material generally need not be disclosed;[55] however, such a determination requires an assessment of materiality. If disclosure is required, generally only the disclosure of facts is required, but not the disclosure of projections, opinions, or interpretations unless otherwise specifically required.[56] The disclosure of information in and by itself does not appear to make that information material.[57]

If disclosure of information is required or is voluntarily or mistakenly made, disclosure of preliminary negations is generally not required;[58] however, such a determination requires an assessment of the progress of the negotiations.[59] It generally has been held that negotiations at least cease to be preliminary when an agreement in principle has been reached (i.e., an agreement as to price and structure).[60] However, negotiations may cease to be preliminary at an earlier time (e.g., in merger of acquisition situations), depending on the magnitude of the proposed transactions and the likelihood the transaction will occur.[61]

Thus, a business needs to evaluate whether nonpublic information is material and other than of preliminary negotiations, whether there is a duty to disclose such as in the case of insider or company trading or in the case of a required filing or report, whether there has been a partial leak of the information by the business, and the required means or place of disclosure, if any.

The general view is that a business need not respond or reply to rumors made by third parties unless the rumors can be attributed to the business or insiders.[62] However, silence or inaction by the business with respect to incorrect third-party rumors may justify a cause of action against the business when the business has some relationship, association, or interaction with the third party or takes some affirmative action that assists or encourages the rumor.[63]

Finally, management needs to consider how to respond to an inquiry by a third party regarding developments or unusual business or stock activity. The holdings of the various authorities are split in this area. It generally appears permissible for a business to reply "no comment" if nonpublic information is not material and is not related to an agreement in principle, the corporation or insiders are not trading in the corporation's stock, and the information is not a rumor or other disclosure attributed to the corporation.[64] The exchanges generally allow a business to issue a reply statement that the business knows of no corporate developments to account for unusual market activity when there is an indication that information regarding developments has not leaked out and there is no insider trading.[65] A similar approach has been adopted by some courts.[66] However, as stated above, if a business decides to provide information, the information provided must be materially correct. Accordingly, the SEC has taken a position contrary to the position of the exchanges. The SEC has held that when material nonpublic information does exist, a statement that the business does not know of any corporate developments to account for unusual market activity may be materially misleading if the business does not disclose the relevant nonpublic information. In one case, the SEC held that it was materially misleading to reply to an inquiry with a "no corporate developments" statement when there had been several meetings or conversations between the business's senior management and senior management of the prospective acquiring corporation, there had been press rumors, and a significant shareholder had expressed his interest in selling his shares.[67] The Supreme Court has at least suggested that the SEC's approach with respect to "no corporate development" statements is appropriate when material nonpublic information exists but has not been disclosed; that is, that a "no corporate development" statement would not be appropriate in that circumstance.[68]

The following outline may be considered when a business is analyzing a disclosure issue:

1. Is the nonpublic information material?
2. Is the information other than of preliminary negotiations?
3. Is the information soft (e.g., opinions, forecasts, projections, or appraisals), requiring greater consideration prior to possible disclosure?
4. Is there a duty of disclosure by the business or an insider (e.g., is there a required filing or report), will there be insider or corporate trading, or has there been a partial leak of the information by the business?
5. If disclosure is required, by what means and when is disclosure required?
6. Does the business want to voluntarily disclose the information?
7. If disclosure is made, was it a full and accurate disclosure of all relevant material nonpublic factual information?
8. How should the business respond to rumors (e.g., by "no comment," "no corporate development," or voluntary disclosure)?
9. How should the business respond to inquiries (e.g., by "no comment," "no corporate development," or voluntary disclosure)?

The business should seriously consider having only one spokesperson. That person should be kept up-to-date. Disclosures should be planned and determined by a committee of senior management and directors. The business should keep a record of all disclosures. The business should strive to disclose material information, whether that information is good or bad. Careful analysis should be made in those circumstances when nondisclosure of material information is considered.

STOCK EXCHANGE DISCLOSURE REQUIREMENTS

In some circumstances, the disclosure requirements of the major exchanges may be more stringent, and generally are more specific, than some of the statutory federal securities disclosure requirements. The New

York Stock Exchange (NYSE) requires listed companies to quickly release all material information to the public, and also to act promptly to dispel unfounded rumors that result in unusual market activity or price variations.[69] However, when the release of information would endanger the company's goals or provide information helpful to a competitor, the NYSE rules state that the company should also weigh the fairness to the present and potential stockholders. The NYSE requires that a statement be sufficiently defined to allow the public to reasonably evaluate the matter. The NYSE generally requires information to be released to Dow Jones, Reuters Economic Services, the Associated Press, United Press International, and at least one New York City newspaper of general circulation.

The American Stock Exchange (AMEX) also requires prompt release of material information, with possible exceptions when the release would prejudice the company's ability to pursue its corporate objectives or the situation is subject to rapid change and is expected to resolve itself in the near future.[70] The AMEX requires that a release contain sufficient quantitative information to allow investors to evaluate its relative importance; use language laypeople can understand; if applicable, explain why effects cannot be assessed; and be factual, or point out reasonable alternative interpretations when the release interprets the disclosed information.

Similarly, issuers of securities traded on the National Association of Securities Dealers, Inc. Automated Quotations (NASDAQ) system are also required to promptly disclose material information.[71]

CHAPTER 4

THE AUDIT COMMITTEE: WORKING WITH CPAs

CHAPTER OBJECTIVE 1: To explain the activities, responsibilities, and limitations of the audit committee.

CHAPTER OBJECTIVE 2: To describe the role of the independent auditors, how they interact with business management, and general independent accountant standards of care.

The services of independent auditors and work of the audit committee are not panaceas for the various maladies that may affect an organization, such as improper accounting systems, bad business decisions, negligence, gross negligence, or fraud. The independent auditors' opinion, within its materiality parameters, lends substantial credence to, but does not guarantee the correctness or integrity of, the entire accounting system. Similarly, although the work of the audit committee may be extremely valuable, the committee is subject to the oversight of the entire board of directors, and the board cannot unreasonably delegate or abandon its responsibility to the committee.

To understand the function of the audit committee, it is useful to review the function of the board of directors. In general, the board of directors may call special meetings of the shareholders; tends to the selection or succession of board members; selects and removes officers; approves mergers, significant acquisitions, consolidations, the sale or disposition of significant corporate assets, and dissolution of the corporation; declares dividends; makes, alters, or repeals bylaws; fixes their own compensation; establishes committees; reviews and approves basic corporate objectives and strategic plans, including business and social objectives and plans; evaluates management's performance; and monitors the performance of the business and the business's compliance with laws.

Creation of an audit committee is generally not required by state or federal law, including regulations of the SEC. However, other rules or regulations often require a business to have an audit committee. For example, the Federal Deposit Insurance Corporation Improvement Act of 1991 requires each depository institution regulated under the act to have an independent audit committee,[72] and the NYSE requires each listed company to have an audit committee comprised solely of directors, each of whom is independent of management and free from any relationships that in the opinion of the corporation's board of directors would interfere with the exercise of independent judgment by the committee member. NYSE rules permit a former officer to be a member of the audit committee if the board determines that person will exercise independent judgment and will materially assist the function of the committee; however, the majority of the committee must be composed of directors who were not formerly officers of the business or its subsidiaries.

As stated above, the audit committee is a subcommittee subject to the oversight of the entire board of directors—the board cannot unreasonably abdicate its responsibility to the committee. Accordingly, the board should exercise care in selecting members of the audit committee; that is, the members should have sufficient, preferably extensive, auditing and accounting qualifications, and presumably should also have relevant business or industry experience. Directors who are not members of the audit committee can rely on reports of the committee only if the nonmember directors reasonably believe the committee warrants confidence—nonmember directors should be familiar with the activities of the audit committee to ensure some basis for confidence in the committee. Generally, the audit committee performs the following functions:

1. Selects the independent auditors.
2. Actively oversees the accounting and financial reporting policies and practices of the organization.
3. Reviews financial statements and may review significant financial press releases prior to issuance.
4. Provides a direct line of communication between the internal auditors and the board of directors (e.g., conducts meetings with the internal auditors, reviews the internal audit report, and attends to the operations of the accounting system).
5. Provides a direct line of communication between the independent auditors and the board of directors, without management interference (e.g., conducts meetings with the independent auditors and reviews reports of the auditors, including—but not limited to—

the audited financial statements, management letter, and reports specially requested by the directors).

In addition to attesting to the conformity of the organization's financial reports, pursuant to the AICPA Statements on Auditing Standards, the independent auditors are required to discuss at least the following matters with the audit committee (or, if there is no audit committee, with those persons on the board who have responsibility for oversight of the financial reporting process):

1. Significant accounting policies used and their application.
2. The process used by management in formulating accounting estimates.
3. Adjustments arising from the audit.
4. Disagreements with management, whether or not resolved.
5. Major issues discussed with management.
6. Internal control.
7. Errors (unintentional mistakes) and irregularities (intentional misstatements, omissions, or fraud)—the audit must include tests designed to detect errors and irregularities that are material to the financial statements.
8. Illegal acts that come to the auditors' attention. Although normally, an audit performed in accordance with GAAS does not include audit procedures specifically designed to detect illegal acts, the auditors are charged with attesting to all items that have a direct and material effect on the financial statements, including illegal acts. Pursuant to SAS 54, for disclosure purposes, the materiality of an illegal act should be evaluated in the same manner as other loss contingencies, which are discussed in Chapter 6 (See also Chapter 3, Facts that Are Material, for a discussion of illegal acts).

At the time this book went to print, the House of Representatives and the Senate both had introduced or passed similar bills generally requiring audits to include procedures designed to (1) uncover illegal acts affecting a business's financial statements, (2) identify related-party transactions, and (3) evaluate whether there is substantial doubt about the business's ability to continue as a going concern—that is, the ability to remain in business—during the following fiscal year. Requirements (2) and (3) are not dissimilar to currently existing audit requirements. If Congress passes the act into law, it remains to be seen how and to what extent auditors are to determine whether acts discovered are illegal. Of course, the range and variation of possible illegal acts is extremely numerous. As the legislation currently exists, unless an illegal act is clearly inconsequential, the auditor is required to disclose the act to the appropriate level of management. Presumably, the auditor will not make a determination as to the illegality of an act, an analysis the auditor may not be qualified to make, or as to the financial consequence of an act, a determination that may be speculative, but will merely report the suspect act to management. If management does not take appropriate remedial action, the auditor must report the suspect act to the board of directors, and to the SEC if the board does not notify the SEC within one day. Again, it remains to be seen how an auditor will make a determination whether management has taken appropriate remedial action.

Generally, the relationship between the audit committee and the independent auditors is businesslike and amicable. However, although hired and paid by the business, independent auditors performing auditing services are technically third parties subject to obligations of independence and objectivity. The audit committee oversees the scheduling, performance, and fees of the independent accountants' audit services. On occasion, the audit committee may strongly disagree with the work proposed or performed by the independent auditors, including possible disagreement regarding application of GAAP. On those occasions, the audit committee should not necessarily adopt the position proposed by the independent auditors. It may be advisable for the committee to obtain independent opinions from other sources, or, in appropriate circumstances, to retain new auditors.

Management should be aware that certain disagreements with and reports or opinions of the independent auditors may be required to be reported to the regulatory authorities. For example, the Federal Deposit Insurance Corporation Improvement Act of 1991 provides in relevant part that an independent public accountant performing an audit who subsequently ceases to be the accountant for the depository institution shall notify the regulatory authorities. The act also provides that the depository institution shall notify the regulatory authorities of the resignation or dismissal of the institution's independent auditor or of the engagement of a new independent auditor, and the institution shall also provide the regulatory authorities with copies of any report or management letter from the institution's independent auditor. Similarly, Regulation S-K, Item 304 (see Chapter 3), requires in relevant part that a business report, at least to the SEC, the dismissal, resignation, or disengagement of its independent auditor, and of the engagement of a new independent auditor. (See also federal securities Form 8-K, Item 4, pertaining to disclosure of changes in independent accountants.) A business may also be required to report and describe disagreements with its former auditors, including disagreements resolved to the former auditors' satisfaction, and certain reports or advice provided by a new independent auditor with respect to accounting, auditing, or financial reporting issues relating to the business.

The audit committee should strive to gain a level of comfort that the audit or other engagement was reasonably performed. Thus, the audit committee should obtain from the auditors a written engagement letter that specifically outlines the procedures and services the auditors will and will not perform. The audit committee should also request recommendations from the independent auditors regarding possible improvements to the corporate accounting system. The audit committee member should inquire whether there is a public document describing the responsbilities and limitations of the committee to assist the courts in assessing whether members of the committee fulfilled their responsibilities.

ACCOUNTANT REGULATION AND STANDARDS OF CARE

A CPA is licensed by the state in which he or she practices. Thus, to a certain extent, rules governing a CPA's ethical obligations and standard of care will vary depending on the state in which he or she practices. However, national entities such as the AICPA, SEC, Financial Accounting Standards Board (FASB), and the U.S. Treasury, through the Internal Revenue Service, also enact or enforce rules and regulations that may govern or apply to a CPA or his or her conduct depending on the type of services he or she performs.

As a general rule, a CPA has a duty to exercise the ordinary skill and competence of members of the accounting profession performing similar services. A CPA performing auditing services generally discharges his or her professional obligations by complying with GAAP and GAAS, but cases have held that in certain circumstances, compliance with GAAP and GAAS will not absolve a CPA of liability. In the performance of tax services, in addition to exercising the skill and competence of members of the profession, a CPA is governed by Treasury Department Circular No. 230 and AICPA Statements on Responsibilities in Tax Practice (SRTP). Although, pursuant to the AICPA, SRTP are not enforceable standards but are intended only to provide guidance to CPAs, in practice, if SRTP are followed by members of the accounting profession they may become more than just unenforceable guidance standards. In the performance of management adviser services, a CPA is governed by AICPA Standards for Management Advisory Services (SSMAS). In the performance of certain other consulting services, such as being an expert witness or consultant, a CPA is governed by the AICPA's recently issued Standards for Consulting Services (CS).

With respect to ethical obligations, in addition to any of the above-mentioned authorities that may apply, statutes and regulations of the state in which the CPA is licensed and the AICPA Code of Professional Conduct govern the CPA's conduct. State statutes and regulations directly govern the CPA's conduct. It may be argued that, because the AICPA is only a voluntary professional organization, the AICPA Code of Professional Conduct technically only governs the conduct of members of the AICPA with respect to their membership in the AICPA. However, similar to AICPA accounting and auditing pronouncements, in practice, in the absence of contrary state authority, the AICPA Code of Professional Conduct may be cited as governing the ethical conduct of all CPAs.

CHAPTER 5

REVIEW OF AUDITING SERVICES/ REPORTS

CHAPTER OBJECTIVE: To provide a summary description of an independent auditor's services and reports.

Generally Accepted Auditing Standards (GAAS) are rules and practices adopted as guides for the independent auditors when preparing, reporting, and auditing the transactions, events, accounts, and financial records of a business. Although most GAAS are not germane to the discussions in this guide, the following discussions should be helpful to management when working with the independent auditors.

AUDITORS' UNQUALIFIED OPINION

Upon completion of the audit fieldwork, the independent auditors issue the results of the engagement in the form of a written report. The standard report or opinion contains three paragraphs:

1. The introductory paragraph states that an audit has been performed and describes the responsibilities of management and the auditors.
2. The second paragraph, the scope paragraph, states that the audit was performed in accordance with GAAS, generally describes the audit procedures performed, and concludes that there is a reasonable basis for the auditors to express an opinion on the financial statements.
3. The third paragraph, the opinion paragraph, states that the financial statements present fairly, in all material respects, the entity's financial position, results of operations, and cash flows in conformity with GAAP.

The following is an example of the standard independent auditor's report.

Board of Directors
XYZ Corporation

We have audited the accompanying balance sheets of XYZ Corporation as of December 31, 19X1 and 19X2, and the related statements of income, retained earnings, and cash flows for the years then ended. These financial statements are the responsibility of the Company's management. Our responsibility is to express an opinion on these financial statements based on our audit.

We conducted our audits in accordance with generally accepted auditing standards. Those standards require that we plan and perform the audit to obtain reasonable assurance about whether the financial statements are free of material misstatement. An audit includes examining, on a test basis, evidence supporting the amounts and disclosures in the financial statements. An audit also includes assessing the accounting principles used and significant estimates made by management, as well as evaluating the overall financial statement presentation. We believe that our audits provide a reasonable basis for our opinion.

In our opinion, the financial statements referred to above present fairly, in all material respects, the financial position of XYZ Corporation as of December 31, 19X1 and 19X2, and the results of its operations and its cash flows for the years then ended in conformity with generally accepted accounting principles.

Dated
CPA

In my opinion, the language used in the various standard auditor opinions or reports could be substantially improved by expanding the description of the services performed or not performed and by using language that is more descriptive to the nonaccountant reader.

DEPARTURE FROM THE STANDARD AUDIT REPORT

Sometimes, the auditors conclude that the issuance of the standard report is not appropriate. In that circumstance, the auditors may issue a modified opinion that nevertheless is unqualified, a qualified opinion, an adverse opinion, or disclaim an opinion. The standard unqualified opinion may still be appropriate if the effects of the departure—for example, a departure from GAAP—are not significant to the fair or material presentation of the financial statements.

A modified unqualified opinion generally states that the audit was conducted in accordance with GAAS and that the financial statements are in conformity with GAAP, except for certain limited GAAS or GAAP departures, such as uncertainties relating to going concern (i.e., the ability of the entity to remain in business, departure from an accounting principle and the auditor agrees with the departure, a change in the reporting entity, a lack of consistency with respect to accounting principles used in different periods; or a change in accounting estimates). In those circumstances, the standard unqualified audit report may be acceptable, or it may be necessary to add an explanatory paragraph to the standard unqualified report.

A qualified opinion generally states that the audit was conducted in accordance with GAAS and the financial statements are in conformity with GAAP, except for the specified and described item or matter that must be disclosed. In a qualified opinion, the effect of the departure is significant to the fair presentation of the financial statements, but does not by itself require the auditors to issue an adverse opinion or to disclaim an opinion as to the financial statements as a whole.

An adverse opinion generally states that the departure from GAAP is so material that, taken as a whole, the financial statements cannot be relied on.

The auditors should disclaim an opinion when it is impossible to collect sufficient audit evidence because the client has limited the scope of the engagement or because of other circumstances, the effects of which are sufficiently material to preclude the issuance of any opinion. For example, inadequate internal controls may preclude the issuance of an opinion.

COMPILATION REPORT

In a compilation, the accountant prepares or assists in preparing the financial statements without expressing any assurance that the statements prepared are accurate, complete, or in conformity with GAAP. A compilation is not an audit: There are no tests of transactions, balances, or financial information. Although the accountant does not express assurance of the financial statements compiled, if the accountant becomes aware of inaccurate information contained in or relating to the statements, and if the client refuses to correct the inaccuracy, the accountant should withdraw from the engagement or in appropriate circumstances may prepare a modified report.

Although it is not common knowledge, even in a compilation report an accountant impliedly expresses an opinion about aspects of the reporting entity based on information that the accountant obtained or should have obtained while completing the compilation or perhaps while performing other prior work for the reporting entity. Other information that may have been obtained or perhaps that should have been obtained typically relates to regard but omitted disclosure, contingent liabilities, going concern issues, departures from GAAP including the use of improv or unsupported estimates, internal control deficiencies and related party tranaction improprieties.

REVIEW REPORT

A review is more extensive than a compilation, but less extensive than an audit. In a review, the accountant performs sufficient inquiry and analytical procedures to state in his or her report that he or she is not aware of any material modifications that should be made to the financial statements for them to conform with GAAP. A review is not an audit: Generally, tests of underlying documentation, specific confirmations and observations, and evaluation of internal control are not required in a review. Many public accountants no longer perform review engagements because juries and courts have had difficulty understanding that the duties of an accountant issuing a review opinion are less onerous than when performing an audit.

MANAGEMENT LETTER

The independent auditors generally prepare a management letter after completion of the audit. The management letter contains the auditors' analysis and recommendations regarding the business's internal control, accounting system, and general operations based on the information the auditors obtained during and within the scope of the financial statement audit. (See also Chapter 2 regarding audit of internal control.) Management letter comments are not necessarily limited by materiality constraints. As internal control issues gain importance because of legislation such as the Foreign Corrupt Practices Act and the Federal Deposit Insurance Corporation Act of 1991, management letter comments take on greater urgency for directors and management.

OTHER REPORTS

Independent auditors often are engaged to prepare reports other than those discussed above. Those reports could include, but are not limited to, reports on financial statements prepared on a basis other than GAAP (e.g., statements prepared on the cash basis); reports regarding application of an accounting principle; special reports on internal control (e.g., reports after a specific audit of internal control); or reports for securities law purposes (e.g., comfort letters or interim financial information). (See also endnote 72 regarding reports required by the Federal Deposit Insurance Corporation Act of 1991.)

RELATED–PARTY TRANSACTIONS

Material related-party transactions should generally be disclosed on audited financial statements. As previously discussed, related-party transaction should also be addressed in the internal control function of the business. Related parties generally constitute all affiliates of an entity, including management members and their immediate families, principal owners and their immediate families, investments accounted for by the equity method, beneficial employee trusts that are managed by the management of the entity, and any party that may, or does, deal with the entity and has ownership of, control over, or can significantly influence the management or operating polices of the entity to the extent that an arm's-length transaction may not be achieved.

ESTIMATES/VALUATIONS/PROJECTIONS/FORECASTS

Estimates and valuations are often used extensively during preparation of the financial statements. Estimates and valuations may be necessary when valuing contingencies, reducing assets to fair market value, or determining asset salvage values and useful lives. Estimates and valuations should be timely and determined by competent individuals.

A financial *forecast* presents an entity's *expected* financial position, results of operations, and changes in financial position. A forecast is based on the entity's course of action it expects to take. A financial *projection* presents an entity's expected financial position, results of operations, and changes in financial position, given one or more hypothetical assumptions; that is, the entity's assumptions reflecting conditions it expects to exist and the course of action it expects to take, *given one or more hypothetical assumptions.* Although a projection based on hypothetical assumptions generally may be considered unreliable, and both forecasts and projections typically contain disclaimers, management should be careful that forecasts and projections are based on reasonable assumptions and business and financial reality.

Pursuant to AICPA Statements on Standards for Attestation Engagements, a CPA issuing an opinion on a forecast must find that the assumptions on which the forecast is based are appropriate and suitably supported (i.e., that there is a reasonable basis for the assumptions). (See Chapter 3 for more discussion about financial disclosures and projections/forecasts as they pertain to securities laws.)

CHAPTER 6

REVIEW OF ACCOUNTING PRINCIPLES

CHAPTER OBJECTIVE: To provide a concise but complete description of accounting basics/conventions and accounting principles.

The primary function of accounting is to provide quantitative financial information about economic entities and their related transactions. Accounting is an art and a science. Although rules, guides, and practices help the accountant quantify financial information, the accountant also must rely on judgment and estimates. Generally Accepted Accounting Principles (GAAP) are rules and practices adopted as guides for measuring, recording, and reporting the financial activities of a business. GAAP originate from many sources, primarily including the AICPA, the Financial Accounting Standards Board, and the SEC. Most GAAP are broadly worded so as to apply to a range of differing transactions. It is common that more than one acceptable GAAP may apply to a particular event or transaction.

CASH VERSUS ACCRUAL BASIS OF ACCOUNTING

GAAP requires that transactions be recorded by the accrual method of accounting. Under the accrual method, revenue is recognized when it is earned; that is, when entitlement to the revenue is reasonably certain (e.g., when a sale on credit is made), although the cash may not have been received. Expenses are recognized when the obligation to pay the liability or other obligation is reasonably assured or due, although actual payment may not have been made. The accrual method also attempts to match expenses incurred in earning the revenue attributed to the particular accounting period. Under the cash method, revenue is recognized when cash is actually received and expenses are recognized when payment is made.

DOUBLE–ENTRY ACCOUNTING

The accounting system is called a double-entry system because every transaction is recorded in two or more accounts such that debits equal credits. If transactions are properly recorded, in accounting terminology, debits always equal credits. Of course, the fact that debits equal credits does not necessarily mean that the correct accounts have been debited and credited. Debits and credits and their relationships to the various accounts are explained in greater detail later in this chapter.

STATEMENTS—BALANCE SHEET, INCOME, CASH FLOWS, AND CHANGES IN EQUITY

The accounting system produces three primary statements or reports: balance sheet, income statement, and statement of cash flows. The statement of changes in equity may also be considered a primary statement, although some people classify it as a supporting schedule. The balance sheet is a picture of the assets, liabilities, and equity of the entity on a specific date, the date of the balance sheet. The income statement discloses the income, expenses, and changes in retained earnings equity during a specified period of time. The statement of cash flows shows the amount of net cash provided or used by the business during a specified period of time. Changes in equity are discussed in detail later in this chapter.

The balance sheet lists three primary account classifications: assets, liabilities, and equity. The income statement lists two primary classifications: income and expenses.

Assets represent items of positive monetary value; liabilities represent debts of the entity; and equity represents the net of the assets and liabilities. Assets may be listed on the left side of the balance sheet, with liabilities listed above equity on the right side; or assets first may be listed on top, followed below by liabilities and then equity. Income is listed first, at the top of the income statement, followed below by expenses. Assets and liabilities commonly are listed as either short term or long term. A short-term asset is one that is expected to be used within one year; a short-term liability is one that is expected to be paid off within one year. All other assets and liabilities are long term.

The income statement and balance sheet present summaries of the various accounts listed therein. For each account listed, it is possible to view the numerous individual transactions—that is, the debits and credits (and documents relating to those debits and credits)—that combined together total the amounts listed on the income statement and balance sheet. Individual transactions are first recorded in journals that combine the recording of similar groups of transactions in one location (e.g., the cash receipts journal, in which all cash receipt transactions are recorded), and then the transactions are recorded in individual ledgers representing the individual accounts. When a transaction is recorded in a journal or ledger (each transaction consisting of at least one debit and one credit, and for each transaction total debits equaling total credits), the debited accounts are recorded above the credited accounts, and with respect to the columns provided for the recording of the dollar amounts, debits are recorded in the left column and credits are recorded in the right column.

Typically, financial statements report comparative balance sheets (the balance sheet for the current year, and at least for the first immediately preceding year). Comparative balance sheets allow for the comparison of the listed accounts but do not necessarily explain how those changes occurred. Beginning and ending retained earnings as reported on the balance sheet can be linked by net income as provided on the income statement. The statement of cash flows tends to complete the information supplied by the income statement and balance sheet by identifying and differentiating account balance changes and transactions that affect cash, as opposed to reporting transactions and changes that may be more intangible or "paper" related. That is, the statement of cash flows shows actual changes in the cash account balances, actual cash in and cash out, as opposed to the income statement, which is prepared on an accrual basis and does not necessarily report cash received or disbursed by the business. The usefulness of the statement of cash flows is discussed further under the fraud discussion in Chapter 2 pertaining to ratio analysis. The statement of cash flows also segregates cash flows resulting from operating activities, investment activities, and financing activities.

ACCOUNT BALANCE CONVENTIONS

Generally, asset (A) and expense accounts have debit balances; that is, increases in these accounts are represented by debit entries. Liability (L), equity (E), and income accounts have credit balances. Accordingly, since debits equal credits, in general, the debit of an asset or expense account correspondingly will cause the credit of a liability, equity, or income account. The sum of the assets will always equal the sum of the liabilities plus equity (referred to as the balance sheet equation: $A = L + E$). The equation also may be stated as follows: $E = A - L$, and $L = A - E$. The balance sheet equation works because, for any specific balance sheet date, income and expense amounts recorded on the income statement are netted together and the net amount is recorded as either an increase (credit for net income) or decrease (debit for net loss) to the equity section of the balance sheet. Thus, for any specific date, all debits and credits flow through to the balance sheet. The following pages contain example transactions and related illustrative income statement, balance sheet, and statement of cash flows. An illustrative statement of stockholders' equity is also provided later in this chapter.

EXAMPLE TRANSACTIONS AND FINANCIAL STATEMENTS

Financial statements for the following transactions are presented in this section.

	Debits	Credits
1. Cash	10,000	
Common Stock		10,000
Sold and issued 1,000 shares of no-par common stock at $10 per share.		
2. Cash	15,000	
Notes Payable		15,000
Borrowed cash with long-term note.		
3. Inventory/Merchandise	5,000	
Accounts Payable		5,000
Purchased inventory on account.		
4. Equipment	3,000	
Accounts Payable		3,000
Purchase equipment 1 on account.		
5. Equipment	2,500	
Cash		2,500
Purchase equipment 2 with cash.		
6. Salary Expense (selling and administrative)	2,000	
Cash		2,000
Paid salary.		
7. Accounts Receivable	4,000	
Sales		4,000
Sale of merchandise on account.		
8. Cash	3,000	
Accounts Receivable		3,000
Receive cash on account from sale of merchandise.		
9. Accounts Payable	5,000	
Cash		5,000
Pay for inventory purchased on account.		
10. Depreciation Expense	300	
Accumulated Depreciation		300
To record depreciation expense on equipment 1.		
11. Depreciation Expense	250	
Accumulated Depreciation		250
To record depreciation expense on equipment 2.		
12. Cash	2,350	
Accumulated Depreciation	250	
Equipment		2,500
Gain on Sale		100
To record sale of equipment 2.		
Column totals	52,650	52,650

Note: Total debits equal total credits.

Income Statement

The following income statement for the first year of operations of XYZ Company arises from the example transactions presented on the preceding pages.

XYZ COMPANY
Income Statement
For the Year Ending XX/XX/19XX

Revenue from sales		$4,000
Cost of goods sold:		
Beginning inventory	$ 0	
Plus purchases	5,000	
Less ending inventory	− 2,500	
Cost of goods sold		2,500
Gross profit from sales		$1,500
Expenses:		
Salaries (selling and administrative)	$2,000	
Depreciation	550	
Total expenses		2,550
Income from operations		$(1,050)
Other revenue		
Gain on disposal of equipment		100
Net income		$(950)

Note: Ending inventory balance is accounted for by an adjusting journal entry (adjusting journal entry not shown).

Net income, or in this case net loss, flows through to the retained earnings/deficit section of the balance sheet on the following page.

If dividends had been paid, that amount would have been listed below net income as a reduction of retained earnings below net income. Note that depending on applicable law, payment of dividends may not be legally permissible due to lack of current net income and retained earnings.

Balance Sheet

The following balance sheet arising from the example transactions presented on the preceding pages shows the assets, liabilities, and capital of XYZ Company as of the last day of its first year of operations.

XYZ COMPANY
Balance Sheet
XX/XX/19XX

Assets

Current assets:		
Cash	$20,850	
Accounts receivable	1,000	
Inventory	$2,500	
Total current assets		$24,350
Plant and equipment:		
Equipment	$3,000	
Less accumulated depreciation	300	
Total plant and equipment		2,700
Total assets		$27,050

Liabilities:

Current liabilities:	
Accounts payable	$3,000
Long-term liabilities:	
Notes payable	15,000
Total liabilities	$18,000

Equity

Common stock	$10,000
Retained earnings/(deficit)	(950)
Total equity	9,050
Total liabilities and equity	$27,050

Note: Total assets equal total liabilities plus equity.

Statement of Cash Flows

The following statement of cash flows for the first year of operations of XYZ Company arises from the example transactions presented on the preceding pages.

XYZ COMPANY
Statement of Cash Flows
For the Year Ending XX/XX/19XX

Cash flows from operating activities:		
Cash received from customers	$3,000	
Cash paid to employee salary	– 2,000	
Cash paid for inventory	– 5,000	
Net cash provided (used) by operating activities		$ – 4,000
Cash flows from investing activities:		
Purchase of equipment	$ – 2,500	
Sale of equipment	2,350	
Net cash provided (used) by investing activities		$ – 150
Cash flows from financing activities:		
Proceeds from sale of stock	$10,000	
Proceeds from long-term borrowing	15,000	
Net cash provided (used) by financing activities		$25,000
Net cash flow provided (used)		$20,850

SPECIFIC PRINCIPLES AND PRACTICES REVIEW

The following section of this guide discusses accounting for specific trans-actions and certain other significant accounting principles and practices. This chapter generally discusses accounting topics that you would expect to cover through college-level intermediate accounting. It is not possible to discuss the following topics with the degree of specificity or detail that might be expected in an accounting class. If you need a more detailed discussion, you should consult an appropriate accounting text or a person who has requisite accounting knowledge.

Many particular industries are governed by specific accounting pro-nouncements and practices that are beyond the scope of this guide. For example, in banking industry accounting, heavily dependent on accounting for loans, in addition to other auditing and accounting practices particular attention should also be paid to recently issued Statement of Financial Accounting Standards 114, requiring certain impaired loans to be valued based on the present value of expected future cash flows discounted at the loan's effective interest rate; Statement of Financial Accounting Standards 15, Troubled Debt Restructurings; Statement of Financial Accounting

Standards 66, pertaining to accounting for profit from the sale of real property; Statement of Financial Accounting Standards 5, pertaining to contingencies; various AICPA Statements of Position; various pronouncements of the Financial Accounting Standards Board Emerging Issues Task Force; various AICPA Practice Guides and Bulletins; pronouncements of the regulatory agencies, including the Federal Home Loan Bank Board; and others. The senior manager should evaluate the extent to which he or she needs to be familiar with accounting pronouncements that are particular to his or her industry.

Historic Values

Assets and liabilities are initially recorded at historic values (i.e., at the values that were present at the time the transaction originated). It has been suggested that the balance sheet reflect price-level or fair-value accounting (i.e., adjusted in accordance with a particular index or to current fair market value or replacement cost). Although balance sheet accounts are not adjusted to reflect increases in value above original cost, certain accounts are reduced when appropriate (i.e., certain assets are depreciated, inventory is carried at the lower of cost or market, marketable securities may be reduced or increased to market but not above original cost, and contra or loss accounts may be established for estimated uncollectible accounts receivable, notes receivable, or loan receivables). The senior manager should be aware that use of historic values will probably result in the balance sheet misrepresenting the current fair value of the entity. This is an area of much discussion and continuing development. Several existing pronouncements already require current value accounting or information disclosure for specific accounts, assets, or transactions. It is possible, and likely, that in the near future increased current value accounting will be required, thereby also increasing the need for estimates and appraisals.

Contingencies

A contingency is an existing situation or set of circumstances that may, through related future events, result in the acquisition or loss of an asset, or in the incurrence or avoidance of a liability. Gain contingencies generally are not recorded until they are actually realized, although they may be disclosed by footnote. (See also Accounting for Income Taxes, later in this chapter, regarding contingencies relating to anticipated tax refunds and future benefits.) Accounting for loss contingencies is based on the probability that the loss will occur. Loss contingencies arise from many different risks, some of which are the uncollectibility of receivables, loss from fire or other hazards, litigation or claims, warranties, returned items, or product defects.

Accounting for contingencies is generally regulated by AICPA Statement of Financial Accounting Standards 5 and Financial Accounting Standards Board Interpretation No. 14. (See also Chapter 3, Environmental Disclosures, for additional discussion of accounting for contingencies with emphasis on environmental contingencies and SEC and accounting regulations.) After the existence of the contingency is established, the probability of the actual loss occurring is estimated as being probable, reasonably possible, or remote. If it is estimated that the actual occurrence of the contingency is probable, and the amount of the contingency is reasonably estimable, the estimated amount of loss arising from the contingency is recorded. If it is reasonably possible the contingency will occur, or it is probable the contingency will occur but the amount of the loss is not reasonably estimable, the loss is not recorded but the financial statements should contain a disclosure describing the nature of the contingency and the estimated minimum and maximum ranges of possible loss, or a statement that no estimate of the loss can be made. Generally, no disclosure is required if occurrence of the contingency is remote. Finally, with respect to an unasserted claim (e.g., an unasserted liability claim), when there is no indication that a potential claimant is aware of the possible claim, disclosure is required if it is probable that a claim will be asserted and there is a reasonable possibility the outcome will be unfavorable.

Hierarchy of GAAP Pronouncements

In SAS 69, the AICPA recently ranked the hierarchy of GAAP, excluding SEC-related pronouncements. That ranking, from most to least prominent, is as follows:

1. FASB Statements and Interpretations, APB Opinions, and AICPA Accounting Research Bulletins.
2. FASB Technical Bulletins, AICPA Industry Audit and Accounting Guides, and AICPA Statements of Position.

3. Consensus positions of the FASB Emerging Issues Task Force and AICPA Practice Bulletins.
4. AICPA accounting interpretations, "Qs and As" published by the FASB staff, and recognized and prevalent industry practices.
5. Other accounting literature.

Completed-Contract Revenue

Because of the length of time required to complete long-term construction contracts, the question arises as to when income should be recognized. Completed-contract and percentage-of-completion generally are the two methods of revenue recognition that are considered for long-term contracts. Under the completed-contract method, income is recognized only upon completion or substantial completion of the contract. The contract is substantially complete when the remaining costs are insignificant. The primary advantage of the completed-contract method is that it is not based on estimates; the disadvantage is that it does not reflect current work performed when the contract extends over more than one accounting period. During the course of the contract, costs and generally overhead are charged or debited to the work-in-progress account, whereas billings or cash received are credited to the work-in-progress account. Losses are immediately recognized in the period they are discovered.

Percentage-of-Completion Revenue

Under the percentage-of-completion method the percentage of income currently recognized is determined by (1) estimating the percentage of estimated total income that incurred costs to date bear in relation to estimated total costs or (2) in proportion to some other reliable measure of work completed such as an engineering estimate of work completed compared to total work required under the contract. Losses are immediately recognized in the period they are discussed. The primary advantage of the percentage-of-completion method is that, with respect to uncompleted contracts, revenue is regularly recognized. The primary disadvantage is the necessity of relying on estimates.

Percentage-of-completion is preferred over completed-contract when the estimated cost to complete and extent of construction in progress are reasonably determinable. The completed-contract method is preferred when estimates are unreliable.

Installment Method of Revenue

Under the installment method of accounting, a portion of each payment received is allocated to cost recovery and the remaining portion is allocated to gross profit. The percentage is determined by the relationship of the cost, gross profit, and sale amount at the time of sale. Use of the installment method requires that separate records be kept by year and product lines for sales, accounts receivable, realized and unrealized profit, and repossessions.

Cost Recovery Revenue

The cost recovery method generally is used when the recovery of costs is questionable or undeterminable. Such a condition may occur when a purchaser has the right to return the item purchased and it is probable the item will be returned, or when the probability a contingency will occur makes income recognition questionable. Under the cost recovery method, gain is not recognized until all costs are recovered. After costs are recovered, additional amounts received are recognized as gain.

Revenue with Right of Return

Pursuant to the realization principle, revenue is earned or recognized when an exchange has taken place and collection of the sales price is reasonably assured. Transactions are often structured, by contractual agreement or industry practice, to give the purchaser a right to return the merchandise for cash, credit, or exchange. The return right may be short or long term. Revenue arising from a sale with right of return may not be recognized in a variety of circumstances. Generally, revenue is recognized when the purchaser has paid for the merchandise or has incurred a determinable obligation and a reasonable estimate can be made of the amount of future return. However, if the occurrence of the return is probable and the amount of the return can be reasonably estimated, the estimated amount of loss arising from the return must also be recorded. If the occurrence of the return is only reasonably possible or remote, the estimated amount of loss is generally not recorded, but footnote disclosure may be required.

Investments—Debt and Equity Securities

AICPA Statement of Financial Accounting Standards (SFAS) 115 (SFAS is also referred to as FASB or FAS), effective for calendar year 1994 financial statements, provides that investments in equity securities that have readily determinable fair values and investments in all debt securities (with readily determinable fair values), except those debt securities classified as held to maturity, shall be valued at fair value and classified as either trading securities (held for current sale) or securities available for sale. Unrealized holding gains and losses for trading securities are included in earnings. Unrealized gains and losses for securities classified as available for sale are excluded from earnings but reported as a net amount in a separate component of shareholders' equity. An investment in debt securities is only classified as held to maturity, and in that case measured at original or amortized cost, if the business owning the security has the positive intent and ability to hold the securities to maturity. Investments in debt securities held to maturity and investments classified as being available for sale are still valued at fair value in the circumstance of an other than temporary loss value. In that circumstance, the loss is included in earnings, with subsequent gains and losses being reported as separate components of equity, except for additional other than temporary losses, which are included in earnings.

Fair value is that amount at which a financial instrument could be exchanged in a current transaction between willing parties, other than in a forced or liquidation sale. SFAS 115 at least implies that fair value can be determined for most if not almost all securities even if it is necessary to make a reasonable estimate of value.

A debt security is any security representing a creditor relationship with an entity, including certain preferred stock, collateralized mortgage obligations, U.S. Treasury securities, municipal securities, corporate bonds, convertible debt, commercial paper, and real estate mortgage investment conduits, but not trade accounts receivables or most loans receivable arising from consumer, commercial, or real estate lending activities of financial institution unless securitized. An equity security is any security representing an ownership interest in an entity, including most common, preferred, and other capital stock.

In addition to the accounting provisions, SFAS 115 also contains provisions requiring various footnote disclosures of additional information relating to fair value, such as aggregate fair value, gross unrealized holding gains, gross unrealized holding loses, and amortized cost by major security type and maturity grouping.

Until application of SFAS 115 (application of SFAS 115 prior to the specific date of mandatory application is allowable), marketable securities held by a business that does not account for those securities by a specialized industry practice are accounted for at lower of original cost or market (i.e., fair market value or replacement cost) for changes in valuation that are considered temporary. Unrealized losses are always reported. Unrealized gains may be reported if a prior loss was reported. Unrealized gains may raise the carrying value to the original cost, but not to exceed original cost. Unrealized losses and allowable unrealized gains in current marketable securities are deducted from or added to net income, respectively. Unrealized losses and allowable unrealized gains in noncurrent marketable securities are deducted from or added to stockholders' equity, respectively. Unrealized losses that are other than temporary, even those unrealized losses in noncurrent marketable securities, are deducted from net income.

In a recent 1993 Enforcement ruling,[73] the SEC held that a business failed to accrue a loss to income for an other than temporary loss in value of securities held by the business. In that ruling, the SEC held in pertinent part that (1) the phrase ''other than temporary'' does not necessarily mean permanent but can be a lesser degree; and (2) in determining whether a decline in value is other than temporary, management should consider the length of time and extent to which market value has been less than cost, the financial condition and estimated near-term prospects of the issuer, the ability of the holder of the securities to retain the investment for a sufficient time to allow any anticipated recovery in value, and gains, losses, or changes in market value after the date of the financial statements but prior to the issuance of those statements.

Receivables—Accounts/Notes/Loans

Receivables generally are reported on financial statements at the gross amount less an estimated allowance for uncollectible accounts. The loss allowance, or contingency is recorded if it is probable that some or all of the receivables have been impaired at the date of the balance sheet and the amount of the loss can be reasonably estimated. The allowance may be estimated based on a variety of factors, which may include the historical loss experience of the entity or of similar entities, debtor ability to pay, or appraisal of economic conditions and trends. (See also the discussion under Contingencies earlier in this chapter.)

Cost Accounting

Cost accounting is often thought of as an accounting field that is separate from financial accounting. Financial accounting is described as being concerned with how accounting can serve external decision makers such as stockholders and creditors. In that sense, this guide is primarily written with a financial accounting viewpoint. Cost accounting is often described as being concerned with how accounting can serve internal decision makers such as directors, officers, and managers. Some people argue that cost accounting is essentially indistinguishable from managerial accounting. However, in a technical sense, the two may be differentiated in that cost accounting generally refers to the gathering, classifying, recording, and reporting of cost information, whereas managerial accounting primarily is concerned with planning and controlling the entity's business activities.

Actual Costs

The use of actual costs in cost accounting involves actual costs just as the name implies. There is a distinction between the use of actual costs and standard costs that will become clearer after the following discussion of standard costs. The use of actual costs can be explained by describing some of the relevant terminology.

Job-order costing involves unique or separate products for which a separate cost account is kept for each such product. Process costing involves mass production, generally on a continuous basis, such that costs are totaled and then divided by units produced to arrive at cost per unit.

Direct costs are those costs that can be directly traced to product production (e.g., materials and labor). Direct costs are allocated to the appropriate products as described above. For example, in job-order costing, direct costs are directly allocated to the various separate products, whereas in process costing, it is necessary to divide the total costs between the total units produced. Typically, in job-order and process costing, if practical, direct labor costs are directly allocated to specific products based on labor time records, whereas in process costing, materials are typically allocated based on units produced.

Indirect or overhead costs are those costs incurred during operation of the business but that cannot necessarily be directly traced to product production (e.g., factory insurance). In job-order costing, indirect costs are often allocated based on direct labor or machine hours per specific product. Since indirect costs are by their very nature not specifically incurred in the production of any one product, even in job-order costing, it is necessary to allocate those costs according to an established measurement formula. In process costing, indirect costs should also be allocated according to an established formula, typically according to floor space, labor, or machinery percentages.

Standard Costs

The application of standard costs takes actual cost allocation one step further by classifying actual costs either as anticipated costs or variances from anticipated costs. Standard costing first requires that estimations be made of the materials, labor, and overhead expected to be used or incurred in the production of a specified unit of the product.

The standard cost for material is estimated by the amount of physical material needed to produce one unit (e.g., x pounds) and the price per unit of material (e.g., $$y$ per pound). The standard cost for labor is estimated by the time necessary to produce one unit (e.g., x hours) and the cost per unit of time (e.g., $$y$ per hour). Indirect standard costs may be estimated before the fact by estimating the amount of overhead time per unit (e.g., x hours) and the cost per unit of time (e.g., $$y$ per hour of overhead), or they may be estimated after the fact first by estimating the cost of overhead per measurement unit (e.g., cost per hour of labor or per hour of machine use) and then by multiplying that cost by the hours of labor or machine use as justified at the end of the period (e.g, per day, week, or month) based on actual output.

Actual cost variances from the estimated standard costs are separately recorded from the standard costs. The total of the standard and variance costs will equal actual cost as described above. Eventually, both the total standard and variance costs will be attributed to inventory or cost of goods sold because combined they total actual costs. Standard costing, although more complicated than actual costing, is extremely useful to management because it allows for the separation of estimated costs from cost variances. Thereafter, management can determine whether or not the original cost standards were correctly estimated and whether or not the variance presents waste that should be corrected.

Activity-Based Costing

Activity-based costing (ABC) has become increasingly popular as a means of allocating costs. Generally, ABC attempts to allocate indirect costs more directly to the specific related product. Thus, for example, instead of allocating the cost of a purchasing department to products based on respective product prices or production labor, the business could identify different types of products or classifications of products, identify various functions within the purchasing department with respect to the product types or classifications, compute the costs associated with each purchasing department function, and then allocate those costs to product type or classification based on actual service provided by the purchasing department function to the respective product types or classifications. ABC obviously requires much greater cost allocation analysis but provides management with better information to analyze product profitability.

Government Contract Cost Accounting

This guide is not designed to be industry specific; however, considering the dollar magnitude of the government contracting entered into with private and quasi-private entities each year, it is appropriate to briefly note that federal government contracting is a separate and distinct accounting area. The majority of government contracts are governed by Cost Accounting Standards (CAS), Federal Acquisition Regulation (FAR), and pronouncements by the appropriate government contracting entity, (e.g., the Department of Defense). Whereas a primary GAAP objective is to match costs with revenue, CAS attempts to match allowable costs with the appropriate accounting period and project. This is so because, more frequently than not, the private or quasi-private entity receives revenue from the government based on the costs that are allocated to the project (e.g., cost-plus-fixed-fee arrangements). Accounting for government contracts should not be confused with GAAP or GAAS.

Business Combinations

Business combinations occur when the resources of one business entity are partially or completely combined with those of another business entity. There are two distinct methods for recording a combination depending on the circumstances of the transaction: the purchase method, sometimes also referred to as an acquisition, and the pooling method.

If the combination does not qualify as a pooling, it is deemed a purchase. Numerous criteria must be met before the combination will qualify as a pooling. Some of the primary criteria are:

1. Each combining business should be autonomous and not a subsidiary or division of the other within the two years prior to initiation of the plan of combination.
2. At the date of initiation and consummation of the combination, each combining business should be independent of the other, ex-

cept that an intercompany investment of 10 percent or less of the outstanding voting common stock is permissible.

3. After initiation, the combination should be completed within one year or a single transaction.

4. Upon consummation, the acquiring business issues its majority class of voting stock for not less than 90 percent of the voting common stock of the corporation being acquired.

In a purchase, the identifiable net assets are valued at fair market value, and the excess of the purchase price over that value is recorded as goodwill. Excess purchase price will frequently be allocated to assets and goodwill differently for tax and accounting purposes. In a pooling, the assets and liabilities of the acquired business are carried forward to the acquiring business at their prior recorded amounts (i.e., book value, not fair market value), no goodwill is recorded, and the excess of the purchase price over net asset and liability recorded values is allocated to the acquiring business's capital account. Only revenues of the acquired business earned after the acquisition date are attributed to the acquiring business.

Use of the pooling method is often preferred if the specific criteria can be met. Under the pooling method, since goodwill is not recognized and assets are carried at prior book value, not fair market value, it is possible that net income subsequent to the combination will be greater than under the purchase method because there is no goodwill to amortize or increased asset value to depreciate. Revenues of the acquired business are attributed to the acquiring business as if the acquired business were a subsidiary for the entire year.

Consolidated Financial Statements

Consolidated financial statements generally must be used when a parent entity directly or indirectly controls the majority voting interest (over 50 percent) of a subsidiary, unless control of the subsidiary is temporary or there is significant doubt regarding the parent entity's ability to control the subsidiary. Combined financial statements for two companies would merely list all the balance sheet account balances and income statement amounts of the two companies, regardless of the transactions that had occurred between the two entities. Consolidated financial statements report the two entities as if they were one entity. Thus, consolidated financial statements require that intercompany transactions be eliminated. For example, if two businesses are reported as one, a debt owed from one business to the other would not be reported as a debt or receivable because to do so would be akin to having the consolidated business report a debt due from itself as a receivable asset. A consolidating accounting entry would be made on the accountant's consolidated work paper to eliminate the advance from the parent to the subsidiary:

Advance from Parent Company	XXX,XXX	
Advance to Subsidiary Company		XXX,XXX

Other typical intercompany transactions that should be eliminated include balance sheet elimination of the parent business investment in the subsidiary and income statement elimination of intercompany sales, costs of goods sold, and expenses.

Inventory

Inventory typically includes the stock of materials used to produce goods for sale, partially finished goods (work in progress), and finished goods. Changes in inventory flow through to the inventory account balance on the balance sheet and the cost of goods sold calculation on the income statements. Cost of goods sold is calculated according to the following formula:

Beginning inventory	$XX.XX
Plus inventory purchases	XX.XX
Less ending inventory	XX.XX
Equal cost of goods sold	XX.XX

Inventory may be valued by several different methods that may have significantly differing effects on balance sheet value, changes in working capital, and computation of income. To determine inventory value, it is necessary to identify what items of inventory are on hand. This is so because at any one time, the business entity may have on hand several different lots of inventory item x that were purchased at different times and at different costs.

In a periodic inventory system, the inventory is physically counted at intervals that are sufficiently frequent for financial and tax reporting. A periodic system allows for the maintenance of less extensive inventory records.

In a perpetual inventory system, the inventory count is kept by regularly maintained inventory records, and each individual inventory transaction should be posted.

Specific Identification Method

Under the specific identification method, inventory cost is determined by specifically identifying the inventory items that have been purchased, are held in work in progress, or have been sold. Such an ability to specifically identify the inventory items is unusual.

First-In, First-Out (FIFO)

The FIFO method assumes that inventory purchased first is used first. Theoretically, FIFO approximates the specific identification method.

Last-In, First-Out (LIFO)

The LIFO method assumes that inventory purchased last is used first. LIFO matches current revenue with the most recently purchased inventory, thereby, arguably, eliminating gains attributed to increases in the inventory being held.

Standard Costs

Inventory may be valued at standard costs to help management identify waste variances. Ultimately, the variance should be closed to cost of goods sold and the inventory should be valued by one of the other methods described herein.

Dollar-Value LIFO

Dollar-value LIFO is a variation of LIFO that is often used when stock lines are constantly being changed (e.g., in retail businesses). A variety of inventory items are treated as a pool of dollars instead of as separate physical units. Inventory purchased in the first year is valued in cost dollars, whereas inventory purchased in later years is valued by applying a selected price index to the original costs.

Weighted-Average

Under the weighted-average method, inventory value is computed by calculating the total cost of beginning inventory plus inventory purchased during the period, dividing that total by the total number of beginning inventory units plus inventory units purchased during the period, to arrive at weighted-average cost per unit. The weighted-average cost is then applied to ending inventory units to calculate the value of ending inventory.

Moving-Average
The moving-average method is a variation of the weighted-average method in which the cost per unit of inventory is recalculated after every inventory purchase. This valuation method can only be used with a perpetual inventory system.

Retail Inventory Method
The retail method is sometimes used when a business has a great variety of inventory. The retail method is difficult to explain and is further complicated by the fact that it may be used in conjunction with other methods such as LIFO and FIFO. The calculation may also differ if the merchandise has had retail price markups or markdowns.

    The objective of the retail method is to calculate what percentage inventory cost is to retail price (generally, the retail price can be thought of as the cost price plus markup) and then to apply that percentage to ending retail-price merchandise inventory to calculate the cost value of the ending merchandise inventory. To calculate the percentage, the total cost of beginning inventory plus inventory purchases during the period is divided by the total retail value of beginning inventory plus the retail value of inventory purchased during the period. The retail value of ending inventory is then multiplied by that percentage to arrive at the cost value of ending inventory.

Example: FIFO versus LIFO

Date	Quantity Purchased	Unit Price	Total
January 5	2,000	$1.40	$2,800
April 11	1,500	1.80	2,700
June 23	4,000	1.60	6,400
September 3	3,000	2.00	6,000
December 16	2,500	2.10	5,250
Total			$23,150

Assume no beginning inventory, sales of $60,000, and ending inventory of 2,700 items.

Under FIFO, the ending inventory, comprised of 2,700 items, would be valued as follows: 2,500 items at $2.10 per item ($5,250), plus 200 items at $2.00 per item ($400), for a total ending inventory of $5,650. Gross profit under FIFO would be $42,500, as detailed below:

Sales		$60,000
Cost of goods sold:		
Beginning inventory	0	
Purchases	23,150	
Ending inventory	5,650	17,500
Gross profit		$42,500

Under LIFO, the ending inventory, comprised of 2,700 items would be valued as follows; 2,000 items at $1.40 per item ($2,800), plus 700 items at $1.80 per item ($1,260), for a total ending inventory of $4,060. Gross profit under LIFO would be $40,910, as detailed below:

Sales		$60,000
Cost of goods sold:		
Beginning inventory	0	
Purchases	23,150	
Ending inventory	4,060	19,090
Gross profit		$40,910

Under the above-presented hypothetical facts, use of FIFO resulted in greater gross profit. This is not to say that FIFO will always result in greater gross profit, only that such was the result in the above fact situation. Use of the weighted-average method generally computes a result between the amount under FIFO and the amount under LIFO.

Regardless of the inventory valuation method selected, inventory should be carried at the lower of cost or market. Accordingly, the value of inventory reported on the balance sheet should be reduced to fair market value if the fair market value is less than the original balance sheet cost amount.

Consistency is a basic accounting concept. Thus, although any one of several alternative inventory valuation methods may be adopted, once a method is adopted, change to one of the other methods is not permitted in the absence of proper authority, disclosure, and restatement of prior accounting reports and/or reporting the cumulative effect of the change on the current financial statements.

The above discussion applies only to financial inventory accounting; calculation of inventory for tax purposes may be different.

Property, Plant, and Equipment

Property, plant, and equipment are recorded at cost. Substantial improvements that increase the operating efficiency or capacity of an asset should be capitalized, not expensed. Direct costs, and certain interest costs of self-constructed fixed assets, should also be capitalized. Generally, overhead costs of self-constructed assets are not capitalized. Equipment repairs are expensed in the period incurred.

Depreciation

A fixed asset is depreciated to match revenues and expenses by systematically and rationally allocating the cost of the asset over its estimated useful life. Accumulated depreciation is listed on the balance sheet as a contra account below the asset to which it relates.

Various depreciation methods are allowable under GAAP, such as straight-line, units of production, sum-of-the-years'-digits, declining balance, and so on. Under the straight-line method, an equal amount of depreciation is expensed per year over the estimated life of the asset. Under the units of production method, depreciation is varied according to actual current period output as compared to total estimated asset lifetime capacity. Under other methods, such as sum-of-the-years'-digits and declining balance, depreciation is accelerated in the early years of an asset's estimated useful life. Different depreciation methods may be used for financial and tax purposes.

Intangible Assets and Goodwill

Intangible assets are, generally, (1) legal rights, such as patents, trademarks, service marks, trade names, copyrights, and franchises, and (2) presumed competitive advantages, such as goodwill. Intangible assets can be acquired or internally developed by the business entity. The cost of an identifiable intangible asset is amortized over the estimated useful life of the asset, not to exceed 40 years in length. Purchased goodwill, a nonidentifiable intangible asset, is also amortized over its estimated useful life, not to exceed 40 years in length. The costs of internally developed nonidentifiable intangible assets are generally completely expensed in the period incurred. Straight-line amortization should be used unless a more appropriate method can be demonstrated.

Equity Investments

An investor entity should account for an investment in the common stock of another entity when the investment, although less than controlling (i.e., less than 50 percent ownership), gives the investor the ability to exercise significant influence over the operating and financial policies of the entity that was invested in. In the absence of evidence to the contrary, the investor is presumed to have the ability to exercise significant influence over the investee with an investment of 20 percent or more of the voting stock of the investee.

There is a presumption that the investment should generally be accounted for under the cost method if the investment in the investee is less than 20 percent. Under the cost method, the investment is recorded at cost and income is recognized from dividends received out of the investee's accumulated earnings earned after the acquisition date.

Under the equity method, the investment is also recorded at cost. Thereafter, the parent entity's consolidated net income includes the parent entity's proportionate share of the net income reported by the investee as generally adjusted for certain transactions, including intercompany transactions. Since the parent entity records its proportionate share of the investee's net income, dividends received from the investee reduce the basis of the investment. Consolidation under the equity method is usually referred to as "one-line consolidation" because the investment is recorded on the balance sheet as one amount, as compared to consolidated financial statements in which actual balance sheet and income statement accounts are combined. Under the equity method, income is recorded as one amount on the income statement, except for extraordinary items and prior period adjustments.

Extraordinary Items

Net income generally includes all items of income and loss that occur during the accounting period. However, extraordinary items or transactions are separately reported on the income statement. Extraordinary items are material in nature, not expected to occur frequently, and not normally associated with the customary business results or activities of the enterprise. Examples of extraordinary items are gains or losses from the sale of discontinued items or operations, gains or losses on the retirement or restructuring of certain obligations, and certain prior period adjustments. Extraordinary items are reported separately on the income statement below net of tax income or loss from continuing operations.

Leases

From a lessee's viewpoint, leases are classified either as operating or capital leases. A capital lease is a lease in which, at least in form, transfer of ownership has occurred. Transfer of ownership has occurred if one or more of the following criteria are met:

1. Ownership of the leased property is transferred to the lessee by the end of the lease term.
2. The lease contains a bargain purchase option (i.e., the lessee has an option to purchase the leased property at a bargain price), making exercise of the option probable.
3. The lease term is equal to at least 75 percent of the useful life of the leased property.
4. At lease inception, the present value of the minimum lease payments is at least equal to 90 percent of the fair value of the leased property.

In an operating lease, the lessor carries the leased asset on its books, depreciates the leased asset, and receives lease income from the lessee. The lessee amortizes the expense of the lease payments over the period that the lessee obtains benefit from the leased property.

In a capital lease, the lessee amortizes the asset over the estimated life of the asset or the lease term. A portion of the lease payments are attributed or imputed to interest expense, the remaining portions of the lease payments are attributed to amortization, and a portion of the asset value is assigned to unamortized residual value. The lessor accounts for the lease either as a sales-type lease in which the lessor's profit is generally recorded, or a direct financing lease in which the lessor's total unearned income is amortized over the term of the lease, with a portion thereof attributed or imputed to interest income.

In addition to the amounts recorded in the financial records, lessors are generally required to make financial statement disclosures both for capital and operating leases. Similarly, lessees are generally also required to make financial statement disclosures for sales-type, direct financing, and operating leases.

The above discussion relates to lease accounting. Portions of the discussion may be significantly different for income tax purposes.

Payables—Accounts/Notes

Payables are legal obligations, or liabilities, that require the future payment of an asset or the future performance of a service. Liabilities are recorded at the cost of the asset or service that will be used to retire the liability. Liabilities are classified either as current or long term. Current liabilities are expected to be retired by current assets within one year. Examples of current liabilities are accounts payable, short-term notes payable, wages, payroll taxes, and unearned revenue in certain circumstances. Long-term liabilities are not expected to be retired within one year. Examples of long-term liabilities are mortgages or deeds of trust, certain leases, and other unconditional obligations.

Generally, an obligation is recorded as a liability when there is an actual transfer of resources, services, or obligations. Commitments for the future exchange of resources, services, or obligations are not recorded until at least part of the commitment is fulfilled. However, footnote disclosure is generally required for unrecorded unconditional obligations that are (1) substantially noncancelable, (2) associated with financing arrangements for facilities or costs related to the contracted for goods or services, and (3) have a remaining term greater than one year. Examples of unrecorded unconditional obligations are output purchase contracts with minimum payments, certain lease obligations that were not discussed above, and capital stock mandatory redemption and sinking fund requirements.

Earnings per Share and Equity

Earnings per Share (EPS)

GAAP requires income statement disclosure of (1) primary earnings or losses per share (i.e., current net income or loss per share) on common stock and certain common stock equivalents, and (2) fully diluted earnings or losses per share for the combined total of common stock, common stock equivalents, and all other securities that could possiby dilute earnings per share if they were converted to common stock. Common stock equivalents are securities that are not common stock but that could be considered common stock because of conversion provisions they contain. Typical examples of common stock equivalents are stock options and warrants (rights to obtain common stock) and debt or preferred stock that is convertible into common stock. Other securities that contain rights or contingent rights to share in the earnings of the corporation but that are not technically classified as common stock equivalents are considered in the fully diluted earnings per share calculation.

Retained Earnings

Retained earnings are the total net income (i.e., net income less net losses) incurred in prior periods plus net income or loss of the current period, less payments from retained earnings (such as dividends paid). GAAP requires the disclosure of retained earnings. Retained earnings that have been set aside for specific uses or contingencies should be distinguished as appropriated or reserved. It is not unusual to have retained earnings and earnings per share disclosed together on a schedule following the calculation of net income on the income statement.

Statement of Stockholders' Equity

GAAP requires that changes in capital be disclosed by separate statement or footnote. In addition to retained earnings, other capital changes requiring disclosure include capital stock, paid-in capital (capital paid by the stockholders in excess of security par value), treasury stock (stock of the corporation reacquired by the corporation itself), and any other capital or equity account maintained by the corporation. For the example transactions described above in this chapter, the corporation would report (1) a $10,000 capital increase arising from the sale of common stock and (2) in conjunction with the statement of retained earnings, a decrease in equity arising from first year net loss of $950.

A schedule of retained earnings and earning per share for the example transactions described above in this chapter may be displayed as follows (alternative formats are acceptable):

Net income/(loss)	$(950)	
Beginning retained earnings	0	
Common stock dividends	0	
Ending retained earnings	$(950)	(actually a reduction of capital)
Earnings per common share:		
Income/(loss)	$(950)	
Preferred stock dividends	0	
Common stock net income/(loss)	(950)	
Earnings/(loss) per share	$(.95)	

Note: If there had been preferred stock and preferred dividends, those dividends would have been subtracted from earnings available to the common stock.

Foreign Operations

The results of foreign operations and transactions that are included in a parent entity's financial statements by consolidation, combination, or the equity method first are reported in accordance with GAAP in the functional currency of the foreign entity and then are restated in the parent entity's functional currency—in this case, the U.S. dollar. If the foreign operation is a direct and integral component or extension of the parent entity, the functional currency of the foreign operation may be the U.S. dollar; otherwise, the functional currency would be a currency other than the U.S. dollar. Gains and losses resulting from translation of the foreign operation into the functional currency of the parent entity are considered unrealized and are reported as a separate component of the stockholders' equity but are not included in current net income.

Generally, gains and losses from foreign currency transactions—transactions that require settlement in a currency other than the functional currency of the reporting entity—are recognized in current income. However, different treatment may be required for hedge or speculative forward exchange contracts and for intercompany transactions between an investor and an investee when the investee is consolidated, combined, or accounted for under the equity method.

Although not covered in this guide, the senior manager should also be aware that in some circumstances, GAAP requires that segments of a business be separately reported. For example, foreign operations and export sales should be reported separately if they are of the required magnitude.

Accounting for Income Taxes

SFAS 109, effective for fiscal years beginning after December 15, 1992, generally provides that:

1. A current liability is recognized for actual and estimated taxes payable.
2. A current asset is recognized for tax refunds or benefits expected in the current year.
3. Deferred liabilities or assets, respectively, are accrued to take into account estimated future liabilities or expected refunds or benefits attributed to tax and financial statement income and expense timing differences and carryforwards. A deferred tax liability or benefit should be accrued if it is more likely than not (greater than 50 percent probability) that the liability or benefit will be realized.

In measuring the tax liability, asset, or benefit, the business should evaluate the probability that the liability, asset, or benefit will occur or be realized, and estimate its value.

It may be expected that accrued tax assets or benefits will be subject to scrutiny by the SEC. Since tax benefits can often be carried back or forward to certain limited years, the amount of expected tax benefit recorded may be extremely subjective based at least on the business's earnings and taxable income histories and forecasts, income tax rate and law changes, and possible tax planning strategies that may be implemented to allow the business to take advantage of the tax benefits. If it is more likely than not (i.e., greater than 50 percent) that all or a part of an expected tax benefit will not be used by the business, an allowance account must be established by the business to offset or reduce the net value of the tax asset recorded on the books.

Income Tax Allocation

It is a basic premise of accrual accounting that revenues should be matched with related expenses. Thus, for financial statement presentation, it is necessary to match revenue and expense items with their related income tax consequences. Under accrual accounting, it is not appropriate to merely report the taxes paid in the accounting period as the appropriate tax expense. Tax allocation is required when material revenue or expenses recorded on the books or financial statements are different than those amounts reported for tax purposes. The following are examples of situations requiring tax allocation:

1. Revenue is recorded in the financial records but is not reported for tax purposes (e.g., a sale on credit is completely reported as revenue in the financial records but as an installment sale for tax purposes).
2. Revenue is reported for tax purposes but is not recorded in the financial records (e.g., payments received as advances).
3. Expenses are recorded in the financial records before being reported for tax purposes (e.g., certain contingent liabilities).
4. Expenses are reported for tax purposes but are not recorded in the financial records (e.g., depreciation reported for tax purposes is accelerated in comparison to depreciation reported for financial statement purposes).

No allocation is required in situations in which the differences between financial recording and tax reporting are permanent, as opposed to merely being timing differences (e.g., an item is revenue for financial statement purposes but is nontaxable income for tax purposes).

Accounting Changes

Accounting changes are generally classified as changes in an accounting principle, changes in an accounting estimate, or changes in the reporting entity.

An accounting principle, once adopted, should generally not be changed for subsequent transactions that are similar in nature to the original transaction. However, an accepted accounting principle can be changed if it is to a preferable principle. Changes in method of accounting for long-term contracts, inventory pricing, and calculating depreciation are examples of accounting changes. An action may not be considered a change in accounting principle if events or transactions have changed in substance, it is first being reported in financial statements, or the principle previously related to immaterial events or transactions. Generally, the cumulative effect of a change in accounting principle is recognized in the net income of the period of the change. However, some changes may be reported by restating prior financial statements (e.g., for certain principle changes relating to inventories, long-term contracts, public offerings, business combinations, and financing).

A change in an accounting estimate (e.g., estimates of contingencies or uncollectible revenues and asset salvage values or useful lives) is generally recognized in the period of the change. A change in an accounting estimate typically occurs because of additional information or a change in conditions. Corrections of errors made on prior financial statements are not classified as changes in accounting estimates. Errors are often mathematical or result from the improper application of accounting principles (e.g., prior use of an unacceptable accounting principle). An error is reported as a prior period adjustment in the period of the change.

Prior year financial statements are generally restated when there is a change in the reporting entity.

Postretirement Costs

SFAS 106 requires the current accrual of the present value of postretirement benefits other than pension plans (e.g., health and other benefits) by the date the employee is eligible to receive the benefits. Most employers currently expense these costs only when actually paid. SFAS 106 is effective for most companies and employees no later than fiscal years beginning after December 15, 1992. For many companies, SFAS 106 will require the accrual of a material expense and the implementation of additional, extensive accounting procedures.

Financial Instruments

SFAS 107 is the second phase of a broad accounting pronouncement project relating to financial instruments and off-balance-sheet financing. The first phase was SFAS 105, which became effective for fiscal years ending after June 15, 1990. SFAS 107 is effective for fiscal years ending after December 15, 1992, except for businesses with less than $150 million in total assets, for which it is effective for fiscal years ending after December 15, 1995.

The senior manager should be aware that SEC Staff Accounting Bulletin 74 generally requires financial statement disclosure of the potential effects of the adoption of new accounting standards that have been issued but are not yet effective, unless management expects that the impact on the business's financial position and results of operations will not be material.

A financial instrument is described as cash, evidence of an ownership interest in an entity, or a contract that obligates one entity (1) to pay another entity in cash, an ownership interest, or another financial instrument (e.g., a cash contractual obligation) or (2) to exchange a financial instrument on potentially unfavorable grounds with another entity; and entitles the other entity to receipt or exchange of the items specified at (1) and (2) above, respectively. Some typical items that may be financial instruments are cash, stock, loans and other receivables, payables, forward contracts, options, and guaranties.

SFAS 107 generally requires, with limited exceptions, fair value *disclosure,* including the methods and significant assumptions used to estimate fair value, of all financial instruments, but it does not change existing recognition, measurement, or classification requirements. Fair value is defined as the value that would be agreed to between willing parties in a current transaction, other than in a forced or liquidation sale. If it is not practicable to estimate fair value (i.e., if fair value cannot be estimated without incurring excessive costs), disclosure is still required of information relating to fair value (e.g., carrying amount, interest rate, and maturity date) and the reasons why it is not practicable to estimate fair value. SFAS 107 does not define the term *excessive costs,* but it does state that in most cases, it is expected that it will be practicable to estimate fair value even when financial instruments are not readily marketable. Management should consider whether it is practicable to estimate the fair values of individual financial instruments, groups of similar financial instruments, or at least a subset of similar financial instruments.

SFAS 105, the first phase of the financial instruments project, generally requires, with certain exceptions, *disclosure* of information about (1) financial instrument that have off-balance-sheet risk and (2) financial instruments that have concentrations of credit risk. Off-balance-sheet risk is the risk that the business is exposed to loss arising from a financial instrument, which loss is an amount *in excess* of the amount recognized on the financial statements for that financial instrument. SFAS 105 addresses off-balance-sheet risk arising from (1) possible market changes or forces (market risk) and (2) the possibility that the other party to a contract will not appropriately perform in accordance with the terms of the contract (credit risk).

With respect to off-balance-sheet risk, SFAS 105 generally requires at least disclosure of the face or contract amount of the financial instrument and information related to the nature of the risk (market and credit risk), instrument cash requirements, and accounting policies relevant to the financial instrument. Additionally, with respect specifically to off-balance-sheet credit risk, SFAS 105 generally requires disclosure of the amount of loss that would be incurred if a party to the financial instrument failed to perform, the amount and nature of related collateral or security, the business's access to that collateral or security, and the business's policy of requiring collateral or security for financial instruments that have credit risk.

Finally, with respect to all financial instruments, whether or not they have off-balance-sheet risk, SFAS 105 requires disclosure of significant concentrations of credit risk from individual or groups of counterparties, including credit risk in a specific industry or geographic region. A group of counterparties is described as a number of counterparties engaged in similar activities and similarly affected by economic or other conditions, such as accounts receivable from several companies in the same industry. SFAS 105 generally requires disclosure of the nature or characteristic of the concentration of credit risk, the amount of loss that would be incurred if the concentrated counterparty or group of counterparties failed to perform, the amount and nature of related collateral or security, the business's access to that collateral or security, and the business's policy of requiring collateral or security for financial instruments that have credit risk.

Postemployment Benefits

Prior to SFAS 112, postemployment benefits were accounted for by many different methods. SFAS 112 requires, for fiscal years beginning after December 15, 1993, that employers account for postemployment benefits by a uniform method.

Postemployment benefits are described as all benefits provided to former or inactive employees, their beneficiaries, and covered dependents, including such items as salary continuation, supplemental unemployment benefits, severance benefits, disability-related benefits, job training and counseling, and continuation of benefits such as health care and insurance. Former and inactive employees include employees who have been laid off and those on disability, regardless of whether they are expected to return to active status. Employees on vacation or who are absent due to illness or holiday are considered active. SFAS 112 does not apply to pension benefits, postretirement benefits covered by SFAS 106, and certain other deferred compensation and contractual or other termination benefits.

SFAS 112 provides that employers shall accrue a liability for postemployment benefits if the obligation is attributable to employees's services already rendered, the obligation relates to rights that vest or accumulate, the payment of the obligation is probable, and the amount of the obligation can be reasonably estimated. If all four of those conditions are not met, the obligation is accounted for as a contingency under SFAS 5 (see Contingencies, previously discussed in this chapter). Pursuant to SFAS 5, the estimated loss from a contingency is accrued if it is probable an asset had been impaired or a liability had been incurred at the date of the financial statements and the amount of the loss can be reasonably estimated. If it is only reasonably likely that an asset had been impaired or that a liability had been incurred at the date of the financial statements, SFAS 5 requires footnote disclosure of the estimated loss contingency but not accrual. Finally, if it is difficult to estimate the amount of contingent loss, SFAS 5 requires that an estimated range of loss be provided, or an explanation why the loss cannot be estimated may be appropriate.

CHAPTER 7

CONCLUSION

For legal and business reasons, it is imperative that the senior manager understand his or her duties relating to the business's accounting function and implement a methodology to help ensure satisfaction of those duties. No text can contain sufficient material that, if followed, would guarantee that the senior manager had satisfied his or her accounting duties—it is impossible to anticipate all the accounting-related circumstances that the senior manager may be required to address, all the legal standards that may apply to the activities of the senior manager, or how a trier of fact may apply the legal standards in a particular circumstance. However, it is possible to structure the business's accounting function and to acquire legal and accounting knowledge such that the senior manager is better prepared to make informed business decisions and has reasonable comfort that he or she has satisfied his or her accounting-related duties.

This guide is a summary of information that could otherwise fill several thousand pages of text; therefore, you are encouraged to consult additional texts or authorities if greater explanation is needed. With the help of this guide and other accounting-related materials, I encourage you to continually work to improve the reliability and responsiveness of the accounting function to the business and its officers, directors, managers, creditors, and stockholders.

APPENDIX A

REGULATION S-K

```
              OMB APPROVAL
OMB Number:        3235-0071
Expires:        March 31, 1995
Estimated average burden
hours per response ..... 1.00
```

UNITED STATES
SECURITIES AND EXCHANGE COMMISSION
Washington, D.C. 20549

REGULATION S-K

TABLE OF CONTENTS

REGULATION S-K

PART 229 — STANDARD INSTRUCTIONS FOR FILING FORMS UNDER SECURITIES ACT OF 1933, SECURITIES EXCHANGE ACT OF 1934 AND ENERGY POLICY AND CONSERVATION ACT OF 1975 — REGULATION S-K

Subpart 229.1 — General

General

Reg. §229.10.

(a) *Application of Regulation S-K.* This part [together with the General Rules and Regulations under the Securities Act of 1933, 15 U.S.C. 77a et seq., as amended ("Securities Act"), and the Securities Exchange Act of 1934, 15 U.S.C. 78a et seq., as amended ("Exchange Act") (Parts 230 and 240 of this chapter), the Interpretative Releases under these Acts (Parts 231 and 241 of this chapter), and the forms under these Acts (Parts 239 and 249 of this chapter)] states the requirements applicable to the content of the non-financial statement portions of:

    (1) Registration statements under the Securities Act (Part 239 of this chapter) to the extent provided in the forms to be used for registration under such Act; and

    (2) Registration statements under section 12 (Subpart C of Part 249 of this chapter), annual or other reports under sections 13 and 15(d) (Subparts D and E of Part 249 of this chapter), annual reports to security holders and proxy and information statements under section 14 of the Exchange Act (Part 240 of this chapter), and any other documents required to be filed under the Exchange Act, to the extent provided in the forms and rules under such Act.

(b) *Commission policy on projections.* The Commission encourages the use in documents specified in Rule 175 under the Securities Act (§230.175 of this chapter) and Rule 3b-6 under the Exchange Act (§240.3b-6 of this chapter) of management's projections of future economic performance that have a reasonable basis and are presented in an appropriate format. The guidelines set forth herein represent the Commission's views on important factors to be considered in formulating and disclosing such projections.

    (1) *Basis for projections.* The Commission believes that management must have the option to present in Commission filings its good faith assessment of a registrant's future performance. Management, however, must have a reasonable basis for such an assessment. Although a history of operations or experience in projecting may be among the factors providing a basis for management's assessment, the Commission does not believe that a registrant always must have had such a history or experience in order to formulate projections with a reasonable basis. An outside review of management's projections may furnish additional support for having a reasonable basis for a projection. If management decides to include a report of such a review in a Commission filing, there also should be disclosure of the qualifications of the reviewer, the extent of the review, the relationship between the reviewer and the registrant, and other material factors concerning the process by which any outside review was sought or obtained. Moreover, in the case of a registration statement under the Securities Act, the reviewer would be deemed an expert and an appropriate consent must be filed with the registration statement.

    (2) *Format for projections.* In determining the appropriate format for projections included in Commission filings, consideration must be given to, among other things, the financial items to be projected, the period to be covered, and the manner of presentation to be used. Although traditionally projections have been given for three financial items generally considered to be of primary importance to investors (revenues, net income (loss) and earnings (loss) per share), projection information need not necessarily be limited to these three items. However, management should take care to assure that the choice of items projected is not susceptible to misleading inferences through selective projection of only favorable items. Revenues, net income (loss) and earnings (loss) per share usually are presented together in order to avoid any misleading inferences that may arise when the individual items reflect contradictory trends. There may be instances, however, when it is appropriate to present earnings (loss) from continuing operations, or income (loss) before extraordinary items in addition to or in lieu of net income (loss). It generally would be misleading to present sales or revenue projections without one of the foregoing measures of income. The period that appropriately may be covered by a projection depends to a large extent on the particular circumstances of the company involved. For certain companies in certain industries, a projection covering a two or three year period may be entirely reasonable. Other companies may not have a reasonable basis for projections beyond the current year. Accordingly, management should select the period most appropriate in the circumstances. In addition, management, in making a projection, should disclose what, in its opinion, is the most probable specific amount or the most reasonable range for each financial item projected based on the selected assumptions. Ranges, however, should not be so wide as to make the disclosures meaningless. Moreover, several projections based on varying assumptions may be judged by management to be more meaningful than a single number or range and would be permitted.

(3) *Investor understanding.*

    (i) When management chooses to include its projections in a Commission filing, the disclosures accompanying the projections should facilitate investor understanding of the basis for and limitations of projections. In this regard investors should be cautioned against attributing undue certainty to management's assessment, and the Commission believes that investors would be aided by a statement indicating management's intention regarding the furnishing of updated projections. The Commission also believes that investor understanding would be enhanced by disclosure of the assumptions which in management's opinion are most significant to the projections or are the key factors upon which the financial results of the enterprise depend and encourages disclosure of assumptions in a manner that will provide a framework for analysis of the projection.

    (ii) Management also should consider whether disclosure of the accuracy or inaccuracy of previous projections would provide investors with important insights into the limitations of projections. In this regard, consideration should be given to presenting the projections in a format that will facilitate subsequent analysis of the reasons for differences between actual and forecast results. An important benefit may arise from the systematic analysis of variances between projected and actual results on a continuing basis, since such disclosure may highlight for investors the most significant risk and profit-sensitive areas in a business operation.

    (iii) With respect to previously issued projections, registrants are reminded of their responsibility to make full and prompt disclosure of material facts, both favorable and unfavorable, regarding their financial condition. This responsibility may extend to situations where management knows or has reason to know that its previously disclosed projects no longer have a reasonable basis.

    (iv) Since a registrant's ability to make projections with relative confidence may vary with all the facts and circumstances, the responsibility for determining whether to discontinue or to resume making projections is best left to management. However, the Commission encourages registrants not to discontinue or to resume projections in Commission filings without a reasonable basis.

(c) *Commission policy on security ratings.* In view of the importance of security ratings ("ratings") to investors and the marketplace, the Commission permits registrants to disclose, on a voluntary basis, ratings assigned by rating organizations to classes of debt securities, convertible debt securities and preferred stock in registration statements and periodic reports. In addition, the Commission permits, pursuant to Rule 134(a)(14) under the Securities Act (§230.134(a)(14) of this chapter), voluntary disclosure of ratings assigned by any nationally recognized statistical rating organizations ("NRSROs") in certain communications deemed not to be a prospectus ("tombstone advertisements").

Set forth herein are the Commission's views on important matters to be considered in disclosing security ratings.

(1) *Securities Act filings.*

    (i) If a registrant includes in a registration statement filed under the Securities Act any rating(s) assigned to a class of securities, it should consider including: (A) any other rating intended for public dissemination assigned to such class by an NRSRO ("additional NRSRO rating") that is available on the date of the initial filing of the document and that is materially different from any rating disclosed; and (B) the name of each rating organization whose rating is disclosed; each such rating organization's definition or description of the category in which it rated the class of securities; the relative rank of each rating within the assigning rating organization's overall classification system; and a statement informing investors that a security rating is not a recommendation to buy, sell or hold securities, that it may be subject to revision or withdrawal at any time by the assigning rating organization and that each rating should be evaluated independently of any other rating. The registrant also should include the written consent of any rating organization that is not an NRSRO whose rating is included. With respect to the written consent of any NRSRO whose rating is included, see Rule 436(g) under the Securities Act (§230.436(g) of this chapter).

    (ii) If a change in a rating already included is available subsequent to the filing of the registration statement, but prior to its effectiveness, the registrant should consider including such rating change in the final prospectus. If the rating change is material or if a materially different rating from any disclosed becomes available during this period, the registrant should consider amending the registration statement to include the rating change or additional rating and recirculating the preliminary prospectus.

    (iii) If a materially different additional NRSRO rating or a material change in a rating already included becomes available during any period in which offers or sales are being made, the registrant should consider disclosing such additional rating or rating change by means of a post-effective amendment or sticker to the prospectus pursuant to Rule 424(b) under the Securities Act (§230.424(b) of this chapter), unless, in the case of a registration statement on Form S-3 (§239.13 of this chapter), it has been disclosed in a document incorporated by reference into the registration statement subsequent to its effectiveness and prior to the termination of the offering.

(2) *Exchange Act filings.*

    (i)   If a registrant includes in a registration statement or periodic report filed under the Exchange Act any rating(s) assigned to a class of securities, it should consider including the information specified in paragraphs (c)(1)(i)(A) and (B) of this section.

    (ii) If there is a material change in the rating(s) assigned by any NRSRO(s) to any outstanding class(es) of securities of a registrant subject to the reporting requirements of section 13(a) or 15(d) of the Exchange Act, the registrant should consider filing a report on Form 8-K (§249.308 of this chapter) or other appropriate report under the Exchange Act disclosing such rating change.

Subpart 229.100 — Business

Description of Business

Reg. §229.101. Item 101.

(a) *General development of business.* Describe the general development of the business of the registrant, its subsidiaries and any predecessor(s) during the past five years, or such shorter period as the registrant may have been engaged in business. Information shall be disclosed for earlier periods if material to an understanding of the general development of the business.

    (1) In describing developments, information shall be given as to matters such as the following: the year in which the registrant was organized and its form of organization; the nature and results of any bankruptcy, receivership or similar proceedings with respect to the registrant or any of its significant subsidiaries; the nature and results of any other material reclassification, merger or consolidation of the registrant or any of its significant subsidiaries; the acquisition or disposition of any material amount of assets otherwise than in the ordinary course of business; and any material changes in the mode of conducting the business.

    (2) Registrants,

        (i)   filing a registration statement on Form S-1 (§239.11 of this chapter) under the Securities Act or on Form 10 (§249.210 of this chapter) under the Exchange Act,

        (ii) not subject to the reporting requirements of section 13(a) or 15(d) of the Exchange Act immediately prior to the filing of such registration statement, and

        (iii) that (including predecessors) have not received revenue from operations during each of the three fiscal years immediately prior to the filing of registration statement, shall provide the following information:

            (A) if the registration statement is filed prior to the end of the registrant's second fiscal quarter, a description of the registrant's plan of operation for the remainder of the fiscal year; or

            (B) if the registration statement is filed subsequent to the end of the registrant's second fiscal quarter, a description of the registrant's plan of operation for the remainder of the fiscal year and for the first six months of the next fiscal year. If such information is not available, the reasons for its not being available shall be stated. Disclosure relating to any plan shall include such matters as:

                (1) In the case of a registration statement on Form S-1, a statement in narrative form indicating the registrant's opinion as to the period of time that the proceeds from the offering will satisfy cash requirements and whether in the next six months it will be necessary to raise additional funds to meet the expenditures required for operating the business of the registrant; the specific reasons for such opinion shall be set forth and categories of expenditures and sources of cash resources shall be identified; however, amounts of expenditures and cash resources need not be provided; in addition, if the narrative statement is based on a cash budget, such budget shall be furnished to the Commission as supplemental information, but not as part of the registration statement;

                (2) An explanation of material product research and development to be performed during the period covered in the plan;

                (3) Any anticipated material acquisition of plant and equipment and the capacity thereof;

                (4) Any anticipated material changes in number of employees in the various departments such as research and development, production, sales or administration; and

                (5) Other material areas which may be peculiar to the registrant's business.

(b) *Financial information about industry segments.* State for each of the registrant's last three fiscal years or for each fiscal year the registrant has been engaged in business, whichever period is shorter, the amounts of revenue (with sales to unaffiliated customers and sales or transfers to other industry segments of the registrant shown separately), operating profit or loss and identifiable assets attributable to each of the registrant's industry segments. (See Appendix A to this Item for a suggested tabular format for presentation of this information.) To the extent that financial information included pursuant to this paragraph (b) complies with generally accepted accounting principles, the registrant may include in its financial statements a cross reference to this data in lieu of presenting duplicative information about its segments in the financial statements; conversely, a registrant may cross reference to the financial statements.

   (1)   The prior period information shall be restated retroactively in the following circumstances, unless not material, with appropriate disclosure of the nature and effect of the restatement:

       (i)   When the financial statements of the registrant as a whole have been restated retroactively; or

      (ii)   when there has been a change in the way the registrant's products or services are grouped into industry segments and such change affects the segment information being reported; restatement is not required when a registrant's reportable segments change solely as a result of a change in the nature of its operations or as a result of a segment losing or gaining in significance.

   (2)   If the registrant includes, or is required by Article 3 of Regulation S-X (17 CFR 210) to include, interim financial statements, discuss any facts relating to the performance of any of the segments during the period which, in the opinion of management, indicate that the three year segment financial data may not be indicative of current or future operations of the segment. Comparative financial information shall be included to the extent necessary to the discussion.

(c) *Narrative description of business.*

   (1)   Describe the business done and intended to be done by the registrant and its subsidiaries, focusing upon the registrant's dominant industry segment or each reportable industry segment about which financial information is presented in the financial statements. To the extent material to an understanding of the registrant's business taken as a whole, the description of each such segment shall include the information specified in paragraphs (c)(1)(i) through (x) of this Item. The matters specified in paragraphs (c)(1)(xi) through (xiii) of this Item shall be discussed with respect to the registrant's business in general; where material, the industry segments to which these matters are significant shall be identified.

       (i)   The principal products produced and services rendered by the registrant in the industry segment and the principal markets for, and methods of distribution of, the segment's principal products and services. In addition, state for each of the last three fiscal years the amount or percentage of total revenue contributed by any class of similar products or services which accounted for 10 percent or more of consolidated revenue in any of the last three fiscal years or 15 percent or more of consolidated revenue, if total revenue did not exceed $50,000,000 during any of such fiscal years.

      (ii)   A description of the status of a product or segment (*e.g.*, whether in the planning stage, whether prototypes exist, the degree to which product design has progressed or whether further engineering is necessary), if there has been a public announcement of, or if the registrant otherwise has made public information about, a new product or industry segment that would require the investment of a material amount of the assets of the registrant or that otherwise is material. This paragraph is not intended to require disclosure of otherwise nonpublic corporate information the disclosure of which would affect adversely the registrant's competitive position.

     (iii)   The sources and availability of raw materials.

     (iv)   The importance to the industry segment and the duration and effect of all patents, trademarks, licenses, franchises and concessions held.

      (v)   The extent to which the business of the industry segment is or may be seasonal.

     (vi)   The practices of the registrant and the industry (respective industries) relating to working capital items (*e.g.*, where the registrant is required to carry significant amounts of inventory to meet rapid delivery requirements of customers or to assure itself of a continuous allotment of goods from suppliers; where the registrant provides rights to return merchandise; or where the registrant has provided extended payment terms to customers).

    (vii)   The dependence of the segment upon a single customer, or a few customers, the loss of any one or more of which would have a material adverse effect on the segment. The name of any customer and its relationship, if any, with the registrant or its subsidiaries shall be disclosed if sales to the customer by one or more segments are made in an aggregate amount equal to 10 percent or more of the registrant's consolidated revenues and the loss of such customer would have a material adverse effect on the registrant and its subsidiaries taken as a whole. The names of other customers may be included, unless in the particular case the effect of including the names would be misleading. For purposes of this paragraph, a group of customers under common control or customers that are affiliates of each other shall be regarded as a single customer.

(viii) The dollar amount of backlog orders believed to be firm, as of a recent date and as of a comparable date in the preceding fiscal year, together with an indication of the portion thereof not reasonably expected to be filled within the current fiscal year, and seasonal or other material aspects of the backlog. (There may be included as firm orders government orders that are firm but not yet funded and contracts awarded but not yet signed, provided an appropriate statement is added to explain the nature of such orders and the amount thereof. The portion of orders already included in sales or operating revenues on the basis of percentage of completion or program accounting shall be excluded.)

(ix) A description of any material portion of the business that may be subject to renegotiation of profits or termination of contracts or subcontracts at the election of the Government.

(x) Competitive conditions in the business involved including, where material, the identity of the particular markets in which the registrant competes, an estimate of the number of competitors and the registrant's competitive position, if known or reasonably available to the registrant. Separate consideration shall be given to the principal products or services or classes of products or services of the segment, if any. Generally, the names of competitors need not be disclosed. The registrant may include such names, unless in the particular case the effect of including the names would be misleading. Where, however, the registrant knows or has reason to know that one or a small number of competitors is dominant in the industry it shall be identified. The principal methods of competition (*e.g.*, price, service, warranty or product performance) shall be identified, and positive and negative factors pertaining to the competitive position of the registrant, to the extent that they exist, shall be explained if known or reasonably available to the registrant.

(xi) If material, the estimated amount spent during each of the last three fiscal years on company-sponsored research and development activities determined in accordance with generally accepted accounting principles. In addition, state, if material, the estimated dollar amount spent during each of such years on customer-sponsored research activities relating to the development of new products, services or techniques or the improvement of existing products, services or techniques.

(xii) Appropriate disclosure also shall be made as to the material effects that compliance with Federal, State and local provisions which have been enacted or adopted regulating the discharge of materials into the environment, or otherwise relating to the protection of the environment, may have upon the capital expenditures, earnings and competitive position of the registrant and its subsidiaries. The registrant shall disclose any material estimated capital expenditures for environmental control facilities for the remainder of its current fiscal year and its succeeding fiscal year and for such further periods as the registrant may deem material.

(xiii) The number of persons employed by the registrant.

(d) *Financial information about foreign and domestic operations and export sales.*

(1) State for each of the registrant's last three fiscal years, or for each fiscal year the registrant has been engaged in business, whichever period is shorter, the amounts of revenue (with sales to unaffiliated customers and sales or transfers to other geographic areas shown separately), operating profit or loss and identifiable assets attributable to each of the registrant's geographic areas and the amount of export sales in the aggregate or by appropriate geographic area to which the sales are made. (See Appendix B to this Item for a suggested tabular format for presentation of this information.) To the extent that financial information included pursuant to this paragraph (d) complies with generally accepted accounting principles, the registrant may include in its financial statements a cross reference to this data in lieu of presenting duplicative data in its financial statements; conversely a registrant may cross-reference to the financial statements. The prior period information shall be retroactively restated in the following circumstances, unless not material, with appropriate disclosure of the nature and effect of the restatement:

(i) When the financial statements of the registrant as a whole have been retroactively restated, or

(ii) When there has been a change in the way a registrant's foreign operations are grouped into geographic areas and such change affects the geographic area information being reported. Restatement is not required when a registrant's geographic areas change as a result of a change in the nature of operations or as a result of an area losing or gaining in significance.

(2) Any risks attendant to the foreign operations and any dependence of one or more of the registrant's industry segments upon such foreign operations shall be described unless it would be more appropriate for this matter to be discussed in connection with the description of one or more of the registrant's industry segments pursuant to paragraph (c) of this Item.

(3) If the registrant includes, or is required by Article 3 of Regulation S-X [17 CFR 210], to include, interim financial statements, discuss any facts relating to the information furnished pursuant to this paragraph (d) that, in the opinion of management, indicate that the three year financial data for foreign and domestic operations or export sales may not be indicative of current or future operations. Comparative information shall be included to the extent necessary to the discussion.

Instructions to Item 101.

1. In determining what information about the industry segments is material to any understanding of the registrant's business taken as a whole and therefore required to be disclosed pursuant to paragraph (c) of this Item, the registrant should take into account both quantitative and qualitative factors such as the significance of the matter to the registrant (*e.g.*, whether a matter with a relatively minor impact on the registrant's business is represented by management to be important to its future profitability), the pervasiveness of the matter (*e.g.*, whether it affects or may affect numerous items in the segment information), and the impact of the matter (*e.g.*, whether it distorts the trends reflected in the segment information). Situations may arise when information should be disclosed about a segment, although the information in quantitative terms may not appear significant to the registrant's business taken as a whole.

2. The determination whether information about foreign and domestic operations and export sales is required in the document for a particular year shall be based upon an evaluation of interperiod comparability. For instance, interperiod comparability most likely would require that foreign and domestic operations and export sales that have been significant in the past and are expected to be significant in the future be regarded as reportable even though they are not significant in the current fiscal year.

3. The Commission, upon written request of the registrant and where consistent with the protection of investors, may permit the omission of any of the information required by this Item or the furnishing in substitution thereof of appropriate information of comparable character.

Appendix A — Industry Segments

The table set forth below is illustrative of the format that might be used for presenting the segment information required by paragraphs (b) and (c)(1)(i) of Item 101 regarding industry segments and classes of similar products or services.

FINANCIAL INFORMATION RELATING TO INDUSTRY SEGMENTS
AND CLASSES OF PRODUCTS OR SERVICES

	Year 1	Year 2	Year 3
Sales to unaffiliated customers:			
Industry segment A:			
Class of product 1			
Class of product 2			
Industry segment B:			
Class of product 1			
Class of product 2			
Industry segment C			
Other industries			
Intersegment sales or transfers:			
Industry segment A			
Industry segment B			
Industry segment C			
Other industries			
Operating profit or loss:			
Industry segment A			
Industry segment B			
Industry segment C			
Other industries			
Identifiable assets:			
Industry segment A			
Industry segment B			
Industry segment C			
Other industries			

Appendix B — Foreign and Domestic Operations and Export Sales

The table set forth below is illustrative of the format that might be used for presenting the segment information required by paragraph (d) of Item 101 regarding foreign and domestic operations and export sales.

FINANCIAL INFORMATION RELATING TO FOREIGN AND DOMESTIC OPERATIONS AND EXPORT SALES

	Year		
	1	2	3
Sales to unaffiliated customers:			
United States[1]			
Geographic area A			
Geographic area B			
Sales or transfers between geographic areas:			
United States			
Geographic area A			
Geographic area B			
Operating profit or loss:[2]			
United States			
Geographic area A			
Geographic area B			
Identifiable assets:			
United States			
Geographic area A			
Geographic area B			
Export sales; United States[3]			

Description of Property

Reg. §229.102. Item 102. State briefly the location and general character of the principal plants, mines and other materially important physical properties of the registrant and its subsidiaries. In addition, identify the industry segment(s) that use the properties described. If any such property is not held in fee or is held subject to any major encumbrance, so state and describe briefly how held.

Instructions to Item 102.

1. What is required is such information as reasonably will inform investors as to the suitability, adequacy, productive capacity and extent of utilization of the facilities by the registrant. Detailed descriptions of the physical characteristics of individual properties or legal descriptions by metes and bounds are not required and shall not be given.

2. In determining whether properties should be described, the registrant should take into account both quantitative and qualitative factors. See Instruction 1 to Item 101 of Regulation S-K (§229.101).

3. In the case of an extractive enterprise, material information shall be given as to production reserves, locations, development and the nature of the registrant's interest. If individual properties are of major significance to an industry segment:

    A. More detailed information concerning these matters shall be furnished; and

    B. Appropriate maps shall be used to disclose location data of significant properties except in cases for which numerous maps would be required.

4. A. If reserve estimates are referred to in the document, the staff of the Office of Engineering, Division of Corporation Finance of the Commission, shall be consulted. That Office may request that a copy of the full report of the engineer or other expert who estimated the reserves be furnished as supplemental information and not as part of the filing. See Rule 418 of Regulation C (§230.418 of this chapter) and Rule 12b-4 of Regulation 12B (§240.12b-4 of this chapter) with respect to the submission to, and return by, the Commission of supplemental information.

    B. If the estimates of reserves, or any estimated valuation thereof, are represented as being based on estimates prepared or reviewed by independent consultants, those independent consultants shall be named in the document.

5. Estimates of oil or gas reserves other than proved or, in the case of other extractive reserves, estimates other than proved or probable reserves, and any estimated values of such reserves shall not be disclosed in any document publicly filed with the Commission, unless such information is required to be disclosed in the document by foreign or state law; provided, however, that where such estimates previously have been provided to a person (or any of its affiliates) that is offering to acquire, merge or consolidate with the registrant or otherwise to acquire the registrant's securities, such estimates may be included in documents relating to such acquisition.

---

1 Or appropriate area of domestic operations
2 Or some other reasonable measure of profitability as used in the financial statements.
3 Identify the geographic areas to which the sales are made, if appropriate.

9

6. The definitions in §210.4-10(a) of Regulation S-X [17 CFR 210] shall apply to this Item with respect to oil and gas operations.

Legal Proceedings

Reg. §229.103. Item 103. Describe briefly any material pending legal proceedings, other than ordinary routine litigation incidental to the business, to which the registrant or any of its subsidiaries is a party or of which any of their property is the subject. Include the name of the court or agency in which the proceedings are pending, the date instituted, the principal parties thereto, a description of the factual basis alleged to underlie the proceeding and the relief sought. Include similar information as to any such proceedings known to be contemplated by governmental authorities.

Instructions to Item 103.

1. If the business ordinarily results in actions for negligence or other claims, no such action or claim need be described unless it departs from the normal kind of such actions.

2. No information need be given with respect to any proceeding that involves primarily a claim for damages if the amount involved, exclusive of interest and costs, does not exceed 10 percent of the current assets of the registrant and its subsidiaries on a consolidated basis. However, if any proceeding presents in large degree the same legal and factual issues as other proceedings pending or known to be contemplated, the amount involved in such other proceedings shall be included in computing such percentage.

3. Notwithstanding Instructions 1 and 2, any material bankruptcy, receivership, or similar proceeding with respect to the registrant or any of its significant subsidiaries shall be described.

4. Any material proceedings to which any director, officer or affiliate of the registrant, any owner of record or beneficially of more than five percent of any class of voting securities of the registrant, or any associate of any such director, officer, affiliate of the registrant, or security holder is a party adverse to the registrant or any of its subsidiaries or has a material interest adverse to the registrant or any of its subsidiaries also shall be described.

5. Notwithstanding the foregoing, an administrative or judicial proceeding (including, for purposes of A and B of this Instruction, proceedings which present in large degree the same issues) arising under any Federal, State or local provisions that have been enacted or adopted regulating the discharge of materials into the environment or primarily for the purpose of protecting the environment shall not be deemed "ordinary routine litigation incidental to the business" and shall be described if:

    A. Such proceeding is material to the business or financial condition of the registrant;

    B. Such proceeding involves primarily a claim for damages, or involves potential monetary sanctions, capital expenditures, deferred charges or charges to income and the amount involved, exclusive of interest and costs, exceeds 10 percent of the current assets of the registrant and its subsidiaries on a consolidated basis; or

    C. A governmental authority is a party to such proceeding and such proceeding involves potential monetary sanctions, unless the registrant reasonably believes that such proceeding will result in no monetary sanctions, or in monetary sanctions, exclusive of interest and costs, of less than $100,000; provided, however, that such proceedings which are similar in nature may be grouped and described generically.

Subpart 229.200 — Securities of the Registrant

Market Price of and Dividends on the Registrant's Common Equity and Related Stockholder Matters

Reg. §229.201. Item 201.

(a) *Market information.*

(1) (i) Identify the principal United States market or markets in which each class of the registrant's common equity is being traded. Where there is no established public trading market for a class of common equity, furnish a statement to that effect. For purposes of this Item the existence of limited or sporadic quotations should not of itself be deemed to constitute an "established public trading market." In the case of foreign registrants, also identify the principal established foreign public trading market, if any, for each class of the registrant's common equity.

(ii) If the principal United States market for such common equity is an exchange, state the high and low sales prices for the equity for each full quarterly period within the two most recent fiscal years and any subsequent interim period for which financial statements are included, or are required to be included by Article 3 of Regulation S-X [17 CFR 210], as reported in the consolidated transaction reporting system or, if not so reported, as reported on the principal exchange market for such equity.

(iii) If the principal United States market for such common equity is not an exchange, state the range of high and low bid information for the equity for each full quarterly period within the two most recent fiscal years and any subsequent interim period for which financial statements are included, or are required to be included by Article 3 of Regulation S-X, as regularly quoted in the automated quotation system of a registered securities association, or where the equity is not

10

quoted in such a system, the range of reported high and low bid quotations, indicating the source of such quotations. Indicate, as applicable, that such over-the-counter market quotations reflect inter-dealer prices, without retail mark-up, mark-down or commission and may not necessarily represent actual transactions. Where there is an absence of an established public trading market, reference to quotations shall be qualified by appropriate explanation.

(iv) Where a foreign registrant has identified a principal established foreign trading market for its common equity pursuant to paragraph (a)(1) of this Item, also provide market price information comparable, to the extent practicable, to that required for the principal United States market, including the source of such information. Such prices shall be stated in the currency in which they are quoted. The registrant may translate such prices into United States currency at the currency exchange rate in effect on the date the price disclosed was reported on the foreign exchange. If the primary United States market for the registrant's common equity trades using American Depositary Receipts, the United States prices disclosed shall be on that basis.

(v) If the information called for by this Item is being presented in a registration statement filed pursuant to the Securities Act or a proxy or information statement filed pursuant to the Exchange Act, the document also shall include price information as of the latest practicable date, and, in the case of securities to be issued in connection with an acquisition, business combination or other reorganization, as of the date immediately prior to the public announcement of such transaction.

(2) If the information called for by this paragraph (a) is being presented in a registration statement on Form S-1 [§239.11 of this chapter] or Form S-18 [§239.28 of this chapter] under the Securities Act or on Form 10 [§249.210 of this chapter] under the Exchange Act relating to a class of common equity for which at the time of filing there is no established United States public trading market, indicate the amount(s) of common equity (i) that is subject to outstanding options or warrants to purchase, or securities convertible into, common equity of the registrant; (ii) that could be sold pursuant to Rule 144 under the Securities Act [§230.144 of this chapter] or that the registrant has agreed to register under the Securities Act for sale by security holders; or (iii) that is being, or has been publicly proposed to be, publicly offered by the registrant (unless such common equity is being offered pursuant to an employee benefit plan or dividend reinvestment plan), the offering of which could have a material effect on the market price of the registrant's common equity.

(b) *Holders.*

(1) Set forth the approximate number of holders of each class of common equity of the registrant as of the latest practicable date.

(2) If the information called for by this paragraph (b) is being presented in a registration statement filed pursuant to the Securities Act or a proxy statement or information statement filed pursuant to the Exchange Act that relates to an acquisition, business combination or other reorganization, indicate the effect of such transaction on the amount and percentage of present holdings of the registrant's common equity owned beneficially by (i) any person (including any group as that term is used in section 13(d)(3) of the Exchange Act) who is known to the registrant to be the beneficial owner of more than five percent of any class of the registrant's common equity and (ii) each director and nominee and (iii) all directors and officers as a group, and the registrant's present commitments to such persons with respect to the issuance of shares of any class of its common equity.

(c) *Dividends.*

(1) State the frequency and amount of any cash dividends declared on each class of its common equity by the registrant for the two most recent fiscal years and any subsequent interim period for which financial statements are required to be presented by §210.3 of Regulation S-X. Where there are restrictions (including, where appropriate, restrictions on the ability of registrant's subsidiaries to transfer funds to the registrant in the form of cash dividends, loans or advances) that currently materially limit the registrant's ability to pay such dividends or that the registrant reasonably believes are likely to limit materially the future payment of dividends on the common equity so state and either (i) describe briefly (where appropriate quantify) such restrictions, or (ii) cross reference to the specific discussion of such restrictions in the Management's Discussion and Analysis of financial condition and operating results prescribed by Item 303 of Regulation S-K (§229.303) and the description of such restrictions required by Regulation S-X in the registrant's financial statements.

(2) Where registrants have a record of paying no cash dividends although earnings indicate an ability to do so, they are encouraged to consider the question of their intention to pay cash dividends in the foreseeable future and, if no such intention exists, to make a statement of that fact in the filing. Registrants which have a history of paying cash dividends also are encouraged to indicate whether they currently expect that comparable cash dividends will continue to be paid in the future and, if not, the nature of the change in the amount or rate of cash dividend payments.

Instructions to Item 201.
1. Registrants, the common equity of which is listed for trading on more than one securities exchange registered under the Exchange Act, are required to indicate each such exchange pursuant to paragraph (a)(1)(i) of this Item; such registrants, however, need only

report one set of price quotations pursuant to paragraph (a)(1)(ii) of this Item; where available, these shall be the prices as reported in the consolidated transaction reporting system and, where the prices are not so reported, the prices on the most significant (in terms of volume) securities exchange for such shares.

2. Market prices and dividends reported pursuant to this Item shall be adjusted to give retroactive effect to material changes resulting from stock dividends, stock splits and reverse stock splits.

3. The computation of the approximate number of holders of registrant's common equity may be based upon the number of record holders or also may include individual participants in security position listings. See Rule 17Ad-8 under the Exchange Act. The method of computation that is chosen shall be indicated.

4. If the registrant is a foreign issuer, describe briefly:

    A. Any governmental laws, decrees or regulations in the country in which the registrant is organized that restrict the export or import of capital, including, but not limited to, foreign exchange controls, or that affect the remittance of dividends or other payments to nonresident holders of the registrant's common equity; and

    B. All taxes, including withholding provisions, to which United States common equity holders are subject under existing laws and regulations of the foreign country in which the registrant is organized. Include a brief description of pertinent provisions of any reciprocal tax treaty between such foreign country and the United States regarding withholding. If there is no such treaty, so state.

5. If the registrant is a foreign private issuer whose common equity of the class being registered is wholly or partially in bearer form, the response to this Item shall so indicate together with as much information as the registrant is able to provide with respect to security holdings in the United States. If the securities being registered trade in the United States in the form of American Depositary Receipts or similar certificates, the response to this Item shall so indicate together with the name of the depositary issuing such receipts and the number of shares or other units of the underlying security representing the trading units in such receipts.

Description of Registrant's Securities

Reg. §229.202. Item 202.

Note — If the securities being described have been accepted for listing on an exchange, the exchange may be identified. The document should not however, convey the impression that the registrant may apply successfully for listing of the securities on an exchange or that, in the case of an underwritten offering, the underwriters may request the registrant to apply for such listing, unless there is reasonable assurance that the securities to be offered will be acceptable to a securities exchange for listing.

(a) *Capital stock.* If capital stock is to be registered, state the title of the class and describe such of the matters listed in paragraphs (a)(1) through (5) as are relevant. A complete legal description of the securities need not be given.

    (1) Outline briefly: (i) dividend rights; (ii) terms of conversion; (iii) sinking fund provisions; (iv) redemption provisions; (v) voting rights, including any provisions specifying the vote required by security holders to take action; (vi) any classification of the Board of Directors, and the impact of such classification where cumulative voting is permitted or required; (vii) liquidation rights; (viii) preemption rights; and (ix) liability to further calls or to assessment by the registrant and for liabilities of the registrant imposed on its stockholders under state statutes (*e.g.*, to laborers, servants or employees of the registrant), unless such disclosure would be immaterial because the financial resources of the registrant or other factors make it improbable that liability under such state statutes would be imposed; (x) any restriction on alienability of the securities to be registered; and (xi) any provision discriminating against any existing or prospective holder of such securities as a result of such security holder owning a substantial amount of securities.

    (2) If the rights of holders of such stock may be modified otherwise than by a vote of a majority or more of the shares outstanding, voting as a class, so state and explain briefly.

    (3) If preferred stock is to be registered, describe briefly any restriction on the repurchase or redemption of shares by the registrant while there is any arrearage in the payment of dividends or sinking fund installments. If there is no such restriction, so state.

    (4) If the rights evidenced by, or amounts payable with respect to, the shares to be registered are, or may be, materially limited or qualified by the rights of any other authorized class of securities, include the information regarding such other securities as will enable investors to understand such limitations or qualifications. No information need be given, however, as to any class of securities all of which will be retired, provided appropriate steps to ensure such retirement will be completed prior to or upon delivery by the registrant of the shares.

    (5) Describe briefly or cross-reference to a description in another part of the document, any provision of the registrant's charter or by-laws that would have an effect of delaying, deferring or preventing a change in control of the registrant and that would

operate only with respect to an extraordinary corporate transaction involving the registrant [or any of its subsidiaries], such as a merger, reorganization, tender offer, sale or transfer of substantially all of its assets, or liquidation. Provisions and arrangements required by law or imposed by governmental or judicial authority need not be described or discussed pursuant to this paragraph (a)(5). Provisions or arrangements adopted by the registrant to effect, or further, compliance with laws or governmental or judicial mandate are not subject to the immediately preceding sentence where such compliance did not require the specific provisions or arrangements adopted.

(b) *Debt securities.* If debt securities are to be registered, state the title of such securities, the principal amount being offered, and, if a series, the total amount authorized and the total amount outstanding as of the most recent practicable date; and describe such of the matter listed in paragraphs (b)(1) through (10) as are relevant. A complete legal description of the securities need not be given. For purposes solely of this Item, debt securities that differ from one another only as to the interest rate or maturity shall be regarded as securities of the same class. Outline briefly:

(1) Provisions with respect to maturity, interest, conversion, redemption, amortization, sinking fund, or retirement;

(2) Provisions with respect to the kind and priority of any lien securing the securities, together with a brief identification of the principal properties subject to such lien;

(3) Provisions with respect to the subordination of the rights of holders of the securities to other security holders or creditors of the registrant; where debt securities are designated as subordinated in accordance with Instruction 1 to this Item, set forth the aggregate amount of outstanding indebtedness as of the most recent practicable date that by the terms of such debt securities would be senior to such subordinated debt and describe briefly any limitation on the issuance of such additional senior indebtedness or state that there is no such limitation;

(4) Provisions restricting the declaration of dividends or requiring the maintenance of any asset ratio or the creation or maintenance of reserves;

(5) Provisions restricting the incurrence of additional debt or the issuance of additional securities; in the case of secured debt, whether the securities being registered are to be issued on the basis of unbonded bondable property, the deposit of cash or otherwise; as of the most recent practicable date, the approximate amount of unbonded bondable property available as a basis for the issuance of bonds; provisions permitting the withdrawal of cash deposited as a basis for the issuance of bonds; and provisions permitting the release or substitution of assets securing the issue; *Provided, however,* That provisions permitting the release of assets upon the deposit of equivalent funds or the pledge of equivalent property, the release of property no longer required in the business, obsolete property, or property taken by eminent domain or the application of insurance moneys, and other similar provisions need not be described;

(6) The general type of event that constitutes a default and whether or not any periodic evidence is required to be furnished as to the absence of default or as to compliance with the terms of the indenture;

(7) Provisions relating to modification of the terms of the security or the rights of security holders;

(8) If the rights evidenced by the securities to be registered are, or may be, materially limited or qualified by the rights of any other authorized class of securities, the information regarding such other securities as will enable investors to understand the rights evidenced by the securities; to the extent not otherwise disclosed pursuant to this Item, no information need be given, however, as to any class of securities all of which will be retired, provided appropriate steps to ensure such retirement will be completed prior to or upon delivery by the registrant of the securities;

(9) If debt securities are to be offered at a price such that they will be deemed to be offered at an "original issue discount" as defined in paragraph (a) of Section 1273 of the Internal Revenue Code (26 U.S.C. 1273), or if a debt security is sold in a package with another security and the allocation of the offering price between the two securities may have the effect of offering the debt security at such an original issue discount, the tax effects thereof pursuant to sections 1271-1278; and

(10) The name of the trustee(s) and the nature of any material relationship with the registrant or with any of its affiliates; the percentage of securities of the class necessary to require the trustee to take action; and what indemnification the trustee may require before proceeding to enforce the lien.

(c) *Warrants and rights.* If the securities described are to be offered pursuant to warrants or rights state:

(1) The amount of securities called for by such warrants or rights;

(2) The period during which and the price at which the warrants or rights are exercisable;

(3) The amount of warrants or rights outstanding;

(4) Provisions for changes to or adjustments in the exercise price; and

(5) Any other material terms of such rights or warrants.

13

(d) *Other securities.* If securities other than capital stock, debt, warrants or rights are to be registered, include a brief description (comparable to that required in paragraphs (a), (b) and (c) of Item 202) of the rights evidenced thereby.

(e) *Market information for securities other than common equity.* If securities other than common equity are to be registered and there is an established public trading market for such securities (as that term is used in Item 201 of Regulation S-K (§229.201 of this chapter)) provide market information with respect to such securities comparable to that required by paragraph (a) of Item 201 of Regulation S-K (§229.201).

(f) *American Depositary Receipts.* If Depositary Shares represented by American Depositary Receipts are being registered, furnish the following information:

   (1)   The name of the depositary and the address of its principal executive office.

   (2)   State the title of the American Depositary Receipts and identify the deposited security. Describe briefly the terms of deposit, including the provisions, if any, with respect to: (i) the amount of deposited securities represented by one unit of American Depositary Receipts; (ii) the procedure for voting, if any, the deposited securities; (iii) the collection and distribution of dividends; (iv) the transmission of notices, reports and proxy soliciting material; (v) the sale or exercise of rights; (vi) the deposit or sale of securities resulting from dividends, splits or plans of reorganization; (vii) amendment, extension or termination of the deposit; (viii) rights of holders of receipts to inspect the transfer books of the depositary and the list of holders of receipts; (ix) restrictions upon the right to deposit or withdraw the underlying securities; (x) limitation upon the liability of the depositary.

   (3)   Describe all fees and charges which may be imposed directly or indirectly against the holder of the American Depositary Receipts, indicating the type of service, the amount of fee or charges and to whom paid.

Instructions to Item 202.

1.   Wherever the title of securities is required to be stated, there shall be given such information as will indicate the type and general character of the securities, including the following:

   A.   In the case of shares, the par or stated value, if any; the rate of dividends, if fixed, and whether cumulative or non-cumulative; a brief indication of the preference, if any; and if convertible or redeemable, a statement to that effect;

   B.   In the case of debt, the rate of interest; the date of maturity or, if the issue matures serially, a brief indication of the serial maturities, such as "maturing serially from 1955 to 1960"; if the payment of principal or interest is contingent, an appropriate indication of such contingency; a brief indication of the priority of the issue; and, if convertible or callable, a statement to that effect; or

   C.   In the case of any other kind of security, appropriate information of comparable character.

2.   If the registrant is a foreign registrant, include (to the extent not disclosed in the document pursuant to Item 201 of Regulation S-K (§229.201) or otherwise) in the description of the securities:

   A.   A brief description of any limitations on the right of nonresident or foreign owners to hold or vote such securities imposed by foreign law or by the charter or other constituent document of the registrant, or if no such limitations are applicable, so state;

   B.   A brief description of any governmental laws, decrees or regulations in the country in which the registrant is organized affecting the remittance of dividends, interest and other payments to nonresident holders of the securities being registered;

   C.   A brief outline of all taxes, including withholding provisions, to which United States security holders are subject under existing laws and regulations of the foreign country in which the registrant is organized; and

   D.   A brief description of pertinent provisions of any reciprocal tax treaty between such foreign country and the United States regarding withholding or, if there is no such treaty, so state.

3.   Section 305(a)(2) of the Trust Indenture Act of 1939, 15 U.S.C. 77aaa et seq., as amended ("Trust Indenture Act"), shall not be deemed to require the inclusion in a registration statement or in a prospectus of any information not required by this Item.

4.   Where convertible securities or stock purchase warrants are being registered that are subject to redemption or call, the description of the conversion terms of the securities or material terms of the warrants shall disclose:

   A.   Whether the right to convert or purchase the securities will be forfeited unless it is exercised before the date specified in a notice of the redemption or call;

   B.   The expiration or termination date of the warrants;

14

C.   The kinds, frequency and timing of notice of the redemption or call, including the cities or newspapers in which notice will be published (where the securities provide for a class of newspapers or group of cities in which the publication may be made at the discretion of the registrant, the registrant should describe such provision); and

D.   In the case of bearer securities, that investors are responsible for making arrangements to prevent loss of the right to convert or purchase in the event of redemption of call, for example, by reading the newspapers in which the notice of redemption or call may be published.

5.   The response to paragraph (f) shall include information with respect to fees and charges in connection with (A) the deposit or substitution of the underlying securities; (B) receipt and distribution of dividends; (C) the sale or exercise of rights; (D) the withdrawal of the underlying security; and (E) the transferring, splitting or grouping of receipts. Information with respect to the right to collect the fees and charges against dividends received and deposited securities shall be included in response to this item.

Subpart 229.300 — Financial Information

Selected Financial Data

Reg. §229.301. Item 301. Furnish in comparative columnar form the selected financial data for the registrant referred to below, for

(a)   Each of the last five fiscal years of the registrant (or for the life of the registrant and its predecessors, if less), and

(b)   Any additional fiscal years necessary to keep the information from being misleading.

Instructions to Item 301.

1.   The purpose of the selected financial data shall be to supply in a convenient and readable format selected financial data which highlight certain significant trends in the registrant's financial condition and results of operations.

2.   Subject to appropriate variation to conform to the nature of the registrant's business, the following items shall be included in the table of financial data; net sales or operating revenues; income (loss) from continuing operations; income (loss) from continuing operations per common share; total assets; long-term obligations and redeemable preferred stock (including long-term debt, capital leases, and redeemable preferred stock as defined in §210.5-02.28(a) of Regulation S-X [17 CFR 210]; and cash dividends declared per common share. Registrants may include additional items which they believe would enhance an understanding of and would highlight other trends in their financial condition and results of operations.

Briefly describe, or cross-reference to a discussion thereof, factors such as accounting changes, business combinations or dispositions of business operations, that materially affect the comparability of the information reflected in selected financial data. Discussion of, or reference to, any material uncertainties should also be included where such matters might cause the data reflected herein not to be indicative of the registrant's future financial condition or results of operations.

3.   All references to the registrant in the table of selected financial data and in this Item shall mean the registrant and its subsidiaries consolidated.

4.   If interim period financial statements are included, or are required to be included by Article 3 of Regulation S-X, registrants should consider whether any or all of the selected financial data need to be updated for such interim periods to reflect a material change in the trends indicated; where such updating information is necessary, registrants shall provide the information on a comparative basis unless not necessary to an understanding of such updating information.

5.   A foreign private issuer shall disclose also the following information in all filings containing financial statements:

A.   In the forepart of the document and as of the latest practicable date, the exchange rate into U.S. currency of the foreign currency in which the financial statements are denominated;

B.   A history of exchange rates for the five most recent years and any subsequent interim period for which financial statements are presented setting forth the rates for period end, the average rates, and the range of high and low rates for each year, and

C.   If equity securities are being registered, a five year summary of dividends per share stated in both the currency in which the financial statements are denominated and United States currency based on the exchange rates at each respective payment date.

6.   A foreign private issuer shall present the selected financial data in the same currency as its financial statements. The issuer may present the selected financial data on the basis of the accounting principles used in its primary financial statements but in such case shall present this data also on the basis of any reconciliations of such data to United States generally accepted accounting principles and Regulation S-X made pursuant to Rule 4-01 of Regulation S-X (§210.4-01 of this chapter).

7.   For purposes of this rule, the rate of exchange means the noon buying rate in New York City for cable transfers in foreign currencies as certified for customs purposes by the Federal Reserve Bank of New York. The average rate means the average of the exchange rates on the last day of each month during a year.

Supplementary Financial Information

Reg. §229.302. Item 302.

(a) *Selected quarterly financial data.* Registrants specified in paragraph (a)(5) of this Item shall provide the information specified below.

    (1) Disclosure shall be made of net sales, gross profit (net sales less cost and expenses associated directly with or allocated to products sold or services rendered), income (loss) before extraordinary items and cumulative effect of a change in accounting, per share data based upon such income (loss), and net income (loss), for each full quarter within the two most recent fiscal years and any subsequent interim period for which financial statements are included or are required to be included by Article 3 of Regulation S-X [17 CFR 210].

    (2) When the data supplied pursuant to this paragraph (a) vary from the amounts previously reported on the Form 10-Q (§249.308a of this chapter) filed for any quarter, such as would be the case when a pooling of interests occurs or where an error is corrected, reconcile the amounts given with those previously reported and describe the reason for the difference.

    (3) Describe the effect of any disposals of segments of a business, and extraordinary, unusual or infrequently occurring items recognized in each full quarter within the two most recent fiscal years and any subsequent interim period for which financial statements are included or are required to be included by Article 3 of Regulation S-X, as well as the aggregate effect and the nature of year-end or other adjustments which are material to the results of that quarter.

    (4) If the financial statements to which this information relates have been reported on by an accountant, appropriate professional standards and procedures, as enumerated in the Statements of Auditing Standards issued by the Auditing Standards Board of the American Institute of Certified Public Accountants, shall be followed by the reporting accountant with regard to the data required by this paragraph (a).

    (5) This paragraph (a) applies to any registrant, except a foreign private issuer that meets both of the following tests:

        (i) First test. The registrant:

            (A) Has securities registered pursuant to section 12(b) of the Exchange Act (other than mutual life insurance companies); or

            (B) Is an insurance company that is subject to the reporting requirements of section 15(d) of the Exchange Act and has securities which also meet the criteria set forth in paragraphs (C)(*1*) and (C)(*2*) immediately following; or

            (C) Has securities registered pursuant to section 12(g) of the Exchange Act which also

                (1) Are quoted on the Nationa! Association of Securities Dealers Automated Quotation System, and

                (2) Meet the following criteria:

        (i) Three or more dealers stand willing to, and do in fact, make a market in such stock, including making regularly published bona fide bids and offers for such stock for their own accounts; or the stock is registered on a securities exchange that is exempted by the Commission from registration as a national securities exchange pursuant to section 5 of the Exchange Act; for purposes of this paragraph, the insertion of quotations into the National Association of Securities Dealers Automated Quotation System by three or more dealers on at least 10 business days during the six month period immediately preceding the fiscal year for which the financial statements are required shall satisfy the requirement that three dealers be making a market;

        (ii) There continue to be 800 or more holders of record, as defined in Rule 12g5-1 (§240.12g5-1 of this chapter), under the Exchange Act, of the stock who are not officers, directors, or beneficial owners of 10 percent or more of the stock;

        (iii) The registrant continues to be a United States corporation;

        (iv) There are 300,000 or more of such securities outstanding in addition to shares held beneficially by officers, directors, or beneficial owners of more than 10 percent of the stock; and

        (v) In addition, the registrant shall meet two of the three following requirements;

            (A) The shares described in paragraph (5)(i)(C)(*2*)(*iv*) of this Item continue to have a market value of at least $2.5 million;

            (B) The minimum representative bid price of such stock is at least $5 per share; or

            (C) The registrant continues to have at least $2.5 million of capital, surplus, and undivided profits.

Instructions to Paragraph (a)(5)(i)(C)(2)(v).

1. The computation required by paragraphs *(v)(A)* and *(v)(B)* shall be based on the average of the closing representative bid prices as reported by the National Association of Securities Dealers Automated Quotation System in accordance with Rule 11Ac1-2 under the Exchange Act (§240.11Ac1-2 of this chapter) for the 20 business days immediately preceding the fiscal year for which the financial statements are required.

2. The computation required by paragraph *v(C)* shall be as at the last business day of the fiscal year immediately preceding the fiscal year for which the financial statements are required.

    (ii) Second test. The registrant and its consolidated subsidiaries (A) have had a net income after taxes but before extraordinary items and the cumulative effect of a change in accounting of at least $250,000 for each of the last three fiscal years; or (B) had total assets of at least $200,000,000 for the last fiscal year-end.

(b) *Information about oil and gas producing activities.* Registrants engaged in oil and gas producing activities shall present the information about oil and gas producing activities (as those activities are defined in Regulation S-X, §210.4-10(a)) specified in paragraphs 9-34 of Statement of Financial Accounting Standards ("SFAS") No. 69, "Disclosures about Oil and Gas Producing Activities," if such oil and gas producing activities are regarded as significant under one or more of the tests set forth in paragraph 8 of SFAS No. 69.

Instructions to Paragraph (b).

1. (a) SFAS No. 69 disclosures that relate to annual periods shall be presented for each annual period for which an income statement is required, (b) SFAS No. 69 disclosures required as of the end of an annual period shall be presented as of the date of each audited balance sheet required, and (c) SFAS No. 69 disclosures required as of the beginning of an annual period shall be presented as of the beginning of each annual period for which an income statement is required.

2. This paragraph, together with §210.4-10 of Regulation S-X, prescribes financial reporting standards for the preparation of accounts by persons engaged, in whole or in part, in the production of crude oil or natural gas in the United States, pursuant to Section 503 of the Energy Policy and Conservation Act of 1975 [42 U.S.C. 6383] ("EPCA") and Section 11(c) of the Energy Supply and Environmental Coordination Act of 1974 [15 U.S.C. 796] ("ESECA") as amended by Section 506 of EPCA. The application of this paragraph to those oil and gas producing operations of companies regulated for ratemaking purposes on an individual-company-cost-of-service basis may, however, give appropriate recognition to differences arising because of the effect of the ratemaking process.

3. Any person exempted by the Department of Energy from any recordkeeping or reporting requirements pursuant to Section 11(c) of ESECA, as amended, is similarly exempted from the related provisions of this paragraph in the preparation of accounts pursuant to EPCA. This exemption does not affect the applicability of this paragraph to filings pursuant to the federal securities laws.

Management's Discussion and Analysis of Financial Condition and Results of Operations

Reg. §229.303. Item 303.

(a) *Full fiscal years.* Discuss registrant's financial condition, changes in financial condition and results of operations. The discussion shall provide information as specified in paragraphs (a)(1), (2) and (3) with respect to liquidity, capital resources and results of operations and also shall provide such other information that the registrant believes to be necessary to an understanding of its financial condition, changes in financial condition and results of operations. Discussions of liquidity and capital resources may be combined whenever the two topics are interrelated. Where in the registrant's judgment a discussion of segment information or of other subdivisions of the registrant's business would be appropriate to an understanding of such business, the discussion shall focus on each relevant, reportable segment or other subdivision of the business and on the registrant as a whole.

    (1) *Liquidity.* Identify any known trends or any known demands, commitments, events or uncertainties that will result in or that are reasonably likely to result in the registrant's liquidity increasing or decreasing in any material way. If a material deficiency is identified, indicate the course of action that the registrant has taken or proposes to take to remedy the deficiency. Also identify and separately describe internal and external sources of liquidity, and briefly discuss any material unused sources of liquid assets.

    (2) *Capital resources.*

        (i) Describe the registrant's material commitments for capital expenditures as of the end of the latest fiscal period, and indicate the general purpose of such commitments and the anticipated source of funds needed to fulfill such commitments.

        (ii) Describe any known material trends, favorable or unfavorable, in the registrant's capital resources. Indicate any expected material changes in the mix and relative cost of such resources. The discussion shall consider changes between equity, debt and any off-balance sheet financing arrangements.

(3) *Results of operations.*

    (i) Describe any unusual or infrequent events or transactions or any significant economic changes that materially affected the amount of reported income from continuing operations and, in each case, indicate the extent to which income was so affected. In addition, describe any other significant components of revenues or expenses that, in the registrant's judgment, should be described in order to understand the registrant's results of operations.

    (ii) Describe any known trends or uncertainties that have had or that the registrant reasonably expects will have a material favorable or unfavorable impact on net sales or revenues or income from continuing operations. If the registrant knows of events that will cause a material change in the relationship between costs and revenues (such as known future increases in costs of labor or materials or price increases or inventory adjustments), the change in the relationship shall be disclosed.

    (iii) To the extent that the financial statements disclose material increases in net sales or revenues, provide a narrative discussion of the extent to which such increases are attributable to increases in prices or to increases in the volume or amount of goods or services being sold or to the introduction of new products or services.

    (iv) For the three most recent fiscal years of the registrant, or for those fiscal years beginning after December 25, 1979, or for those fiscal years in which the registrant has been engaged in business, whichever period is shortest, discuss the impact of inflation and changing prices on the registrant's net sales and revenues and on income from continuing operations.

Instructions to Paragraph 303(a).

1. The registrant's discussion and analysis shall be of the financial statements and of other statistical data that the registrant believes will enhance a reader's understanding of its financial condition, changes in financial condition and results of operations Generally, the discussion shall cover the three year period covered by the financial statements and shall use year-to-year comparisons or any other formats that in the registrant's judgment enhance a reader's understanding. However, where trend information is relevant, reference to the five year selected financial data appearing pursuant to Item 301 of Regulation S-K (§229.301) may be necessary.

2. The purpose of the discussion and analysis shall be to provide to investors and other users information relevant to an assessment of the financial condition and results of operations of the registrant as determined by evaluating the amounts and certainty of cash flows from operations and from outside sources. The information provided pursuant to this Item need only include that which is available to the registrant without undue effort or expense and which does not clearly appear in the registrant's financial statements.

3. The discussion and analysis shall focus specifically on material events and uncertainties known to management that would cause reported financial information not to be necessarily indicative of future operating results or of future financial condition. This would include descriptions and amounts of (A) matters that would have an impact on future operations and have not had an impact in the past, and (B) matters that have had an impact on reported operations and are not expected to have an impact upon future operations.

4. Where the consolidated financial statements reveal material changes from year to year in one or more line items, the causes for the changes shall be described to the extent necessary to an understanding of the registrant's businesses as a whole; *Provided, however,* That if the causes for a change in one line item also relate to other line items, no repetition is required and a line-by-line analysis of the financial statements as a whole is not required or generally appropriate. Registrants need not recite the amounts of changes from year to year which are readily computable from the financial statements. The discussion shall not merely repeat numerical data contained in the consolidated financial statements.

5. The term "liquidity" as used in this Item refers to the ability of an enterprise to generate adequate amounts of cash to meet the enterprise's needs for cash. Except where it is otherwise clear from the discussion, the registrant shall indicate those balance sheet conditions or income or cash flow items which the registrant believes may be indicators of its liquidity condition. Liquidity generally shall be discussed on both a long-term and short-term basis. The issue of liquidity shall be discussed in the context of the registrant's own business or businesses. For example a discussion of working capital may be appropriate for certain manufacturing, industrial or related operations but might be inappropriate for a bank or public utility.

6. Where financial statements presented or incorporated by reference in the registration statement are required by §210.4-08(e)(3) of Regulation S-X [17 CFR Part 210] to include disclosure of restrictions on the ability of both consolidated and unconsolidated subsidiaries to transfer funds to the registrant in the form of cash dividends, loans or advances, the discussion of liquidity shall include a discussion of the nature and extent of such restrictions and the impact such restrictions have had and are expected to have on the ability of the parent company to meet its cash obligations.

7. Registrants are encouraged, but not required, to supply forward-looking information. This is to be distinguished from presently known data which will impact upon future operating results, such as known future increases in costs of labor or materials. This lat-

ter data may be required to be disclosed. Any forward-looking information supplied is expressly covered by the safe harbor rule for projections. See Rule 175 under the Securities Act [17 CFR 230.175], Rule 3b-6 under the Exchange Act [17 CFR 240.3b-6] and Securities Act Release No. 6084 (June 25, 1979) (44 FR 33810).

8. Registrants are only required to discuss the effects of inflation and other changes in prices when considered material. This discussion may be made in whatever manner appears appropriate under the circumstances. All that is required is a brief textual presentation of management's views. No specific numerical financial data need be presented except as Rule 3-20(c) of Regulation S-X (§210.3-20(c) of this chapter) otherwise requires. However, registrants may elect to voluntarily disclose supplemental information on the effects of changing prices as provided for in Statement of Financial Accounting Standards No. 89, "Financial Reporting and Changing Prices" or through other supplemental disclosures. The Commission encourages experimentation with these disclosures in order to provide the most meaningful presentation of the impact of price changes on the registrant's financial statements.

9. Registrants that elect to disclose supplementary information on the effects of changing prices as specified by SFAS No. 89, "Financial Reporting and Changing Prices," may combine such explanations with the discussion and analysis required pursuant to this Item or may supply such information separately with appropriate cross reference.

10. All references to the registrant in the discussion and in this Item shall mean the registrant and its subsidiaries consolidated.

11. Foreign private registrants also shall discuss briefly any pertinent governmental economic, fiscal, monetary, or potential policies or factors that have materially affected or could materially affect, directly or indirectly, their operations or investments by United States nationals.

12. If the registrant is a foreign private issuer, the discussion shall focus on the primary financial statements presented in the registration statement or report. There shall be a reference to the reconciliation to United States generally accepted accounting principles, and a discussion of any aspects of the difference between foreign and United States generally accepted accounting principles, not discussed in the reconciliation, that the registrant believes is necessary for an understanding of the financial statements as a whole.

(b) *Interim periods.* If interim period financial statements are included or are required to be included by Article 3 of Regulations S-X (17 CFR 210), a management's discussion and analysis of the financial condition and results of operations shall be provided so as to enable the reader to assess material changes in financial condition and results of operations between the periods specified in paragraphs (b)(1) and (2) of this Item. The discussion and analysis shall include a discussion of material changes in those items specifically listed in paragraph (a) of this Item, except that the impact of inflation and changing prices on operations for interim periods need not be addressed.

(1) *Material changes in financial condition.* Discuss any material changes in financial condition from the end of the preceding fiscal year to the date of the most recent interim balance sheet provided. If the interim financial statements include an interim balance sheet as of the corresponding interim date of the preceding fiscal year, any material changes in financial condition from that date to the date of the most recent interim balance sheet provided also shall be discussed. If discussions of changes from both the end and the corresponding interim date of the preceding fiscal year are required, the discussions may be combined at the discretion of the registrant.

(2) *Material changes in results of operations.* Discuss any material changes in the registrant's results of operations with respect to the most recent fiscal year-to-date period for which an income statement is provided and the corresponding year-to-date period of the preceding fiscal year. If the registrant is required to or has elected to provide an income statement for the most recent fiscal quarter, such discussion also shall cover material changes with respect to that fiscal quarter and the corresponding fiscal quarter in the preceding fiscal year. In addition, if the registrant has elected to provide an income statement for the twelve-month period ended as of the date of the most recent interim balance sheet provided, the discussion also shall cover material changes with respect to that twelve-month and the twelve-month period ended as of the corresponding interim balance sheet date of the preceding fiscal year. Notwithstanding the above, if for purposes of a registration statement a registrant subject to paragraph (b) of §210.3-03 of Regulation S-X provides a statement of income for the twelve-month period ended as of the date of the most recent interim balance sheet provided in lieu of the interim income statements otherwise required, the discussion of material changes in that twelve-month period will be in respect to the preceding fiscal year rather than the corresponding preceding period.

Instructions to Paragraph (b) of Item 303.

1. If interim financial statements are presented together with financial statements for full fiscal years, the discussion of the interim financial information shall be prepared pursuant to this paragraph (b) and the discussion of the full fiscal year's information shall be prepared pursuant to paragraph (a) of this Item. Such discussions may be combined.

2. In preparing the discussion and analysis required by this paragraph (b), the registrant may presume that users of the interim financial information have read or have access to the discussion and analysis required by paragraph (a) for the preceding fiscal year.

3. The discussion and analysis required by this paragraph (b) is required to focus only on material changes. Where the interim financial statements reveal material changes from period to period in one or more significant line items, the causes for the changes shall

be described if they have not already been disclosed; Provided, however, That if the causes for a change in one line item also relate to other line items, no repetition is required. Registrants need not recite the amounts of changes from period to period which are readily computable from the financial statements. The discussion shall not merely repeat numerical data contained in the financial statements. The information provided shall include that which is available to the registrant without undue effort or expense and which does not clearly appear in the registrant's condensed interim financial statements.

4. The registrant's discussion of material changes in results of operations shall identify any significant elements of the registrant's income or loss from continuing operations which do not arise from or are not necessarily representative of the registrant's ongoing business.

5. The registrant shall discuss any seasonal aspects of its business which have had a material effect upon its financial condition or results of operation.

6. Registrants are encouraged but are not required to discuss forward-looking information. Any forward-looking information supplied is expressly covered by the safe harbor rule for projections. See Rule 175 under the Securities Act (17 CFR 230.175), Rule 3b-6 under the Exchange Act (17 CFR 249.3b-6) and Securities Act Release No. 6084 (June 25, 1979) (44 FR 38810).

Changes in and Disagreements with Accountants on Accounting and Financial Disclosure

Reg. §229.304. Item 304.

(a) (1) If during the registrant's two most recent fiscal years or any subsequent interim period, an independent accountant who was previously engaged as the principal accountant to audit the registrant's financial statements, or an independent accountant who was previously engaged to audit a significant subsidiary and on whom the principal accountant expressed reliance in its report, has resigned (or indicated it has declined to stand for re-election after the completion of the current audit) or was dismissed, then the registrant shall:

   (i) State whether the former accountant resigned, declined to stand for re-election or was dismissed and the date thereof.

   (ii) State whether the principal accountant's report on the financial statement for either of the past two years contained an adverse opinion or a disclaimer of opinion, or was qualified or modified as to uncertainty, audit scope, or accounting principles; and also describe the nature of each such adverse opinion, disclaimer of opinion, modification, or qualification.

   (iii) State whether the decision to change accountants was recommended or approved by:

      (A) any audit or similar committee of the board of directors, if the issuer has such a committee; or

      (B) the board of directors, if the issuer has no such committee.

   (iv) State whether during the registrant's two most recent fiscal years and any subsequent interim-period preceding such resignation, declination or dismissal there were any disagreements with the former accountant on any matter of accounting principles or practices, financial statement disclosure, or auditing scope of procedure, which disagreement(s), if not resolved to the satisfaction of the former accountant, would have caused it to make reference to the subject matter of the disagreement(s) in connection with its report. Also, (A) describe each such disagreement; (B) state whether any audit or similar committee of the board of directors, or the board of directors, discussed the subject matter of each of such disagreements with the former accountant; and (C) state whether the registrant has authorized the former accountant to respond fully to the inquiries of the successor accountant concerning the subject matter of each of such disagreements and, if not, describe the nature of any limitation thereon and the reason therefore. The disagreements required to be reported in response to this Item include both those resolved to the former accountant's satisfaction and those not resolved to the former accountant's satisfaction. Disagreements contemplated by this Item are those that occur at the decision-making level, i.e., between personnel of the registrant responsible for presentation of its financial statements and personnel of the accounting firm responsible for rendering its report.

   (v) Provide the information required by paragraphs (a)(1)(iv) of this Item for each of the kinds of events (even though the registrant and the former accountant did not express a difference of opinion regarding the event) listed in paragraphs (A) through (D) below, that occurred within the registrant's two most recent fiscal years and any subsequent interim period preceding the former accountant's resignation, declination to stand for re-election, or dismissal ("reportable events"). If the event led to a disagreement or difference of opinion, then the event should be reported as a disagreement under paragraph (a)(1)(iv) and need not be repeated under this paragraph.

      (A) The accountant's having advised the registrant that the internal controls necessary for the registrant to develop reliable financial statements do not exist;

(B) the accountant's having advised the registrant that information has come to the accountant's attention that has led it to no longer be able to rely on management's representations, or that has made it unwilling to be associated with the financial statements prepared by management;

(C) *(1)* the accountant's having advised the registrant of the need to expand significantly the scope of its audit, or that information has come to the accountant's attention during the time period covered by Item 304(a)(1)(iv), that if further investigated may *(i)* materially impact the fairness or reliability of either: a previously issued audit report or the underlying financial statements; or the financial statements issued or to be issued covering the fiscal period(s) subsequent to the date of the most recent financial statements covered by an audit report (including information that may prevent it from rendering an unqualified audit report on those financial statements), or *(ii)* cause it to be unwilling to rely on management's representations or be associated with the registrant's financial statements, and *(2)* due to the accountant's resignation (due to audit scope limitations or otherwise) or dismissal, or for any other reason, the accountant did not so expand the scope of its audit or conduct such further investigation; or

(D) *(1)* the accountant's having advised the registrant that information has come to the accountant's attention that it has concluded materially impacts the fairness or reliability of either *(i)* a previously issued audit report or the underlying financial statements, or *(ii)* the financial statements issued or to be issued covering the fiscal period(s) subsequent to the date of the most recent financial statements covered by an audit report (including information that, unless resolved to the accountant's satisfaction, would prevent it from rendering an unqualified audit report on those financial statements), and *(2)* due to the accountant's resignation, dismissal or declination to stand for re-election, or for any other reason, the issue has not been resolved to the accountant's satisfaction prior to its resignation, dismissal or declination to stand for re-election.

(2) If during the registrant's two most recent fiscal years or any subsequent interim period, a new independent accountant has been engaged as either the principal accountant to audit the registrant's financial statements, or as an independent accountant to audit a significant subsidiary and on whom the principal accountant is expected to express reliance in its report, then the registrant shall identify the newly engaged accountant and indicate the date of such accountant's engagement. In addition, if during the registrant's two most recent fiscal years, and any subsequent interim period prior to engaging that accountant, the registrant (or someone on its behalf) consulted the newly engaged accountant regarding (i) either: the application of accounting principles to a specified transaction, either completed or proposed; or the type of audit opinion that might be rendered on the registrant's financial statements, and either a written report was provided to the registrant or oral advice was provided that the new accountant concluded was an important factor considered by the registrant in reaching a decision as to the accounting, auditing or financial reporting issue; or (ii) any matter that was either the subject of a disagreement (as defined in paragraph 304(a)(1)(iv) and the related instructions to this item) or a reportable event (as described in paragraph 304(a)(1)(v)), then the registrant shall:

(A) so state and identify the issues that were the subjects of those consultations;

(B) briefly describe the views of the newly engaged accountant as expressed orally or in writing to the registrant on each such issue and, if written views were received by the registrant, file them as an exhibit to the report or registration statement requiring compliance with this Item 304(a);

(C) state whether the former accountant was consulted by the registrant regarding any such issues, and if so, provide a summary of the former accountant's views; and

(D) request the newly engaged accountant to review the disclosure required by this Item 304(a) before it is filed with the Commission and provide the new accountant the opportunity to furnish the registrant with a letter addressed to the Commission containing any new information, clarification of the registrant's expression of its views, or the respects in which it does not agree with the statements made by the registrant in response to Item 304(a). The registrant shall file any such letter as an exhibit to the report or registration statement containing the disclosure required by this Item.

(3) The registrant shall provide the former accountant with a copy of the disclosures it is making in response to this Item 304(a) that the former accountant shall receive no later than the day that the disclosures are filed with the Commission. The registrant shall request the former accountant to furnish the registrant with a letter addressed to the Commission stating whether it agrees with the statements made by the registrant in response to this Item 304(a) and, if not, stating the respects in which it does not agree. The registrant shall file the former accountant's letter as an exhibit to the report or registration statement containing this disclosure. If the former accountant's letter is unavailable at the time of filing such report or registration statement. Notwithstanding the ten business day period, the registrant shall file the letter by amendment within two business days of receipt; if the letter is received on a Saturday, Sunday or holiday on which the Commission is not open for business, then the two business day period shall begin to run on and shall include the first business day thereafter. The former accountant may provide the registrant with an interim letter highlighting specific areas of concern and indicating that

a more detailed letter will be forthcoming within the ten business day period noted above. If not filed with the report or registration statement containing the registrant's disclosure under this Item 304 (a), then the interim letter, if any, shall be filed by the registrant by amendment within two business days of receipt.

(b) If, (1) in connection with a change in accountants subject to paragraph (a) of this Item 304, there was any disagreement of the type described in paragraph (a)(1)(iv) or any reportable event as described in paragraph (a)(1)(v) of this Item; (2) during the fiscal year in which the change in accountants took place or during the subsequent fiscal year, there have been any transactions or events similar to those which involved such disagreement or reportable event and (3) such transactions or events were material and were accounted for or disclosed in a manner different from that which the former accountants apparently would have concluded was required, the registrant shall state the existence and nature of the disagreement or reportable event and also state the effect on the financial statements if the method had been followed which the former accountants apparently would have concluded was required. These disclosures need not be made if the method asserted by the former accountants ceases to be generally accepted because of authoritative standards or interpretations subsequently issued.

Instructions to Item 304.

1. The disclosure called for by paragraph (a) of this Item need not be provided if it has been previously reported (as that term is defined in Rule 12b-2 under the Exchange Act (§240.12b-2 of this chapter); the disclosure called for by paragraph (a) must be provided, however, notwithstanding prior disclosure, if required pursuant to Item 9 of Schedule 14A (§240.14a-101 of this chapter). The disclosure called for by paragraph (b) of this section must be furnished, where required, notwithstanding any prior disclosure about accountant changes or disagreements.

2. When disclosure is required by paragraph (a) of this section in an annual report to security holders pursuant to Rule 14a-3 (§240.14a-3 of this chapter) or Rule 14c-3 (§240.14c-3 of this chapter), or in a proxy or information statement filed pursuant to the requirements of Schedule 14A or 14C (§240.14a-101 or §240.14c-101 of this chapter), in lieu of a letter pursuant to paragraph (a)(2)(D) or (a)(3), prior to filing such materials with or furnishing such materials to the Commission, the registrant shall furnish the disclosure required by paragraph (a) of this section to any former accountant engaged by the registrant during the period set forth in paragraph (a) of this section and to the newly engaged accountant. If any such accountant believes that the statements made in response to paragraph (a) of this section are incorrect or incomplete, it may present its views in a brief statement, ordinarily expected not to exceed 200 words, to be included in the annual report or proxy or information statement. This statement shall be submitted to the registrant within ten business days of the date the accountant receives the registrant's disclosure. Further, unless the written views of the newly engaged accountant required to be filed as an exhibit by paragraph (a)(2)(B) of this Item 304 have been previously filed with the Commission the registrant shall file a Form 8-K concurrently with the annual report or proxy or information statement for the purpose of filing the written views as exhibits thereto.

3. The information required by Item 304(a) need not be provided for a company being acquired by the registrant that is not subject to the filing requirements of either section 13(a) or 15(d) of the Exchange Act, or, because of section 12(i) of the Exchange Act, has not furnished an annual report to security holders pursuant to Rule 14a-3 or Rule 14c-3 for its latest fiscal year.

4. The term 'disagreements' as used in this Item shall be interpreted broadly, to include any difference of opinion concerning any matter of accounting principles or practices, financial statements disclosure, or auditing scope or procedure which (if not resolved to the satisfaction of the former accountant) would have caused it to make reference to the subject matter of the disagreement in connection with its report. It is not necessary for there to have been an argument to have had a disagreement, merely a difference of opinion. For purposes of this Item, however, the term disagreements does not include initial differences of opinion based on incomplete facts or preliminary information that were later resolved to the former accountant's satisfaction by, and providing the registrant and the accountant do not continue to have a difference of opinion upon, obtaining additional relevant facts or information.

5. In determining whether any disagreement or reportable event has occurred, an oral communication from the engagement partner or another person responsible for rendering the accounting firm's opinion (or their designee) will generally suffice as the accountant advising the registrant of a reportable event or as a statement of a disagreement at the "decision-making level" within the accounting firm and require disclosure under this Item.

Subpart 229.400 — Management and Certain Security Holders

Directors, Executive Officers, Promoters and Control Persons

Reg. §229.401. Item 401.

(a) *Identification of directors.* List the names and ages of all directors of the registrant and all persons nominated or chosen to become directors; indicate all positions and offices with the registrant held by each such person; state his term of office as director and any period(s) during which he has served as such; describe briefly any arrangement or understanding between him and any other person(s) (naming such person(s)) pursuant to which he was or is to be selected as a director or nominee.

Instructions to Paragraph (a) of Item 401.

1. Do not include arrangements or understandings with directors or officers of the registrant acting solely in their capacities as such.

2. No nominee or person chosen to become a director who has not consented to act as such shall be named in response to this Item. In this regard, with respect to proxy statements, see Rule 14a-4(d) under the Exchange Act (§240.14a-4(d) of this chapter).

3. If the information called for by this paragraph (a) is being presented in a proxy or information statement, no information need be given respecting any director whose term of office as a director will not continue after the meeting to which the statement relates.

4. With regard to proxy statements in connection with action to be taken concerning the election of directors, if fewer nominees are named than the number fixed by or pursuant to the governing instruments, state the reasons for this procedure and that the proxies cannot be voted for a greater number of persons than the number of nominees named.

5. With regard to proxy statements in connection with action to be taken concerning the election of directors, if the solicitation is made by persons other than management, information shall be given as to nominees of the persons making the solicitation. In all other instances, information shall be given as to directors and persons nominated for election or chosen by management to become directors.

(b) *Identification of executive officers.* List the names and ages of all executive officers of the registrant and all persons chosen to become executive officers; indicate all positions and offices with the registrant held by each such person; state his term of office as officer and the period during which he has served as such and describe briefly any arrangement or understanding between him and any other person(s) (naming such person(s)) pursuant to which he was or is to be selected as an officer.

Instructions to Paragraph (b) of Item 401.

1. Do not include arrangements or understandings with directors or officers of the registrant acting solely in their capacities as such.

2. No person chosen to become an executive officer who has not consented to act as such shall be named in response to this Item.

3. The information regarding executive officers called for by this Item need not be furnished in proxy or information statements prepared in accordance with Schedule 14A under the Exchange Act (§240.14a-101 of this chapter) by those registrants relying on General Instruction G of Form 10-K under the Exchange Act (§249.310 of this chapter), *Provided,* That such information is furnished in a separate item captioned "Executive officers of the registrant" and included in Part I of the registrant's annual report on Form 10-K.

(c) *Identification of certain significant employees.* Where the registrant employs persons such as production managers, sales managers, or research scientists who are not executive officers but who make or are expected to make significant contributions to the business of the registrant, such persons shall be identified and their background disclosed to the same extent as in the case of executive officers. Such disclosure need not be made if the registrant was subject to section 13(a) or 15(d) of the Exchange Act or was exempt from section 13(a) by section 12(g)(2)(G) of such Act immediately prior to the filing of the registration statement, report, or statement to which this Item is applicable.

(d) *Family relationships.* State the nature of any family relationship between any director, executive officer, or person nominated or chosen by the registrant to become a director or executive officer.

Instructions to Paragraph (d) of Item 401. The term "family relationship" means any relationship by blood, marriage, or adoption, not more remote than first cousin.

(e) *Business experience.*

(1) *Background.* Briefly describe the business experience during the past five years of each director, executive officer, person nominated or chosen to become a director or executive officer, and each person named in answer to paragraph (c) of Item 401, including: each person's principal occupations and employment during the past five years; the name and principal business of any corporation or other organization in which such occupations and employment were carried on; and whether such corporation or organization is a parent, subsidiary or other affiliate of the registrant. When an executive officer or person named in response to paragraph (c) of Item 401 has been employed by the registrant or a subsidiary of the registrant for less than five years, a brief explanation shall be included as to the nature of the responsibility undertaken by the individual in prior positions to provide adequate disclosure of his prior business experience. What is required is information relating to the level of his professional competence, which may include, depending upon the circumstances, such specific information as the size of the operation supervised.

(2) *Directorships.* Indicate any other directorships held by each director or person nominated or chosen to become a director in any company with a class of securities registered pursuant to section 12 of the Exchange Act or subject to the requirements of section 15(d) of such Act or any company registered as an investment company under the Investment Company Act of 1940, 15 U.S.C. 80a-1, et seq., as amended, naming such company.

23

(f) *Involvement in certain legal proceedings.* Describe any of the following events that occurred during the past five years and that are material to an evaluation of the ability or integrity of any director, person nominated to become a director or executive officer of the registrant:

(1) A petition under the Federal bankruptcy laws or any state insolvency law was filed by or against, or a receiver, fiscal agent or similar officer was appointed by a court for the business or property of such person, or any partnership in which he was a general partner at or within two years before the time of such filing, or any corporation or business association of which he was an executive officer at or within two years before the time of such filing;

(2) Such person was convicted in a criminal proceeding or is a named subject of a pending criminal proceeding (excluding traffic violations and other minor offenses);

(3) Such person was the subject of any order, judgment, or decree, not subsequently reversed, suspended or vacated, of any court of competent jurisdiction, permanently or temporarily enjoining him from, or otherwise limiting, the following activities:

    (i) Acting as a futures commission merchant, introducing broker, commodity trading advisor, commodity pool operator, floor broker, leverage transaction merchant, any other person regulated by the Commodity Futures Trading Commission, or an associated person of any of the foregoing, or as an investment adviser, underwriter, broker or dealer in securities, or as an affiliated person, director or employee of any investment company, bank, savings and loan association or insurance company, or engaging in or continuing any conduct or practice in connection with such activity;

    (ii) Engaging in any type of business practice; or

    (iii) Engaging in any activity in connection with the purchase or sale of any security or commodity or in connection with any violation of Federal or State securities laws or Federal commodities laws;

(4) Such person was the subject of any order, judgment or decree, not subsequently reversed, suspended or vacated, of any Federal or State authority barring, suspending or otherwise limiting for more than 60 days the right of such person to engage in any activity described in paragraph (f)(3)(i) of this Item, or to be associated with persons engaged in any such activity; or

(5) Such person was found by a court of competent jurisdiction in a civil action or by the Commission to have violated any Federal or State securities law, and the judgment in such civil action or finding by the Commission has not been subsequently reversed, suspended, or vacated.

(6) Such person was found by a court of competent jurisdiction in a civil action or by the Commodity Futures Trading Commission to have violated any Federal commodities law, and the judgment in such civil action or finding by the Commodity Futures Trading Commission has not been subsequently reversed, suspended or vacated.

Instructions to Paragraph (f) of Item 401.

1. For purposes of computing the five year period referred to in this paragraph, the date of a reportable event shall be deemed the date on which the final order, judgment or decree was entered, or the date on which any rights of appeal from preliminary orders, judgments, or decrees have lapsed. With respect to bankruptcy petitions, the computation date shall be the date of filing for uncontested petitions or the date upon which approval of a contested petition became final.

2. If any event specified in this paragraph (f) has occurred and information in regard thereto is omitted on the grounds that it is not material, the registrant may furnish to the Commission, at time of filing (or at the time preliminary materials are filed pursuant to Rule 14a-6 or 14c-5 under the Exchange Act (§§240.14a-6 and 240.14c-5 of this chapter), as supplemental information and not as part of the registration statement, report, or proxy or information statement, materials to which the omission relates, a description of the event and a statement of the reasons for the omission of information in regard thereto.

3. The registrant is permitted to explain any mitigating circumstances associated with events reported pursuant to this paragraph.

4. If the information called for by this paragraph (f) is being presented in a proxy or information statement, no information need be given respecting any director whose term of office as a director will not continue after the meeting to which the statement relates.

(g) *Promoters and control persons*

(1) Registrants, which have not been subject to the reporting requirements of Section 13(a) or 15(d) of the Exchange Act for the twelve months immediately prior to the filing of the registration statement, report, or statement to which this Item is applicable, and which were organized within the last five years, shall describe with respect to any promoter, any of the events enumerated in paragraphs (f)(1) through (f)(6) of this section that occurred during the past five years and that are material to a voting or investment decision.

(2) Registrants, which have not been subject to the reporting requirements of Section 13(a) or 15(d) of the Exchange Act for the twelve months immediately prior to the filing of the registration statement, report, or statement to which this Item is ap-

plicable, shall describe with respect to any control person, any of the events enumerated in paragraphs (f)(1) through (f)(6) of this section that occurred during the past five years and that are material to a voting or investment decision.

Instructions to Paragraph (g) of Item 401.

1. Instructions 1. through 3. to paragraph (f) shall apply to this paragraph (g).

2. Paragraph (g) shall not apply to any subsidiary of a registrant which has been reporting pursuant to Section 13(a) or 15(d) of the Exchange Act for the twelve months immediately prior to the filing of the registration statement, report or statement.

Executive Compensation

Reg. §229.402. Item 402.

(a) (1) *Cash compensation.* Furnish in substantially the tabular form specified, all cash compensation paid to the following persons through the latest practicable date for services rendered in all capacities to the registrant and its subsidiaries during the registrant's last fiscal year.

   (i) *Five executive officers.* Each of the registrant's five most highly compensated executive officers whose cash compensation required to be disclosed pursuant to this paragraph exceeds $60,000, naming each such person; and

   (ii) *All executive officers.* All executive officers as a group, stating the number of persons in the group without naming them.

(2) *Bonuses and deferred compensation.* The Cash Compensation Table also shall include:

   (i) All cash bonuses to be paid to the named individuals and group for services rendered in all capacities to the registrant and its subsidiaries during the last fiscal year unless such amounts have not been allocated at such time as compensation disclosure is filed;

   (ii) All cash bonuses paid during the last fiscal year for services rendered in all capacities to the registrant and its subsidiaries in a previous fiscal year, less any amount relating to the same contract, agreement, plan or arrangement included in the Cash Compensation Table for a prior fiscal year and less any amount that would have been so included but for the fact that the individual was not included in the Cash Compensation Table; as a named individual or as a member of the group, for such prior fiscal year; and

   (iii) All compensation that would have been paid in cash to the named individuals and group for services rendered in all capacities to the registrant and its subsidiaries during the last fiscal year but for the fact that the payment of such compensation was deferred.

Cash Compensation Table

(A) Name of Individual or Number in Group	(B) Capacities in Which Served	(C) Cash Compensation

Instructions to Item 402(a).

1. *Cash Compensation Table.*

   (A) The registrant may include additional columns in the Cash Compensation Table. For example, the registrant may segregate cash bonuses and deferred compensation from cash salaries and fees.

   (B) Amounts deferred pursuant to Section 401(k) of the Internal Revenue Code are to be included in paragraph (a) for the fiscal year during which they are accrued.

   (C) Registrants need list in Column (B) of the Cash Compensation Table only those principal capacities served by each of the identified individuals. The cash compensation disclosed, however, must include cash compensation received in all capacities.

2. *Persons covered.*

   (A) Paragraph (a) of this section applies to any individual who was an executive officer of the registrant at any time during the last fiscal year. Information need not be disclosed, however, for any portion of the period during which such individual was not an executive officer of the registrant, provided a statement to that effect is made. With respect to an individual who becomes for the first time an individual whose compensation is to be reported in the Cash Compensation Table, it is not necessary to report compensation that would have been reported in the Table had the individual been included in prior years.

(B) Registrants should be flexible in determining which individuals should be named in the Cash Compensation Table in order to ensure that disclosure is made with respect to key policy making members of management. Consideration should be given to the question of whether an individual's level of executive responsibilities, viewed in conjunction with such individual's actual level of cash compensation is such that the registrant reasonably may conclude that the person is among its five most highly compensated, key policy making executive officers. Under this standard, it may be appropriate, in certain circumstances, to include an executive officer of a subsidiary in the Cash Compensation Table.

(C) In certain circumstances, it may be appropriate for a registrant not to include in the Cash Compensation Table an individual who is one of the registrant's five most highly compensated executive officers. Among the factors that should be considered in determining not to name an individual are: (i) The distribution or accrual of an unusually large amount of cash compensation (such as a bonus or commission) that is not part of a recurring arrangement and is unlikely to continue, and (ii) the payment of amounts of cash compensation relating to overseas assignments that may be attributed predominantly to such assignments.

(b) (1) *Compensation pursuant to plans.* Describe briefly all plans, pursuant to which cash or non-cash compensation was paid or distributed during the last fiscal year, or is proposed to be paid or distributed in the future, to the named individuals and group specified in paragraph (a) of this section. Information need not be given with respect to any group life, health, hospitalization, medical reimbursement or relocation plans that do not discriminate, in scope, terms, or operation, in favor of officers or directors of the registrant and that are available generally to all salaried employees. The description of each plan shall include the following, except that the description of any defined benefit or actuarial plans need not include the information specified in paragraphs (b)(1)(vi) and (b)(1)(vii) of this section and the description of any stock option and stock appreciation right plan need not include the information specified in paragraph (b)(1)(vii) of this section:

(i) A summary of how the plan operates and who is covered by the plan;

(ii) The criteria used to determine amounts payable, including any performance formula or measure;

(iii) The time periods over which the measurement of benefits will be determined;

(iv) Payment schedules;

(v) Any recent material amendments to the plan;

(vi) Amounts paid or distributed pursuant to the plan to the named individuals and the group during the last fiscal year less any amount relating to the same plan which previously has been disclosed as accrued pursuant to paragraph (b)(1)(vii) of this section or a predecessor provision; and

(vii) Amounts accrued pursuant to the plan for the accounts of the named individuals and group during the last fiscal year, the distribution or unconditional vesting of which are not subject to future events.

(2) *Pension table.* As to defined benefit and actuarial plans, other than any defined benefit or actuarial plan under which benefits are not determined primarily by final compensation (or average final compensation) and years of service, include, as the payment schedule required by paragraph (b)(1)(iv) of this section, a separate Pension Table showing estimated annual benefits payable upon retirement (including amounts attributable to any defined benefit supplementary or excess pension award plans) in specified compensation and years-of-service classifications. In addition, in furnishing the information required by paragraphs (b)(1)(i)-(v) of this section, include:

(i) The compensation covered by the plan, including the relationship of such covered compensation to the compensation reported in the Cash Compensation Table pursuant to paragraph (a) of this section, and state the current compensation covered by the plan for any individuals named in the Cash Compensation Table whose covered compensation differs substantially (by more than 10 percent) from that set forth in the Cash Compensation Table;

(ii) The estimated credited years of service for each of the individuals named in the Cash Compensation Table; and

(iii) A statement as to the basis upon which benefits are computed (e.g., straight life annuity amounts) and whether or not the benefits listed in the Pension Table are subject to any deduction for Social Security or other offset amounts.

Example of Pension Table

Remuneration	Years of Service				
	15	20	25	30	35
125,000	xxx	xxx	xxx	xxx	xxx
150,000	xxx	xxx	xxx	xxx	xxx
175,000	xxx	xxx	xxx	xxx	xxx
200,000	xxx	xxx	xxx	xxx	xxx
225,000	xxx	xxx	xxx	xxx	xxx

(3) *Alternative pension plan disclosure.* In furnishing the information required by paragraphs (b)(1)(i)-(v) of this section with respect to defined benefit or actuarial plans under which benefits are not determined primarily by final compensation (or average final compensation) and years of service, include:

    (i) The formula by which benefits are determined; and

    (ii) The estimated annual benefits payable upon retirement at normal retirement age for each of the individuals named in the Cash Compensation Table pursuant to paragraph (a) of this section.

(4) *Stock option and stock appreciation right plans.* In addition to providing the information required by paragraphs (b)(1)(i)-(vi) of this section, furnish:

    (i) With respect to stock options granted during the last fiscal year: (A) the title and aggregate amount of securities subject to options; (B) the average per share exercise price; and (C) if such option exercise price was less than 100 percent of the market value of the security on the date of grant, such fact and the market price on such date. The title and aggregate amount of such securities subject to options, if any, which are in tandem with stock appreciation rights should be set forth separately.

    (ii) With respect to the exercise or realization of options or stock appreciation rights held in tandem with options, state the net value of securities (market value less any exercise price) or cash realized during the last fiscal year.

    (iii) With respect to plans pursuant to which stock appreciation rights not in tandem with options were granted during the last fiscal year: (A) the number of rights granted; and (B) the average per share base price thereof.

    (iv) With respect to the exercise or realization of stock appreciation rights not in tandem with options, state the net value of the shares (market price) or cash realized during the last fiscal year.

Instructions to Item 402(b).

1. *Format.* With the exception of those pension plans disclosed pursuant to paragraph 402(b)(2), the registrant may use either a narrative, tabular or other format or combination of formats provided the information so disclosed is clear and understandable. Disclosure required by paragraph (b)(2), pertaining to certain defined benefit and actuarial plans, is required to be presented in the Pension Table format set forth in that paragraph.

2. *Cash paid pursuant to plans.* The cash compensation paid pursuant to a plan need not be disclosed as amounts paid or distributed pursuant to paragraph (b)(1)(vi) of this section if such compensation was included in the Cash Compensation Table pursuant to paragraph (a) of this section and a statement to that effect is made. Similarly, the cash compensation deferred under a deferred compensation plan need not be disclosed as amounts accrued pursuant to paragraph (b)(1)(vii) of this section if such compensation was included in the Cash Compensation Table and a statement to that effect is made.

3. *Definition of "plan."* The term "plan" includes, but is not limited to the following: any plan, contract, authorization or arrangement, whether or not set forth in any formal documents, pursuant to which the following may be received: cash, stock, restricted stock, phantom stock, stock options, stock appreciation rights, stock options in tandem with stock appreciation rights, warrants, convertible securities, performance units and performance shares. A plan may be applicable to one person.

4. *Pension levels.* Compensation set forth in the Pension Table pursuant to paragraph (b)(2) of this section shall allow for reasonable increases in existing compensation levels; alternatively, registrants may present as the highest compensation level in the Pension Table an amount equal to 120 percent of the amount of covered compensation of the most highly compensated individual named in the Cash Compensation Table pursuant to paragraph (a) of this section.

5. *Definition of "normal retirement age."* The term "normal retirement age" means normal retirement age as defined in a pension or similar plan or, if not defined therein, the earliest time at which a participant may retire without any benefit reduction because of age.

(c) *Other compensation.* Describe, stating amounts, any other compensation not covered by paragraphs (a) or (b) of this section that was paid or distributed during the last fiscal year to the named individuals and group specified in paragraph (a) of this section unless:

    (1) With respect to any named individual, the aggregate amount of such other compensation is the lesser of $25,000 or 10 percent of the compensation reported in the Cash Compensation Table for such person pursuant to paragraph (a) of this section or

    (2) With respect to the group, the aggregate amount of such other compensation is the lesser of $25,000 times the number of persons in the group or 10 percent of the compensation reported in the Cash Compensation Table for the group pursuant to paragraph (a) of this section and a statement to that effect is made.

Instructions to Item 402(c).

1. *Scope.* Compensation to be disclosed pursuant to this paragraph may include, among other things: (a) personal benefits or; (b) securities or property that were paid or distributed other than pursuant to a plan. It does not, in any event, include cash, which is to be disclosed pursuant to either paragraph (a) or (b).

2. *Threshold.* If the amount of other compensation for a named individual or group exceeds the established thresholds, the entire amount of such other compensation must be disclosed pursuant to this paragraph.

3. *Valuation.* Compensation within paragraph (c) shall be valued on the basis of the registrant's and subsidiaries' aggregate incremental cost.

(d) *Compensation of directors.*

(1) *Standard arrangements.* Describe any standard arrangement, stating amounts, pursuant to which directors of the registrant are compensated for all services as a director, including any additional amounts payable for committee participation or special assignments.

(2) *Other arrangements.* Describe any other arrangements pursuant to which any director of the registrant was compensated during the registrant's last fiscal year for services as a director, stating the amount paid and the name of the director.

(e) *Termination of employment and change of control arrangement.* Describe any compensatory plan or arrangement, including payments to be received from the registrant, with respect to any individual named in the Cash Compensation Table pursuant to paragraph (a) of this section for the latest or then next preceding fiscal year if such a plan or arrangement results or will result from the resignation, retirement or any other termination of such individual's employment with the registrant and its subsidiaries or from a change in control of the registrant or a change in the individual's responsibilities following a change in control and the amount involved, including all periodic payments or installments, exceeds $60,000.

General Instructions to Item 402.

1. *Foreign private issuers.* A foreign private issuer may respond to all of Item 402 by indicating the aggregate payments or benefits paid or to be paid to all executive officers as a group unless such registrants disclose to their security holders or otherwise make public the information specified in this section for individually named executive officers, in which case such information also shall be disclosed.

2. *Transactions with third parties.* This section includes transactions between the registrant and a third party where the primary purpose of the transaction is to furnish compensation to any named individual or the group specified in paragraph (a) of this section. No information need be given in response to any paragraph of this section as to any such transaction if the transaction has been reported in response to Item 404 of Regulation S-K (§229.404 of this chapter).

3. *Exclusions.* No information need be given pursuant to this Item with respect to interest on deferred compensation provided that the rate of interest does not exceed prevailing market interest rates either: (1) at the time the interest is accrued or (2) at the time the plan pursuant to which the compensation is deferred was established. Similarly, dividends awarded on restricted stock need not be disclosed provided that the restricted stock is not of a particular class available only to certain employees on a discriminatory basis.

Security Ownership of Certain Beneficial Owners and Management

Reg. §229.403. Item 403.

(a) *Security ownership of certain beneficial owners.* Furnish the following information, as of the most recent practicable date, in substantially the tabular form indicated, with respect to any person (including any "group" as that term is used in section 13(d)(3) of the Exchange Act) who is known to the registrant to be the beneficial owner of more than five percent of any class of the registrant's voting securities. The address given in column (2) may be a business, mailing or residence address. Show in column (3) the total number of shares beneficially owned and in column (4) the percentage of class so owned. Of the number of shares shown in column (3), indicate by footnote or otherwise the amount known to be shares with respect to which such listed beneficial owner has the right to acquire beneficial ownership, as specified in Rule 13d-3(d)(1) under the Exchange Act (§240.13d-3(d)(1) of this chapter).

(1) Title of Class	(2) Name and Address of Beneficial Owner	(3) Amount and Nature of Beneficial Owner	(4) Percent of Class

(b) *Security ownership of management.* Furnish the following information, as of the most recent practicable date, in substantially the tabular form indicated, as to each class of equity securities of the registrant or any of its parents or subsidiaries other than directors' qualifying shares, beneficially owned by all directors and nominees, naming them, and directors and officers of the registrant as a group, without naming them. Show in column (3) the total number of shares beneficially owned and in column (4) the percent of class so owned. Of the number of shares shown in column (3), indicate, by footnote or otherwise, the amount of

28

shares with respect to which such persons have the right to acquire beneficial ownership as specified in Rule 13d-3(d)(1) under the Exchange Act.

(1)	(2)	(3)	(4)
	Name and Address	Amount and Nature	
Title of Class	of Beneficial Owner	of Beneficial Owner	Percent of Class

(c) Changes in control. Describe any arrangements, known to the registrant, including any pledge by any person of securities of the registrant or any of its parents, the operation of which may at a subsequent date result in a change in control of the registrant.

Instructions to Item 403.

1. The percentages are to be calculated on the basis of the amount of outstanding securities, excluding securities held by or for the account of the registrant or its subsidiaries, plus securities deemed outstanding pursuant to Rule 13d-3(d)(1) under the Exchange Act [17 CFR 240.13d-3(d)(1)]. For purposes of paragraph (b), if the percentage of shares beneficially owned by any director or nominee, or by all directors and officers of the registrant as a group, does not exceed one percent of the class so owned, the registrant may, in lieu of furnishing a precise percentage, indicate this fact by means of an asterisk and explanatory footnote or other similar means.

2. For the purposes of this Item, beneficial ownership shall be determined in accordance with Rule 13d-3 under the Exchange Act (§240.13d-3 of this chapter). Include such additional subcolumns or other appropriate explanation of column (3) necessary to reflect amounts as to which the beneficial owner has (A) sole voting power, (B) shared voting power, (C) sole investment power, or (D) shared investment power.

3. The registrant shall be deemed to know the contents of any statements filed with the Commission pursuant to section 13(d) or 13(g) of the Exchange Act. When applicable, a registrant may rely upon information set forth in such statements unless the registrant knows or has reason to believe that such information is not complete or accurate or that a statement or amendment should have been filed and was not.

4. For purposes of furnishing information pursuant to paragraph (a) of this Item, the registrant may indicate the source and date of such information.

5. Where more than one beneficial owner is known to be listed for the same securities, appropriate disclosure should be made to avoid confusion. For purposes of paragraph (b), in computing the aggregate number of shares owned by directors and officers of the registrant as a group, the same shares shall not be counted more than once.

6. Paragraph (c) of this Item does not require a description of ordinary default provisions contained in the charter, trust indentures or other governing instruments relating to securities of the registrant.

7. Where the holder(s) of voting securities reported pursuant to paragraph (a) hold more than five percent of any class of voting securities of the registrant pursuant to any voting trust or similar agreement, state the title of such securities, the amount held or to be held pursuant to the trust or agreement (if not clear from the table) and the duration of the agreement. Give the names and addresses of the voting trustees and outline briefly their voting rights and other powers under the trust or agreement.

Certain Relationships and Related Transactions

Reg. §229.404. Item 404.

(a) *Transactions with management and others.* Describe briefly any transaction, or series of similar transactions, since the beginning of the registrant's last fiscal year, or any currently proposed transaction, or series of similar transactions, to which the registrant or any of its subsidiaries was or is to be a party, in which the amount involved exceeds $60,000 and in which any of the following persons had, or will have, a direct or indirect material interest, naming such person and indicating the person's relationship to the registrant, the nature of such person's interest in the transaction(s), the amount of such transaction(s) and, where practicable, the amount of such person's interest in the transaction(s):

   (1)   Any director or executive officer of the registrant;

   (2)   Any nominee for election as a director;

   (3)   Any security holder who is known to the registrant to own of record or beneficially more than five percent of any class of the registrant's voting securities; and

   (4)   Any member of the immediate family of any of the foregoing persons.

Instructions to Paragraph (a) of Item 404.

1. The materiality of any interest is to be determined on the basis of the significance of the information to investors in light of all the circumstances of the particular case. The importance of the interest to the person having the interest, the relationship of the parties

to the transaction with each other and the amount involved in the transactions are among the factors to be considered in determining the significance of the information to investors.

2. For purposes of paragraph (a), a person's immediate family shall include such person's spouse; parents; children; siblings; mothers and fathers-in-law; sons and daughters-in-law; and brothers and sisters-in-law.

3. In computing the amount involved in the transaction or series of similar transactions, include all periodic installments in the case of any lease or other agreement providing for periodic payments or installments.

4. The amount of the interest of any person specified in paragraphs (a)(1) through (4) shall be computed without regard to the amount of the profit or loss involved in the transaction(s).

5. In describing any transaction involving the purchase or sale of assets by or to the registrant or any of its subsidiaries, otherwise than in the ordinary course of business, state the cost of the assets to the purchaser and, if acquired by the seller within two years prior to the transaction, the cost thereof to the seller. Indicate the principal followed in determining the registrant's purchase or sale price and the name of the person making such determination.

6. Information shall be furnished in answer to paragraph (a) with respect to transactions that involve remuneration from the registrant or its subsidiaries, directly or indirectly, to any of the persons specified in paragraphs (a)(1) through (4) for services in any capacity unless the interest of such person arises solely from the ownership individually and in the aggregate of less than ten percent of any class of equity securities of another corporation furnishing the services to the registrant or its subsidiaries.

7. No information need be given in answer to paragraph (a) as to any transaction where:

   A. The rates or charges involved in the transaction are determined by competitive bids, or the transaction involves the rendering of services as a common or contract carrier, or public utility, at rates or charges fixed in conformity with law or governmental authority;

   B. The transaction involves services as a bank depositary of funds, transfer agent, registrar, trustee under a trust indenture, or similar services; or

   C. The interest of the person specified in paragraphs (a)(1) through (4) arises solely from the ownership of securities of the registrant and such person receives no extra or special benefit not shared on a pro rata basis.

8. Paragraph (a) requires disclosure of indirect, as well as direct, material interests in transactions. A person who has a position or relationship with a firm, corporation, or other entity that engages in a transaction with the registrant or its subsidiaries may have an indirect interest in such transaction by reason of such position or relationship. Such an interest, however, shall not be deemed "material" within the meaning of paragraph (a) where:

   A. The interest arises only (i) from such person's position as a director of another corporation or organization which is a party to the transaction; or (ii) from the direct or indirect ownership by such person and all other persons specified in paragraphs (a)(1) through (4), in the aggregate, of less than a ten percent equity interest in another person (other than a partnership) which is a party to the transaction; or (iii) from both such position and ownership;

   B. The interest arises only from such person's position as a limited partner in a partnership in which the person and all other persons specified in paragraphs (a)(1) through (4) have an interest of less than ten percent; or

   C. The interest of such person arises solely from the holding of an equity interest (including a limited partnership interest, but excluding a general partnership interest) or a creditor interest in another person that is a party to the transaction with the registrant or any of its subsidiaries, and the transaction is not material to such other person.

9. There may be situations where, although these instructions do not expressly authorize nondisclosure, the interest of a person specified in paragraphs (a)(1) through (4) in a particular transaction or series of transactions is not a direct or indirect material interest. In that case, information regarding such interest and transaction is not required to be disclosed in response to this paragraph.

(b) *Certain business relationships.* Describe any of the following relationships regarding directors or nominees for director that exist, or have existed during the registrant's last fiscal year, indicating the identity of the entity with which the registrant has such a relationship, the name of the nominee or director affiliated with such entity and the nature of such nominee's or director's affiliation, the relationship between such entity and the registrant and the amount of the business done between the registrant and the entity during the registrant's last full fiscal year or proposed to be done during the registrant's current fiscal year:

   (1) If the nominee or director is, or during the last fiscal year has been, an executive officer of, or owns, or during the last fiscal year has owned, of record or beneficially in excess of ten percent equity interest in, any business or professional entity that has made during the registrant's last full fiscal year, or proposes to make during the registrant's current fiscal year, payments to the registrant or its subsidiaries for property or services in excess of five percent of (i) the registrant's consolidated gross revenues for its last full fiscal year, or (ii) the other entity's consolidated gross revenues for its last full fiscal year;

30

(2) If the nominee or director is, or during the last fiscal year has been, an executive officer of, or owns, or during the last fiscal year has owned, of record or beneficially in excess of ten percent equity interest in, any business or professional entity to which the registrant or its subsidiaries has made during the registrant's last full fiscal year, or proposes to make during the registrant's current fiscal year, payments for property or services in excess of five percent of (i) the registrant's consolidated gross revenues for its last full fiscal year, or (ii) the other entity's consolidated gross revenues for its last full fiscal year;

(3) If the nominee or director is, or during the last fiscal year has been, an executive officer of, or owns, or during the last fiscal year has owned, of record or beneficially in excess of ten percent equity interest in, any business or professional entity to which the registrant or its subsidiaries was indebted at the end of the registrant's last full fiscal year in an aggregate amount in excess of five percent of the registrant's total consolidated assets at the end of such fiscal year;

(4) If the nominee or director is, or during the last fiscal year has been, a member of, or of counsel to, a law firm that the issuer has retained during the last fiscal year or proposes to retain during the current fiscal year; *Provided, however,* that the dollar amount of fees paid to a law firm by the registrant need not be disclosed if such amount does not exceed five percent of the law firm's gross revenues for that firm's last full fiscal year;

(5) If the nominee or director is, or during the last fiscal year has been, a partner or executive officer of any investment banking firm that has performed services for the registrant, other than as a participating underwriter in a syndicate, during the last fiscal year or that the registrant proposes to have perform services during the current year; *Provided, however,* that the dollar amount of compensation received by an investment banking firm need not be disclosed if such amount does not exceed five percent of the investment banking firm's consolidated gross revenues for that firm's last full fiscal year; or

(6) Any other relationships that the registrant is aware of between the nominee or director and the registrant that are substantially similar in nature and scope to those relationships listed in paragraphs (b)(1) through (5).

Instructions to Paragraph (b) of Item 404.
1. In order to determine whether payments or indebtedness exceed five percent of the consolidated gross revenues of any entity, other than the registrant, it is appropriate to rely on information provided by the nominee or director.

2. In calculating payments for property and services the following may be excluded:

   A. Payments where the rates or charges involved in the transaction are determined by competitive bids, or the transaction involves the rendering of services as a common contract carrier, or public utility, at rates or charges fixed in conformity with law or governmental authority;

   B. Payments that arise solely from the ownership of securities of the registrant and no extra or special benefit not shared on a pro rata basis by all holders of the class of securities is received; or

   C. Payments made or received by subsidiaries other than significant subsidiaries as defined in Rule 1-02(v) of Regulation S-X [§210.1-02(v) of this chapter], provided that all such subsidiaries making or receiving payments, when considered in the aggregate as a single subsidiary, would not constitute a significant subsidiary as defined in Rule 1-02(v).

3. In calculating indebtedness the following may be excluded:

   A. Debt securities that have been publicly offered, admitted to trading on a national securities exchange, or quoted on the automated quotation system of a registered securities association;

   B. Amounts due for purchases subject to the usual trade terms; or

   C. Indebtedness incurred by subsidiaries other than significant subsidiaries as defined in Rule 1-02(v) of Regulation S-X [§210.1-02(v) of this chapter], provided that all such subsidiaries incurring indebtedness, when considered in the aggregate as a single subsidiary, would not constitute a significant subsidiary as defined in Rule 1-02(v).

4. No information called for by paragraph (b) need be given respecting any director who is no longer a director at the time of filing the registration statement or report containing such disclosure. If such information is being presented in a proxy or information statement, no information need be given respecting any director whose term of office as a director will not continue after the meeting to which the statement relates.

(c) *Indebtedness of management.* If any of the following persons has been indebted to the registrant or its subsidiaries at any time since the beginning of the registrant's last fiscal year in an amount in excess of $60,000, indicate the name of such person, the nature of the person's relationship by reason of which such person's indebtedness is required to be described, the largest aggregate amount of indebtedness outstanding at any time during such period, the nature of the indebtedness and of the transaction in which it was incurred, the amount thereof outstanding as of the latest practicable date and the rate of interest paid or charged thereon:

(1) Any director or executive officer of the registrant;

(2) Any nominee for election as a director;

(3) Any member of the immediate family of the persons specified in paragraph (c)(1) or (2);

(4) Any corporation or organization (other than the registrant or a majority-owned subsidiary of the registrant) of which any of the persons specified in paragraphs (c)(1) or (2) is an executive officer or partner or is, directly or indirectly, the beneficial owner of ten percent or more of any class of equity securities; and

(5) Any trust or other estate in which any of the persons specified in paragraph (c)(1) or (2) has a substantial beneficial interest or as to which such person serves as a trustee or in a similar capacity.

Instructions to Paragraph (c) of Item 404.

1. For purposes of paragraph (c), the members of a person's immediate family are those persons specified in Instruction 2 to Item 404(a).

2. Exclude from the determination of the amount of indebtedness all amounts due from the particular person for purchases subject to usual trade terms, for ordinary travel and expense payments and for other transactions in the ordinary course of business.

3. If the lender is a bank, savings and loan association, or broker-dealer extending credit under Federal Reserve Regulation T [12 CFR Part 220] and the loans are not disclosed as nonaccrual, past due, restructured or potential problems (see Item III.C.1. and 2. of Industry Guide 3, Statistical Disclosure by Bank Holding Companies), disclosure may consist of a statement, if such is the case, that the loans to such persons (A) were made in the ordinary course of business, (B) were made on substantially the same terms, including interest rates and collateral, as those prevailing at the time for comparable transactions with other persons, and (C) did not involve more than the normal risk of collectibility or present other unfavorable features.

4. If any indebtedness required to be described arose under Section 16(b) of the Exchange Act and has not been discharged by payment, state the amount of any profit realized, that such profit will inure to the benefit of the registrant or its subsidiaries and whether suit will be brought or other steps taken to recover such profit. If, in the opinion of counsel, a question reasonably exists as to the recoverability of such profit, it will suffice to state all facts necessary to describe the transactions, including the prices and number of shares involved.

(d) *Transactions with promoters.* Registrants that have been organized within the past five years and that are filing a registration statement on Form S-1 under the Securities Act (§239.11 of this chapter) or on Form 10 under the Exchange Act (§249.210 of this chapter) shall:

(1) State the names of the promoters, the nature and amount of anything of value (including money, property, contracts, options or rights of any kind) received or to be received by each promoter, directly or indirectly, from the registrant and the nature and amount of any assets, services or other consideration therefor received or to be received by the registrant; and

(2) As to any assets acquired or to be acquired by the registrant from a promoter, state the amount at which the assets were acquired or are to be acquired and the principle followed or to be followed in determining such amount and identify the persons making the determination and their relationship, if any, with the registrant or any promoter. If the assets were acquired by the promoter within two years prior to their transfer to the registrant, also state the cost thereof to the promoter.

Instructions to Item 404.

1. No information need be given in response to any paragraph of Item 404 as to any compensation or other transaction reported in response to any other paragraph of Item 404 or to Item 402 of Regulation S-K (§229.402 of this chapter) or as to any compensation with respect to which information may be omitted pursuant to Item 402.

2. If the information called for by Item 404 is being presented in a registration statement filed pursuant to the Securities Act or the Exchange Act, information shall be given for the periods specified in this Item and, in addition, for the two fiscal years preceding the registrant's last fiscal year.

3. A foreign private issuer may respond to Item 404 only to the extent that the registrant discloses to its security holders or otherwise makes public the information specified in that Item.

Compliance With Section 16(a) of the Exchange Act

Reg §229.405. Item 405. Every registrant having a class of equity securities registered pursuant to Section 12 of the Exchange Act (15 U.S.C. 78l), every closed-end investment company registered under the Investment Company Act of 1940 (15 U.S.C. § 80a-1 *et seq.*), and every holding company registered pursuant to the Public Utility Holding Company Act of 1935 (15 U.S.C. § 79a *et seq.*) shall:

(a) Based solely upon a review of Forms 3 (§ 249.103) and 4 (§ 249.104) and amendments thereto furnished to the registrant pursuant to § 240.16a-3(e) during its most recent fiscal year and Forms 5 and amendments thereto (§ 249.105) furnished to the registrant with respect to its most recent fiscal year, and any written representation referred to in (b)(2)(i) below:

(1) Identify each person who, at any time during the fiscal year, was a director, officer, beneficial owner of more than ten percent of any class of equity securities of the registrant registered pursuant to Section 12 of the Exchange Act, or any other person subject to Section 16 of the Exchange Act with respect to the registrant because of the requirements of Section 30 of

32

the Investment Company Act or Section 17 of the Public Utility Holding Company Act ("reporting person") that failed to file on a timely basis, as disclosed in the above Forms, reports required by Section 16(a) of the Exchange Act during the most recent fiscal year or prior fiscal years.

(2) For each such person, set forth the number of late reports, the number of transactions that were not reported on a timely basis, and any known failure to file a required Form.

Note: The disclosure requirement is based on a review of the forms submitted to the registrant during and with respect to its most recent fiscal year, as specified above. Accordingly, a failure to file timely need only be disclosed once. For example, if in the most recently concluded fiscal year a reporting person filed a Form 4 disclosing a transaction that took place in the prior fiscal year, and should have been reported in that year, the registrant should disclose that late filing and transaction pursuant to this Item 405 with respect to the most recently concluded fiscal year, but not in material filed with respect to subsequent years.

(b) With respect to the disclosure required by paragraph (a) of this Item:

(1) A form received by the registrant within three calendar days of the required filing date may be presumed to have been filed with the Commission by the required filing date.

(2) If the registrant (i) receives a written representation from the reporting person that no Form 5 is required; and (ii) maintains the representation for two years, making a copy available to the Commission or its staff upon request, the registrant need not identify such reporting person pursuant to paragraph (a) as having failed to file a Form 5 with respect to that fiscal year.

Subpart 229.500 — Registration Statement and Prospectus Provisions

Forepart of Registration Statement and Outside Front Cover Page of Prospectus

Reg. §229.501. Item 501.

(a) *Facing page.* The facing page of every registration statement shall set forth the approximate date of proposed sale to the public and, where appropriate, the delaying amendment legend as set forth in Regulation C.

(b) *Cross-reference sheet.* Immediately following such facing page, there shall be included a cross reference sheet showing the location in the prospectus of the information required to be included in the prospectus in response to the items of the form. If any such item is inapplicable, or the answer thereto is in the negative and is omitted from the prospectus, a statement to that effect shall be made in the cross reference sheet. The cross reference sheet need not be included in the prospectus.

(c) *Outside front cover page of prospectus.* The following information (to the extent appropriate) shall appear on the outside front cover page of the prospectus with appropriate cross references to more detailed discussion elsewhere in the prospectus:

(1) Name of the registrant and, in the case of a foreign private registrant, an English translation of such name. Where the name of the registrant is the same as that of another well-known company and it appears likely that the registrant may be confused with the other company, or where the name indicates a line of business in which the registrant is not engaged or is engaged to only a limited extent, a statement may be necessary to prevent the confusion of the two companies or to remove a misleading inference that may be drawn from the name as to the nature of the registrant's business. In some circumstances, however, disclosure may not be sufficient, and a change of name may be the only way to preclude confusion of the companies or misleading inferences from registrant's name. Such disclosure or name change is not necessary in the case of an established registrant that over a period of years has changed the general character of its business and the investing public is aware generally of the change and the character of the registrant's present business;

(2) Title and amount of securities offered and a brief description of such securities (unless not necessary to indicate the material terms of the securities, as in the case of an issue of common stock with full voting rights and the dividend and liquidation rights usually associated with common stock);

(3) Where any of the securities to be registered are to be offered for the account of security holders, a statement to that effect;

(4) Cross reference, where applicable to the discussion in the prospectus prescribed by Item 503 of Regulation S-K (§229.503), of material risks in connection with the purchase of the securities, printed in bold-face roman type at least as high as ten-point modern type and at least two points leaded:

(5) The following statement in capital letters printed in bold-face roman type at least as high as ten-point modern type and at least two points leaded:

THESE SECURITIES HAVE NOT BEEN APPROVED OR DISAPPROVED BY THE SECURITIES AND EXCHANGE COMMISSION NOR HAS THE COMMISSION PASSED UPON THE ACCURACY OR ADEQUACY OF THIS PROSPECTUS. ANY REPRESENTATION TO THE CONTRARY IS A CRIMINAL OFFENSE;

(6) In the case of any preliminary prospectus that is circulated by registrants not subject to the reporting provisions of section 13(a) or 15(d) of the Exchange Act immediately prior to the filing of the registration statement, a bona fide estimate of the range of the maximum offering price and maximum number of shares or other units of securities to be offered, or a bona fide estimate of the principal amount of debt securities to be offered;

(7) Where securities are to be offered for cash, other than on a registration statement on Form S-8 (§239.16b of this chapter), the information called for by the following table, in substantially the tabular form indicated, as to all securities to be registered (estimated, if necessary):

	Price to Public	Underwriting Discounts and Commissions	Proceeds to Issuer or Other Persons
Per unit			
Total			

(8) In the case of any prospectus to be used before the effective date of the registration statement (or, in the case of any prospectus that omits information as permitted by Rule 430A under the Securities Act [§230.430A of this chapter], prior to the determination of the initial public offering price), in red ink, the caption "Subject to Completion," the date of its issuance, and the following statement printed in type as large as that generally used in the body of the prospectus:

Information contained herein is subject to completion or amendment. A registration statement relating to these securities has been filed with the Securities and Exchange Commission. These securities may not be sold nor may offers to buy be accepted prior to the time the registration statement becomes effective. This prospectus shall not constitute an offer to sell or the solicitation of an offer to buy nor shall there be any sale of these securities in any State in which such offer, solicitation or sale would be unlawful prior to registration or qualification under the securities laws of any such state.

(9) Any legend or information required by the law of any State in which the securities are to be offered; and

(10) The date of the prospectus.

Instructions to Item 501.

1. The term "commissions" is defined in paragraph (17) of Schedule A of the Securities Act. Only commissions paid by the registrant or selling security holders in cash are to be included in the table. Commissions paid by other persons, and other consideration to the underwriters, shall be set forth in a note to the table with a reference thereto in the second column of the table. Any finder's fee or similar payments shall be disclosed appropriately.

2. If it is impracticable to state the price to the public, the method by which it is to be determined shall be explained. In addition, if the securities are to be offered at the market, or if the offering price is to be determined by a formula related to market prices, indicate the market involved and the market price as of the latest practicable date.

3. If the securities are to be offered on a best efforts basis, set forth the termination date of the offering, any minimum required purchase and any arrangements to place the funds received in an escrow, trust, or similar arrangement. If no such arrangements have been made, so state. The following tabular presentation of the total maximum and minimum securities to be offered shall be combined with the table required above:

	Price to Public	Underwriting Discount and Commissions	Proceeds to Issuer or Other Persons
Total minimum			
Total maximum			

4. Where an underwriter has received an over-allotment option, maximum-minimum information shall be presented in the price table, or in a note thereto, based on the purchase of all or none of the shares subject to the option. The terms of the option may be described in response to Item 508 of Regulation S-K (§229.508) rather than on the cover page of the prospectus.

5. The total of "other expenses of issuance and distribution" called for by Item 511 of Regulation S-K (§229.511), states separately for the registrant and for the selling security holders, if any, shall be set forth in a note to the proceeds column of the distribution table.

Inside Front and Outside Back Cover Pages of Prospectus

Reg. §229.502. Item 502. The following information, to the extent applicable, shall appear on the inside front cover page of the prospectus (except that the information required by paragraphs (e) and (g) of this Item may be set forth on the outside back cover page).

(a) *Available information.* Registrants subject to the reporting requirements of section 13(a) or 15(d) of the Exchange Act immediately prior to the filing of the registration statement shall:

    (1) State that the registrant is subject to the informational requirements of the Exchange Act and in accordance therewith files reports and other information with the Securities and Exchange commission;

    (2) State that reports (and where registrant is subject to sections 14(a) and 14(c) of the Exchange Act proxy and information statements) and other information filed by the registrant can be inspected and copied at the public reference facilities maintained by the Commission in Washington, D.C., and at certain of its Regional Offices, and state the current address of each such facility (see §§200.11(b) and 200.80(c)(1) of this chapter), and the copies of such material can be obtained from the Public Reference Section of the Commission, Washington,D.C. 20549 at prescribed rates; and

    (3) Name any national securities exchange on which the registrant's securities are listed and state that reports (and where registrant is subject to sections 14(a) and 14(c) of the Exchange Act proxy and information statements), and other information concerning the registrant can be inspected at such exchanges.

(b) *Reports to security holders.* Where a registrant may not be required to deliver an annual report to security holders (or holders of American depository receipts) pursuant to section 14 of the Exchange Act or stock exchange requirements, describe briefly the nature and frequency of reports that will be given to such holders in such event, specifying whether or not such reports will contain financial information that has been examined and reported upon, with an opinion expressed by, an independent public or certified public accountant, and, in the case of the reports of a foreign private registrant that will not contain financial information prepared in accordance with United States generally accepted accounting principles, state whether the report will include a reconciliation of such information with such accounting principles.

(c) *Incorporation by reference.* Where any document or part thereof is incorporated by reference in the prospectus but not delivered therewith, include an undertaking to provide without charge to each person, including any beneficial owner, to whom a prospectus is delivered, upon written or oral request of such person, a copy of any and all of the information that has been incorporated by reference in the prospectus (not including exhibits to that information that is incorporated by reference unless such exhibits are specifically incorporated by reference into the information that the prospectus incorporates), and the address (including title or department) and telephone number to which such a request is to be directed.

(d) *Stabilization.*

    (1) If the registrant or any of the underwriters knows or has reason to believe that there is an intention to over-allot or that the price of any security may be stabilized to facilitate the offering of the registered securities, set forth a statement in substantially the following form, subject to appropriate modification where circumstances require. Such statement shall be in capital letters, printed in bold-face roman type at least as large as ten-point modern type and at least two points leaded:

    IN CONNECTION WITH THIS· OFFERING, THE UNDERWRITERS MAY OVER-ALLOT OR EFFECT TRANSACTIONS WHICH STABILIZE OR MAINTAIN THE MARKET PRICE OF (IDENTIFY EACH CLASS OF SECURITIES IN WHICH SUCH TRANSACTIONS MAY BE EFFECTED) AT A LEVEL ABOVE THAT WHICH MIGHT OTHERWISE PREVAIL IN THE OPEN MARKET. SUCH TRANSACTIONS MAY BE EFFECTED ON (IDENTIFY EACH EXCHANGE ON WHICH STABILIZING TRANSACTIONS MAY BE EFFECTED; IF NONE, OMIT THIS SENTENCE.) SUCH STABILIZING, IF COMMENCED, MAY BE DISCONTINUED AT ANY TIME.

    (2) If the stabilizing began prior to the effective date of the registration statement, set forth the amount of securities bought, the prices at which they were bought and the period within which they were bought. In the event that Rule 430A under the Securities Act [§230.430A of this chapter] is used, the prospectus filed pursuant to Rule 424(b) [§230.424(b) of this chapter] or included in a post-effective amendment must include information as to stabilizing transportations effected prior to the determination of the public offering price set forth in such prospectus.

    (3) If the securities being registered are to be offered to existing security holders pursuant to warrants or rights and any securities not taken by security holders are to be reoffered to the public after the expiration of the rights offering period, there shall be set forth, by supplement or otherwise, in the prospectus used in connection with such reoffering:

        (i) the amount of securities bought in stabilization activities during the rights offering period and the price or range of prices at which such securities were bought,

        (ii) the amount of the offered securities subscribed for during such period,

        (iii) the amount of the offered securities subscribed for by the underwriters during such period,

        (iv) the amount of the offered securities sold during such period by the underwriters and the price, or range of prices, at which such securities were sold, and

(v) the amount of the offered securities to be reoffered to the public and the public offering price.

(e) *Delivery of prospectuses by dealers.* The legend below shall be set forth inserting the expiration date of the period prescribed by section 4(3) of the Securities Act and Rule 174 thereunder (§230.174 of this chapter) except that this legend need not be included if, pursuant to Rule 174, dealers are not required to deliver a prospectus, or if the exemption provided by section 4(3) of the Securities Act is not applicable because of the provisions of section 24(d) of the Investment Company Act. If such expiration date is not known on the effective date of the registration statement it shall be included in the prospectus, copies of which are required to be filed pursuant to Rule 424(b) under the Securities Act (§230.424(b) of this chapter). The following legend shall be printed in bold-face or italic type at least as large as eight-point modern type and at least two points leaded:

Until (insert date) all dealers effecting transactions in the registered securities, whether or not participating in this distribution, may be required to deliver a prospectus. This is in addition to the obligation of dealers to deliver a prospectus when acting as underwriters and with respect to their unsold allotments or subscriptions.

(f) *Enforceability of civil liabilities against foreign persons.* In the case of a foreign private registrant, a statement of how the enforcement by investors of civil liabilities under the Federal securities laws may be affected by the fact that the registrant is located in a foreign country, that certain of its officers and directors are residents of a foreign country, that certain underwriters or experts named in the registration statement are residents of a foreign country, and that all or a substantial portion of the assets of the registrant and of said persons are located outside the United States. Such disclosure need not be included on the inside front cover page of the prospectus, if it is included, under appropriate caption, elsewhere in the forepart of the prospectus.

(1) Such disclosure shall indicate:

(i) Whether investors will be able to effect service of process within the United States upon such persons;

(ii) Whether investors will be able to enforce, in United States courts, judgments against such persons obtained in such courts predicated upon the civil liability provisions of the Federal securities laws;

(iii) Whether the appropriate foreign courts would enforce judgments of United States courts obtained in actions against such persons predicated upon the civil liability provisions of the Federal securities laws; and

(iv) Whether the appropriate foreign courts would enforce, in original actions, liabilities against such persons predicated solely upon the Federal securities laws.

(2) If any portions of such disclosures are stated to be based upon an opinion of counsel, such counsel shall be named in the prospectus and an appropriate manually signed consent to the use of such name and opinion shall be included as an exhibit to the registration statement.

(g) *Table of contents.* Include a reasonably detailed table of contents showing the subject matter of the various sections or subdivisions of the prospectus and the page number on which each such section or subdivision begins.

Summary Information, Risk Factors and Ratio of Earnings to Fixed Charges

Reg. §229.503. Item 503.

(a) *Summary.* Registrants should include a summary of the information contained in the prospectus where the length or complexity of the prospectus makes such a summary appropriate.

(b) *Address and telephone number.* Registrants shall include in the forepart of the prospectus the complete mailing address, including zip code, and the telephone number, including area code, of their principal executive offices.

(c) *Risk factors.* Registrants, where appropriate, shall set forth on the page immediately following the cover page of the prospectus (or following the summary, if included) under an appropriate caption, a discussion of the principal factors that make the offering speculative or one of high risk; these factors may be due, among other things, to such matters as an absence of an operating history of the registrant, an absence of profitable operations in recent periods, the financial position of the registrant, the nature of the business in which the registrant is engaged or proposes to engage, or, if common equity or securities convertible into or exercisable for common equity are being offered, the absence of a previous market for the registrant's common equity.

(d) *Ratio of earnings to fixed charges.* The ratio of earnings to fixed charges or the ratio of earnings to combined fixed charges and preferred stock dividends (the "ratio") should be disclosed pursuant to the following rules and definitions:

(1) (i) Furnish in registration statements filed under the Securities Act of 1933 (A) the ratio of earnings to fixed charges if debt securities are being registered; or (B) the ratio of earnings to combined fixed charges and preferred stock dividends if preferred stock is being registered. Disclosure of both ratios is permitted in registration statements relating to debt or preferred stock and either ratio or both ratios may be disclosed in other filings.

(ii) The ratio shall be disclosed for the following periods:

(A) Each of the last five fiscal years of the registrant (or for the life of the registrant and its predecessors, if less), and

(B) The latest interim period for which financial statements are presented.

(2) The ratio shall be computed using the amounts for the enterprise as a whole including (i) the registrant, (ii) its majority-owned subsidiaries, whether or not consolidated, (iii) its proportionate share of any fifty-percent-owned persons, and (iv) any income received (but not undistributed amounts) from less-than-fifty-percent-owned persons.

(3) The term "earnings" shall be defined as pretax income from continuing operations with the following adjustments:

(i) Add to pretax income the amount of fixed charges computed pursuant to paragraph (d)(4) of this section, adjusted to exclude (A) the amount of any interest capitalized during the period and (B) the actual amount of any preferred stock dividend requirements of majority-owned subsidiaries and fifty-percent-owned persons which were included in such fixed charges amount but not deducted in the determination of pretax income.

(ii) Only the registrant's share in the income of majority-owned subsidiaries and the distributed income of less-than-fifty-percent-owned persons shall be included in earnings, except that a registrant may include the minority interest in the income of majority-owned subsidiaries that have fixed charges.

(iii) The full amount of losses of majority-owned subsidiaries shall be considered in the computation of earnings.

(iv) Where an investment in a less-than-fifty-percent-owned person accounted for under the equity method results in the recognition of a loss, such loss shall not be considered in the computation of the ratio except where the registrant has guaranteed or otherwise undertaken, directly or indirectly to service the debt of such person. In the latter case, the registrant's equity in the loss shall be included in earnings and the fixed charges shall include the interest expense related to the guaranteed debt.

(v) Registrants other than public utilities may add to earnings the amount of previously capitalized interest amortized during the period.

(vi) A registrant which is a rate-regulated public utility shall not reduce fixed charges (see paragraph (4) below) by any allowance for funds used during construction, but rather shall include any such allowance in the determination of earnings under this paragraph.

(4) (i) The term "fixed charges" shall mean the total of (A) interest, whether expensed or capitalized; (B) amortization of debt expense and discount or premium relating to any indebtedness, whether expensed or capitalized; (C) such portion of rental expense as can be demonstrated to be representative of the interest factor in the particular case; and (D) preferred stock dividend requirements of majority-owned subsidiaries and fifty-percent-owned persons, excluding in all cases items which would be or are eliminated in consolidation.

(ii) If the registrant is a guarantor of debt of a less than fifty-percent-owned person or of an unaffiliated person (such as a supplier), the amount of fixed charges associated with such debt should not be included in the computation of the ratio unless the registrant has been required to satisfy the guarantee or it is probable that the registrant will be required to honor the guarantee and the amount can reasonably be estimated. A footnote to the ratio should disclose the existence of any such guarantee and the amount of the associated fixed charges and state whether or not such amount is included in the computation of the ratio.

(5) The term "preferred stock" shall include all types of preferred and preference stocks.

(6) For purposes of paragraph (4)(i)(D) above and computation of the combined ratio, the preferred stock dividend requirements shall be increased to an amount representing the pre-tax earnings which would be required to cover such dividend requirements. Therefore, the increased amount =

$$\frac{\text{Preferred Stock Dividend Requirements}}{100\% - \text{Income Tax Rate}}$$

The tax rate shall be based on the relationship of the provision for income tax expense applicable to income from continuing operations to the amount of pre-tax income from continuing operations.

(7) If either ratio computation indicates a less than one-to-one coverage, state that earnings are inadequate to cover fixed charges and disclose the dollar amount of the coverage deficiency.

(8) If the level of the registrant's ratio is maintained by its parent, for example, in order to meet the minimum borrowing standards of agencies of various states, or if the registrant's parent is guaranteeing the registrant's debt securities or preferred stock, the parent's ratio as well as the registrant's ratio shall be disclosed.

37

(9) A pro forma ratio shall be presented in the prospectus of any registration statement filed to register debt or preferred stock to be used in a refinancing if the effect of the refinancing changes the historical ratio by ten percent or more.

    (i) A "refinancing" is defined as the extinguishment of one or more specific issues of debt with the proceeds from the sale of additional debt, or the extinguishment of one or more specific issues of preferred stock with the proceeds from the sale of additional preferred stock.

    (ii) The only adjustments which shall be made to the corresponding historical ratio are to give effect to the net increase or decrease in interest expense or preferred stock dividends resulting from (A) the proposed issuance of new debt or preferred stock and (B) the corresponding retirement of any debt or preferred stock presently outstanding (but only for the period of time outstanding) which will be retired with the proceeds from the proposed offering. If only a portion of the proceeds will be used to retire presently outstanding debt or preferred stock, only a related portion of the interest or preferred dividend should be used in the pro forma adjustment.

    (iii) The pro forma ratio, if applicable, shall be presented for only the most recent fiscal year and the latest interim period or, at the option of the registrant, the most recent twelve months.

(10) If the registrant is a foreign private issuer, the ratio shall be computed on the basis of the primary financial statements and, if materially different, their reconciliations.

Use of Proceeds

Reg. §229.504. Item 504. State the principal purposes for which the net proceeds to the registrant from the securities to be offered are intended to be used and the approximate amount intended to be used for each such purpose. Where registrant has no current specific plan for the proceeds, or a significant portion thereof, the registrant shall so state and discuss the principal reasons for the offering.

Instructions to Item 504.

1. Where less than all the securities to be offered may be sold and more than one use is listed for the proceeds, indicate the order of priority of such purposes and discuss the registrant's plans if substantially less than the maximum proceeds are obtained. Such discussion need not be included if underwriting arrangements with respect to such securities are such that, if any securities are sold to the public, it reasonably can be expected that the actual proceeds will not be substantially less than the aggregate proceeds to the registrant shown pursuant to Item 501 of Regulation S-K (§229.501).

2. Details of proposed expenditures need not be given; for example, there need be furnished only a brief outline of any program of construction or addition of equipment. Consideration should be given as to the need to include a discussion of certain matters addressed in the discussion and analysis of registrant's financial condition and results of operations, such as liquidity and capital expenditures.

3. If any material amounts of other funds are necessary to accomplish the specified purposes for which the proceeds are to be obtained, state the amounts and sources of such other funds needed for each such specified purpose and the sources thereof.

4. If any material part of the proceeds is to be used to discharge indebtedness, set forth the interest rate and maturity of such indebtedness. If the indebtedness to be discharged was incurred within one year, describe the use of the proceeds of such indebtedness other than short-term borrowings used for working capital.

5. If any material amount of the proceeds is to be used to acquire assets, otherwise than in the ordinary course of business, describe briefly and state the cost of the assets and, where such assets are to be acquired from affiliates of the registrant or their associates, give the names of the persons from whom they are to be acquired and set forth the principal followed in determining the cost to the registrant.

6. Where the registrant indicates that the proceeds may, or will, be used to finance acquisitions of other businesses, the identity of such businesses, if known, or, if not known, the nature of the businesses to be sought, the status of any negotiations with respect to the acquisition, and a brief description of such business shall be included. Where, however, pro forma financial statements reflecting such acquisition are not required by Regulation S-X to be included in the registration statement, the possible terms of any transaction, the identification of the parties thereto or the nature of the business sought need not be disclosed, to the extent that the registrant reasonably determines that public disclosure of such information would jeopardize the acquisition. Where Regulation S-X [17 CFR 210] would require financial statements of the business to be acquired to be included, the description of the business to be acquired shall be more detailed.

7. The registrant may reserve the right to change the use of proceeds, provided that such reservation is due to certain contingencies that are discussed specifically and the alternatives to such use in that event are indicated.

Determination of Offering Price

Reg. §229.505. Item 505.

(a) *Common equity.* Where common equity is being registered for which there is no established public trading market for purposes of paragraph (a) of Item 201 of Regulation S-K [§229.201(a)] or where there is a material disparity between the offering price of the common equity being registered and the market price of outstanding shares of the same class, describe the various factors considered in determining such offering price.

(b) *Warrants, rights and convertible securities.* Where warrants, rights or convertible securities exercisable for common equity for which there is no established public trading market for purposes of paragraph (a) of Item 201 of Regulation S-K [§229.201(a)] are being registered, describe the various factors considered in determining their exercise or conversion price.

Dilution

Reg. §229.506. Item 506.

Where common equity securities are being registered and there is a substantial disparity between the public offering price and the effective cash cost to officers, directors, promoters and affiliated persons of common equity acquired by them in transactions during the past five years, or which they have the right to acquire, and the registrant is not subject to the reporting requirements of section 13(a) or 15(d) of the Exchange Act immediately prior to filing of the registration statement, there shall be included a comparison of the public contribution under the proposed public offering and the effective cash contribution of such persons. In such cases, and in other instances where common equity securities are being registered by a registrant that has had losses in each of its last three fiscal years and there is a material dilution of the purchasers' equity interest, the following shall be disclosed:

(a) The net tangible book value per share before and after the distribution;

(b) The amount of the increase in such net tangible book value per share attributable to the cash payments made by purchasers of the shares being offered; and

(c) The amount of the immediate dilution from the public offering price which will be absorbed by such purchasers.

Selling Security Holders

Reg. §229.507. Item 507.

If any of the securities to be registered are to be offered for the account of security holders, name each such security holder, indicate the nature of any position, office, or other material relationship which the selling security holder has had within the past three years with the registrant or any of its predecessors or affiliates, and state the amount of securities of the class owned by such security holder prior to the offering, the amount to be offered for the security holder's account, the amount and (if one percent or more) the percentage of the class to be owned by such security holder after completion of the offering.

Plan of Distribution

Reg. §229.508. Item 508.

(a) *Underwriters and underwriting obligation.* If the securities are to be offered through underwriters, name the principal underwriters, and state the respective amounts underwritten. Identify each such underwriter having a material relationship with the registrant and state the nature of the relationship. State briefly the nature of the obligation of the underwriter(s) to take the securities.

Instruction to Paragraph 508(a). All that is required as to the nature of the underwriters' obligation is whether the underwriters are or will be committed to take and to pay for all of the securities if any are taken, or whether it is merely an agency or the type of "best efforts" arrangement under which the underwriters are required to take and to pay for only such securities as they may sell to the public. Conditions precedent to the underwriters' taking the securities, including "market-outs," need not be described except in the case of an agency or "best efforts" arrangement.

(b) *New underwriters.* Where securities being registered are those of a registrant that has not previously been required to file reports pursuant to section 13(a) or 15(d) of the Exchange Act, or where a prospectus is required to include reference on its cover page to material risks pursuant to Item 501 of Regulation S-K (§229.501), and any one or more of the managing underwriter(s) (or where there are no managing underwriters, a majority of the principal underwriters) has been organized, reactivated, or first registered as a broker-dealer within the past three years, these facts concerning such underwriter(s) shall be disclosed in the prospectus together with, where applicable, the disclosures that the principal business function of such underwriter(s) will be to sell the securities to be registered, or that the promoters of the registrant have a material relationship with such underwriter(s). Sufficient details shall be given to allow full appreciation of such underwriter(s) experience and its relationship with the registrant, promoters and their controlling persons.

(c) *Other distributions.* Outline briefly the plan of distribution of any securities to be registered that are to be offered otherwise than through underwriters.

    (1)   If any securities are to be offered pursuant to a dividend or interest reinvestment plan the terms of which provide for the purchase of some securities on the market, state whether the registrant or the participant pays fees, commissions, and expenses incurred in connection with the plan. If the participant will pay such fees, commissions and expenses, state the anticipated cost to participants by transaction or other convenient reference.

    (2)   If the securities are to be offered through the selling efforts of brokers or dealers, describe the plan of distribution and the terms of any agreement, arrangement, or understanding entered into with broker(s) or dealer(s) prior to the effective date of the registration statement, including volume limitations on sales, parties to the agreement and the conditions under which the agreement may be terminated. If known, identify the broker(s) or dealer(s) which will participate in the offering and state the amount to be offered through each.

    (3)   If any of the securities being registered are to be offered otherwise than for cash, state briefly the general purposes of the distribution, the basis upon which the securities are to be offered, the amount of compensation and other expenses of distribution, and by whom they are to be borne. If the distribution is to be made pursuant to a plan of acquisition, reorganization, readjustment or succession, describe briefly the general effect of the plan and state when it became or is to become operative. As to any material amount of assets to be acquired under the plan, furnish information corresponding to that required by Instruction 5 of Item 504 of Regulation S-K (§229.504).

(d) *Offerings on exchange.* If the securities are to be offered on an exchange, indicate the exchange. If the registered securities are to be offered in connection with the writing of exchange-traded call options, describe briefly such transactions.

(e) *Underwriters' compensation.* To the extent not set forth on the cover page of the prospectus, describe the discounts and commissions to be allowed or paid to the underwriters, and all other items that would be deemed by the National Association of Securities Dealers to constitute underwriting compensation for purposes of the Association's Rule of Fair Practice.

(f) *Underwriter's representative on board of directors.* Describe any arrangement whereby the underwriter has the right to designate or nominate a member or members of the board of directors of the registrant. The registrant shall disclose the identity of any director so designated or nominated, and indicate whether or not a person so designated or nominated, or allowed to be designated or nominated by the underwriter is or may be a director, officer, partner, employee or affiliate of the underwriter.

(g) *Indemnification of underwriters.* If the underwriting agreement provides for indemnification by the registrant of the underwriters or their controlling persons against any liability arising under the Securities Act, furnish a brief description of such indemnification provisions.

(h) *Dealers' compensation.* State briefly the discounts and commissions to be allowed or paid to dealers, including all cash, securities, contracts or other considerations to be received by any dealer in connection with the sale of the securities. If any dealers are to act in the capacity of sub-underwriters and are to be allowed or paid any additional discounts or commissions for acting in such capacity, a general statement to that effect will suffice without giving the additional amounts to be sold.

(i) *Finders.* Identify any finder and, if applicable, describe the nature of any material relationship between such finder and the registrant, its officers, directors, principal stockholders, finders or promoters or the principal underwriter(s), or if there is a managing underwriter(s), the managing underwriter(s) (including, in each case, affiliates or associates thereof).

(j) *Discretionary accounts.* If the registrant was not, immediately prior to the filing of the registration statement, subject to the requirements of section 13(a) or 15(d) of the Exchange Act, identify any principal underwriter that intends to sell to any accounts over which it exercises discretionary authority and include an estimate of the amount of securities so intended to be sold. The response to this paragraph shall be contained in a pre-effective amendment which shall be circulated if the information is not available when the registration statement is filed.

Interests of Named Experts and Counsel

Reg. §229.509. Item 509.

    If (a) any expert named in the registration statement as having prepared or certified any part thereof (or is named as having prepared or certified a report or valuation for use in connection with the registration statement), or (b) counsel for the registrant, underwriters or selling security holders named in the prospectus as having given an opinion upon the validity of the securities being registered or upon other legal matters in connection with the registration or offering of such securities, was employed for such purpose on a contingent basis, or at the time of such preparation, certification or opinion or at any time thereafter through the date of effectiveness of the registration statement or that part of the registration statement to which such preparation, certification or opinion relates, had, or is to receive in connection with the offering, a substantial interest, direct or indirect, in the registrant or any of its parents or subsidiaries or was connected with the registrant or any of its parents or subsidiaries as a promoter, managing underwriter (or any principal underwriter, if there are no managing underwriters), voting trustee, director, officer, or employee, furnish a brief statement of the nature of such contingent basis, interest, or connection.

Instructions to Item 509.

1. The interest of an expert (other than an accountant) or counsel will not be deemed substantial and need not be disclosed if the interest, including the fair market value of all securities of the registrant owned, received and to be received, or subject to options, warrants or rights received or to be received by the expert or counsel does not exceed $50,000. For the purpose of this Instruction, the term "expert" or counsel includes the firm, corporation, partnership or other entity, if any, by which such expert or counsel is employed or of which he is a member or of counsel to and all attorneys in the case of counsel, and all nonclerical personnel in the case of named experts, participating in such matter on behalf of such firm, corporation, partnership or entity.

2. Accountants, providing a report on the financial statements, presented or incorporated by reference in the registration statement, should note §210.2-01 of Regulation S-X (17 CFR 210) for the Commission's requirements regarding "Qualification of Accountants" which discusses disqualifying interests.

Disclosure of Commission Position on Indemnification for Securities Act Liabilities

Reg. §229.510. Item 510. In addition to the disclosure prescribed by Item 702 of Regulation S-K (§229.702), if the undertaking required by paragraph (h) of Item 512 of Regulation S-K (§229.512) is not required to be included in the registration statement because acceleration of the effective date of the registration statement is not being requested, and if waivers have not been obtained comparable to those specified in paragraph (h), a brief description of the indemnification provisions relating to directors, officers and controlling persons of the registrant against liability arising under the Securities Act (including any provision of the underwriting agreement which relates to indemnification of the underwriter or its controlling persons by the registrant against such liabilities where a director, officer or controlling person of the registrant is such an underwriter or controlling person thereof or a member of any firm which is such an underwriter) shall be included in the prospectus, together with a statement in substantially the following form:

> Insofar as indemnification for liabilities arising under the Securities Act of 1933 may be permitted to directors, officers or persons controlling the registrant pursuant to the foregoing provisions, the registrant has been informed that in the opinion of the Securities and Exchange Commission such indemnification is against public policy as expressed in the Act and is therefore unenforceable.

Other Expenses of Issuance and Distribution

Reg. §229.511. Item 511. Furnish a reasonably itemized statement of all expenses in connection with the issuance and distribution of the securities to be registered, other than underwriting discounts and commissions. If any of the securities to be registered are to be offered for the account of security holders, indicate the portion of such expenses to be borne by such security holder.

Instruction to Item 511. Insofar as practicable, registration fees, Federal taxes, States taxes and fees, trustees' and transfer agents' fees, costs of printing and engraving, and legal, accounting, and engineering fees shall be itemized separately. Include as a separate item any premium paid by the registrant or any selling security holder on any policy obtained in connection with the offering and sale of the securities being registered which insures or indemnifies directors or officers against any liabilities they may incur in connection with the registration, offering, or sale of such securities. The information may be given as subject to future contingencies. If the amounts of any items are not known, estimates, identified as such, shall be given.

Undertakings

Reg. §229.512. Item 512. Include each of the following undertakings that is applicable to the offering being registered.

(a) *Rule 415 offering.*[1] Include the following if the securities are registered pursuant to Rule 415 under the Securities Act (§230.415 of this chapter):

The undersigned registrant hereby undertakes:

    (1) To file, during any period in which offers or sales are being made, a post-effective amendment to this registration statement:

        (i) To include any prospectus required by section 10(a)(3) of the Securities Act of 1933;

        (ii) To reflect in the prospectus any facts or events arising after the effective date of the registration statement (or the most recent post-effective amendment thereof) which, individually or in the aggregate, represent a fundamental change in the information in the registration statement;

        (iii) To include any material information with respect to the plan of distribution not previously disclosed in the registration statement or any material change to such information in the registration statement;

---

1   Paragraph (a) reflects proposals made in Securities Act Release No. 6334 (Aug. 6, 1981).

Provided, however, that paragraphs (a)(1)(i) and (a)(1)(ii) do not apply if the registration statement is on Form S-3 (§239.13 of this chapter) or Form S-8 (§239.16b of this chapter), and the information required to be included in a post-effective amendment by those paragraphs is contained in periodic reports filed by the registrant pursuant to section 13 or section 15(d) of the Securities Exchange Act of 1934 that are incorporated by reference in the registration statement.

(2) That, for the purpose of determining any liability under the Securities Act of 1933, each such post-effective amendment shall be deemed to be a new registration statement relating to the securities offered therein, and the offering of such securities at that time shall be deemed to be the initial bona fide offering thereof.

(3) To remove from registration by means of a post-effective amendment any of the securities being registered which remain unsold at the termination of the offering.

(4) If the registration is a foreign private issuer, to file a post-effective amendment to the registration statement to include any financial statements required by 3-19 of Regulation S-X (§210.3-19 of this chapter) at the start of any delayed offering or throughout a continuous offering.

(b) *Filings incorporating subsequent Exchange Act documents by reference.* Include the following if the registration statement incorporates by reference any Exchange Act document filed subsequent to the effective date of the registration statement:

The undersigned registrant hereby undertakes that, for purposes of determining any liability under the Securities Act of 1933, each filing of the registrant's annual report pursuant to section 13(a) or section 15(d) of the Securities Exchange Act of 1934 (and, where applicable, each filing of an employee benefit plan's annual report pursuant to section 15(d) of the Securities Exchange Act of 1934) that is incorporated by reference in the registration statement shall be deemed to be a new registration statement relating to the securities offered therein, and the offering of such securities at that time shall be deemed to be the initial bona fide offering thereof.

(c) *Warrants and rights offerings.* Include the following, with appropriate modifications to suit the particular case, if the securities to be registered are to be offered to existing security holders pursuant to warrants or rights and any securities not taken by security holders are to be reoffered to the public:

The undersigned registrant hereby undertakes to supplement the prospectus, after the expiration of the subscription period, to set forth the results of the subscription offer, the transactions by the underwriters during the subscription period, the amount of unsubscribed securities to be purchased by the underwriters, and the terms of any subsequent reoffering thereof. If any public offering by the underwriters is to be made on terms differing from those set forth on the cover page of the prospectus, a post-effective amendment will be filed to set forth the terms of such offering.

(d) *Competitive bids.* Include the following, with appropriate modifications to suit the particular case, if the securities to be registered are to be offered at competitive bidding:

The undersigned registrant hereby undertakes (1) to use its best efforts to distribute prior to the opening of bids, to prospective bidders, underwriters, and dealers, a reasonable number of copies of a prospectus which at that time meets the requirements of section 10(a) of the Act, and relating to the securities offered at competitive bidding, as contained in the registration statement, together with any supplements thereto, and (2) to file an amendment to the registration statement reflecting the results of bidding, the terms of the reoffering and related matters to the extent required by the applicable form, not later than the first use, authorized by the issuer after the opening bids, of a prospectus relating to the securities offered at competitive bidding, unless no further public offering of such securities by the issuer and no reoffering of such securities by the purchasers is proposed to be made.

(e) *Incorporated annual and quarterly reports.* Include the following if the registration statement specifically incorporates by reference (other than by indirect incorporation by reference through a Form 10-K (§249.310 of this chapter) report) in the prospectus all or any part of the annual report to security holders meeting the requirements of Rule 14a-3 or Rule 14c-3 under the Exchange Act (§240.14a-3 and 240.14c-3 of this chapter):

The undersigned registrant hereby undertakes to deliver or cause to be delivered with the prospectus, to each person to whom the prospectus is sent or given, the latest annual report to security holders that is incorporated by reference in the prospectus and furnished pursuant to and meeting the requirements of Rule 14a-3 or Rule 14c-3 under the Securities Exchange Act of 1934; and, where interim financial information required to be presented by Article 3 of Regulation S-X are not set forth in the prospectus, to deliver, or cause to be delivered to each person to whom the prospectus is sent or given, the latest quarterly report that is specifically incorporated by reference in the prospectus to provide such interim financial information.

(f) *Equity offerings of nonreporting registrants.* Include the following if equity securities of a registrant that prior to the offering had no obligation to file reports with the Commission pursuant to section 13(a) or 15(d) of the Exchange Act are being registered for sale in an underwritten offering:

The undersigned registrant hereby undertakes to provide to the underwriter at the closing specified in the underwriting agreements certificates in such denominations and registered in such names as required by the underwriter to permit prompt delivery to each purchaser.

(g) *Registration on Form S-4 or F-4 of securities offered for resale.* Include the following if the securities are being registered on Form S-4 or F-4 (§239.25 or 34 of this chapter) in connection with a transaction specified in paragraph (a) of Rule 145 (§230.145 of this chapter).

    (1) The undersigned registrant hereby undertakes as follows: that prior to any public reoffering of the securities registered hereunder through use of a prospectus which is a part of this registration statement, by any person or party who is deemed to be an underwriter within the meaning of Rule 145(c), the issuer undertakes that such reoffering prospectus will contain the information called for by the applicable registration form with respect to reofferings by persons who may be deemed underwriters, in addition to the information called for by the other Items of the applicable form.

    (2) The registrant undertakes that every prospectus (i) that is filed pursuant to paragraph (1) immediately preceding, or (ii) that purports to meet the requirements of section 10(a)(3) of the Act and is used in connection with an offering of securities subject to Rule 415 (§230.415 of this chapter), will be filed as a part of an amendment to the registration statement and will not be used until such amendment is effective, and that, for purposes of determining any liability under the Securities Act of 1933, each such post-effective amendment shall be deemed to be a new registration statement relating to the securities offered therein, and the offering of such securities at that time shall be deemed to be the initial bona fide offering thereof.

(h) *Request for acceleration of effective date or filing of registration statement on Form S-8.* Include the following if acceleration is requested of the effective date of the registration statement pursuant to Rule 461 under the Securities Act (§230.461 of this chapter), or, if the registration statement is filed on Form S-8, and (1) any provision or arrangement exists whereby the registrant may indemnify a director, officer or controlling person of the registrant against liabilities arising under the Securities Act, or (2) the underwriting agreement contains a provision whereby the registrant indemnifies the underwriter or controlling persons of the underwriter against such liabilities and a director, officer or controlling person of the registrant is such an underwriter or controlling person thereof or a member of any firm which is such an underwriter, and (3) the benefits of such indemnification are not waived by such persons:

    Insofar as indemnification for liabilities arising under the Securities Act of 1933 may be permitted to directors, officers and controlling persons of the registrant pursuant to the foregoing provisions, or otherwise, the registrant has been advised that in the opinion of the Securities and Exchange Commission such indemnification is against public policy as expressed in the Act and is, therefore, unenforceable. In the event that a claim for indemnification against such liabilities (other than the payment by the registrant of expenses incurred or paid by a director, officer or controlling person of the registrant in the successful defense of any action, suit or proceeding) is asserted by such director, officer or controlling person in connection with the securities being registered, the registrant will, unless in the opinion of its counsel the matter has been settled by controlling precedent, submit to a court of appropriate jurisdiction the question whether such indemnification by it is against public policy as expressed in the Act and will be governed by the final adjudication of such issue.

(i) Include the following in a registration statement permitted by Rule 430A under the Securities Act of 1933 (§230.430A of this chapter):

The undersigned registrant hereby undertakes that:

    (1) For purposes of determining any liability under the Securities Act of 1933, the information omitted from the form of prospectus filed as part of this registration statement in reliance upon Rule 430A and contained in a form of prospectus filed by the registrant pursuant to Rule 424(b)(1) or (4) or 497(h) under the Securities Act shall be deemed to be part of this registration statement as of the time it was declared effective.

    (2) For the purpose of determining any liability under the Securities Act of 1933, each post-effective amendment that contains a form of prospectus shall be deemed to be a new registration statement relating to the securities offered therein, and the offering of such securities at that time shall be deemed to be the initial bona fide offering thereof.

Subpart 229.600 — Exhibits

Exhibits

Reg. §229.601. Item 601.

(a) *Exhibits and index required.*

    (1) Subject to Rule 411(c) (§230.411(c) of this chapter) under the Securities Act and Rule 12b-32 (§240.12b-32 of this chapter) under the Exchange Act regarding incorporation of exhibits by reference, the exhibits required by the exhibit table shall be filed as indicated, as part of the registration statement or report.

    (2) Each registration statement or report shall contain an exhibit index, which shall precede immediately the exhibits filed with such registration statement. For convenient reference, each exhibit shall be listed in the exhibit index according to the number assigned to it in the exhibit table. The exhibit index shall indicate, by handwritten, typed, printed, or other legible form of notation in the manually signed original registration statement or report, the page number in the sequential numbering system where such exhibit can be found. Where exhibits are incorporated by reference, this fact shall be noted in the exhibit index referred to in the preceding sentence. Further, the first page of the manually signed registration statement shall list the page in the filing where the exhibit index is located. For a description of each of the exhibits included in the exhibit table, see paragraph (b) of this Item.

    (3) This Item applies only to the forms specified in the exhibit table. With regard to forms not listed in that table, reference shall be made to the appropriate form for the specific exhibit filing requirements applicable thereto.

Instructions to Item 601.

1. If an exhibit to a registration statement (other than an opinion or consent), filed in preliminary form, has been changed only (A) to insert information as to interest, dividend or conversion rates, redemption or conversion prices, purchase or offering prices, underwriters' or dealers' commissions, names, addresses or participation of underwriters or similar matters, which information appears elsewhere in an amendment to the registration statement or a prospectus filed pursuant to Rule 424(b) under the Securities Act [§230.424(b) of this chapter], or (B) to correct typographical errors, insert signatures or make other similar immaterial changes, then, notwithstanding any contrary requirement of any rule or form, the registrant need not refile such exhibit as so amended. Any such incomplete exhibit may not, however, be incorporated by reference in any subsequent filing under any Act administered by the Commission.

2. In any case where two or more indentures, contracts, franchises, or other documents required to be filed as exhibits are substantially identical in all material respects except as to the parties thereto, the dates of execution, or other details, the registrant need file a copy of only one of such documents, with a schedule identifying the other documents omitted and setting forth the material details in which such documents differ from the document a copy of which is filed. The Commission may at any time in its discretion require filing of copies of any documents so omitted.

3. Only copies, rather than originals, need be filed of each exhibit required except as otherwise specifically noted.

Exhibit Table

Instructions to the Exhibit Table.

1. The exhibit table indicates those documents that must be filed as exhibits to the respective forms listed.

2. The "X" designation indicates the documents which are required to be filed with each form even if filed previously with another document. Provided, however, that such previously filed documents may be incorporated by reference to satisfy the filing requirements.

3. The number used in the far left column of the table refers to the appropriate subsection in paragraph (b) where a description of the exhibit can be found. Whenever necessary, alphabetical or numerical subparts may be used.

(b) *Description of exhibits.* Set forth below is a description of each document listed in the exhibit tables.

    (1) *Underwriting agreement* — Each underwriting contract or agreement with a principal underwriter pursuant to which the securities being registered are to be distributed; if the terms of such documents have not been determined, the proposed forms thereof. Such agreement may be filed as an exhibit to a report on Form 8-K (§249.308 of this chapter) which is incorporated by reference into a registration statement subsequent to its effectiveness.

    (2) *Plan of acquisition, reorganization, arrangement, liquidation or succession* — Any material plan of acquisition, disposition, reorganization, readjustment, succession, liquidation or arrangement and any amendments thereto described in the statement or report. Schedules (or similar attachments) to these exhibits shall not be filed unless such schedules contain information which is material to an investment decision and which is not otherwise disclosed in the agreement or the disclosure docu-

Exhibit Table

	Securities Act forms											Exchange Act forms			
	S-1	S-2	S-3	S-4[3]	S-8	S-11	S-18	F-1	F-2	F-3	F-4[3]	10	8-K	10-Q	10-K
(1) Underwriting agreement	X	X	X	X		X	X	X	X	X	X		X		
(2) Plan of acquisition, reorganization arrangement, liquidation or succession	X	X	X	X		X	X	X	X	X	X	X	X	X	X
(3) Articles of Incorporation and by-laws	X	X		X		X		X	X		X	X		X	X
(4) Instruments defining the rights of security holders, including indentures	X	X	X	X	X	X	X	X	X	X	X	X	X	X	X
(5) Opinion re legality	X	X	X	X	X	X	X	X	X	X	X				
(6) Opinion re discount on capital shares	X	X		X		X	X	X	X		X				
(7) Opinion re liquidation preference	X	X		X		X	X	X	X		X	X			X
(8) Opinion re tax matters	X	X	X	X		X	X	X	X	X	X				
(9) Voting trust agreement	X			X		X	X	X	X		X	X			X
(10) Material contracts	X	X	X	X		X	X	X	X	X	X	X		X	X
(11) Statement re computation of per share earnings	X	X	X	X		X		X	X	X	X	X		X	X
(12) Statements re computation of ratios	X	X	X	X		X		X	X	X	X	X			
(13) Annual report to security holders, Form 10-Q or quarterly report to security holders[1]															
(14) Material foreign patents	X	X		X				X			X	X			X
(15) Letter re unaudited interim financial information	X	X	X	X		X	X	X	X	X	X	X			
(16) Letter re change in certifying accountant	X[4]	X[4]		X[4]		X[4]	X[4]	X			X	X[4]	X	X	X[4]
(17) Letter re director resignation															
(18) Letter re change in accounting principles														X	X
(19) Previously unfiled documents														X	X
(20) Report furnished to security holders															
(21) Other documents or statements to security holders													X		
(22) Subsidiaries of the registrant	X			X		X		X			X	X	X		X
(23) Published report regarding matters submitted to vote of security holders														X	X
(24) Consents of experts and counsel	X	X	X	X		X	X	X	X	X	X			X[2]	X[2]
(25) Power of attorney	X	X	X	X		X	X	X	X	X	X	X	X[2]	X[2]	X[2]
(26) Statement of eligibility of trustee	X	X	X	X	X	X	X	X	X	X	X		X	X	X
(27) Invitations for competitive bids	X	X	X	X											
(28) Additional exhibits	X	X	X	X	X	X	X	X	X	X	X	X	X	X	X
(29) Information from reports furnished to state insurance regulatory authorities	X			X	X	X						X			X

[1] Where incorporated by reference into the text of the prospectus and delivered to security holders along with the prospectus as permitted by the registration statement; or, in the case of the Form 10-K, where the annual report to security holders is incorporated by reference into the text of the Form 10-K.

[2] An exhibit need not be provided about a company if (1) with respect to such company an election has been made under Forms S-4 or F-4 to provide information about such company at a level prescribed by Forms S-2, S-3, F-2 or F-3 and (2) the form, the level of which has been elected under Forms S-4 or F-4, would not require such company to provide such exhibit if it were registering a primary offering.

[3] Where the opinion of the expert or counsel has been incorporated by reference into a previously filed Securities Act registration statement.

[4] If required pursuant to Item 304 of Regulation S-K.

ment. The plan filed shall contain a list briefly identifying the contents of all omitted schedules, together with an agreement to furnish supplementally a copy of any omitted schedule to the Commission upon request.

(3) *Articles of incorporation and by-laws* — The articles of incorporation and by-laws of the registrant or instruments corresponding thereto as currently in effect and any amendments thereto. Whenever amendments to the articles or by-laws of the registrant are filed, there shall also be filed a complete copy of the articles or by-laws as amended. Where it is impracticable for the registrant to file a charter amendment authorizing new securities with the appropriate state authority prior to the effective date of the registration statement registering such securities, the registrant may file as an exhibit to the registration statement the form of amendment to be filed with the state authority; and in such a case, if material changes are made after the copy is filed, the registrant must also file the changed copy.

(4) *Instruments defining the rights of security holders, including indentures* —

(i) All instruments defining the rights of holders of the equity or debt securities being registered including, where applicable, the relevant portion of the articles of incorporation or by-laws of the registrant.

(ii) Except as set forth in (iii) below, for filings on Forms S-1, S-11, S-14 and F-4 under the Securities Act (§§239.1, 25, 18, 23 and 34 of this chapter) and Forms 10 and 10-K (§§249.210 and 310 of this chapter) under the Exchange Act all instruments defining the rights of holders of long-term debt of the registrant and its consolidated subsidiaries and for any of its unconsolidated subsidiaries for which financial statements are required to be filed.

(iii) Where the instrument defines the rights of holders of long-term debt of the registrant and its consolidated subsidiaries and for any of its unconsolidated subsidiaries for which financial statements are required to be filed, there need not be filed (A) any instrument with respect to long-term debt not being registered if the total amount of securities authorized thereunder does not exceed 10 percent of the total assets of the registrant and its subsidiaries on a consolidated basis and if there is filed an agreement to furnish a copy of such agreement to the Commission upon request; (B) any instrument with respect to any class of securities if appropriate steps to assure the redemption of retirement of such class will be taken prior to or upon delivery by the registrant of the securities being registered; or (C) copies of instruments evidencing scrip certificates for fractions of shares.

(iv) If any of the securities being registered are, or will be, issued under an indenture to be qualified under the Trust Indenture Act, the copy of such indenture which is filed as an exhibit shall include or be accompanied by (A) a reasonably itemized and informative table of contents; and (B) a cross-reference sheet showing the location in the indenture of the provisions inserted pursuant to sections 310 through 318(a) inclusive of the Trust Indenture Act of 1939.

(v) With respect to Forms 8-K and 10-Q under the Exchange Act which are filed and which disclose, in the text of Form 10-Q, the interim financial statements, or the footnotes thereto, the creation of a new class of securities or indebtedness or the modification of existing rights of security holders, file all instruments defining the rights of holders of these securities or indebtedness. However, there need not be filed any instrument with respect to long-term debt not being registered which meets the exclusion set forth above in paragraph (b)(4)(iii)(A).

Instruction. There need not be filed any instrument which defines the rights of participants (not as security holders) pursuant to an employee benefit plan.

(5) *Opinion re legality* —

(i) An opinion of counsel as to the legality of the securities being registered, indicating whether they will, when sold, be legally issued, fully paid and non-assessable, and, if debt securities, whether they will be binding obligations of the registrant.

(ii) If the securities being registered are issued under a plan and the plan is subject to the requirements of ERISA furnish either:

(A) An opinion of counsel which confirms compliance of the provisions of the written documents constituting the plan with the requirements of ERISA pertaining to such provisions; or

(B) A copy of the Internal Revenue Service determination letter that the plan is qualified under section 401 of the Internal Revenue Code; or

(iii) If the securities being registered are issued under a plan which is subject to the requirements of ERISA and the plan has been amended subsequent to the filing of (ii)(A) or (B) above, furnish either:

(A) An opinion of counsel which confirms compliance of the amended provisions of the plan with the requirements of ERISA pertaining to such provisions; or

(B) A copy of the Internal Revenue Service determination letter that the amended plan is qualified under section 401 of the Internal Revenue Code.

Note: Attention is directed to Item 8 of Form S-8 for exemptions to this exhibit requirement applicable to that Form.

(6) *Opinion re discount on capital shares* — If any discount on capital shares is shown as a deduction from capital shares on the most recent balance sheet being filed for the registrant, there shall be filed a statement of the circumstances under which such discount arose and an opinion of counsel as to the legality of the issuance of the shares to which such discount relates. The opinion shall set forth, or specifically refer to, any applicable constitutional and statutory provisions and shall cite any decisions which in the opinion of counsel are controlling.

(7) *Opinion re liquidation preference* — If the registrant has any shares the preference of which upon involuntary liquidation exceeds the par or stated value thereof, there shall be filed an opinion of counsel as to whether there are any restrictions upon surplus by reason of such excess and also as to any remedies available to security holders before or after payment of any dividend that would reduce surplus to an amount less than the amount of such excess. The opinion shall set forth, or specifically refer to, any applicable constitutional and statutory provisions and shall cite any decisions which, in the opinion of counsel, are controlling.

(8) *Opinion re tax matters* — For filings on Form S-11 under the Securities Act (§239.18) or those to which Securities Act Industry Guide 5 applies, an opinion of counsel or of an independent public or certified public accountant or, in lieu thereof, a revenue ruling from the Internal Revenue Service, supporting the tax matters and consequences to the shareholders as described in the filing when such tax matters are material to the transaction for which the registration statement is being filed. This exhibit otherwise need only be filed with the other applicable registration forms where the tax consequences are material to an investor and a representation as to tax consequences is set forth in the filing. If a tax opinion is set forth in full in the filing, an indication that such is the case may be made in lieu of filing the otherwise required exhibit. Such tax opinions may be conditioned or may be qualified, so long as such conditions and qualifications are adequately described in the filing.

(9) *Voting trust agreement* — Any voting trust agreements and amendments thereto.

(10) *Material contracts* —

    (i) Every contract not made in the ordinary course of business which is material to the registrant and is to be performed in whole or in part at or after the filing of the registration statement or report or was entered into not more than two years before such filing. Only contracts need be filed as to which the registrant or subsidiary of the registrant is a party or has succeeded to a party by assumption or assignment or in which the registrant or such subsidiary has a beneficial interest.

    (ii) If the contract is such as ordinarily accompanies the kind of business conducted by the registrant and its subsidiaries, it will be deemed to have been made in the ordinary course of business and need not be filed unless it falls within one or more of the following categories, in which case it shall be filed except where immaterial in amount or significance:

        (A) Any contract to which directors, officers, promoters, voting trustees, security holders named in the registration statement or report, or underwriters are parties other than contracts involving only the purchase or sale of current assets having a determinable market price, at such market price;

        (B) Any contract upon which the registrant's business is substantially dependent, as in the case of continuing contracts to sell the major part of registrant's products or services or to purchase the major part of registrant's requirements of goods, services or raw materials or any franchise or license or other agreement to use a patent, formula, trade secret, process or trade name upon which registrant's business depends to a material extent;

        (C) Any contract calling for the acquisition or sale of any property, plant or equipment for a consideration exceeding 15 percent of such fixed assets of the registrant on a consolidated basis; or

        (D) Any material lease under which a part of the property described in the registration statement or report is held by the registrant.

    (iii) (A) Any management contract or any compensatory plan, contract or arrangement, including but not limited to plans relating to options, warrants or rights, pension, retirement or deferred compensation or bonus, incentive or profit sharing (or if not set forth in any formal document, a written description thereof) in which any director or any of the five most highly compensated executive officers of the registrant participates shall be deemed material and shall be filed; and any other management contract or any compensatory plan, contract, or arrangement in which any other executive officer of the registrant participates shall be filed unless immaterial in amount or significance.

        (B) Notwithstanding paragraph (iii)(A) above, the following management contracts or compensatory plans, contracts or arrangements need not be filed:

            (1) Ordinary purchase and sales agency agreements.

(2) Agreements with managers of stores in a chain organization or similar organization.

(3) Contracts providing for labor or salesmen's bonuses or payments to a class of security holders, as such.

(4) Any compensatory plan, contract or arrangement which pursuant to its terms is available to employees, officers or directors generally and which in operation provides for the same method of allocation of benefits between management and nonmanagement participants.

(5) Any compensatory plan, contract or arrangement if the registrant is a foreign private issuer that furnishes compensatory information on an aggregate basis as permitted by General Instruction 1 to Item 402 (§229.402).

(6) Any compensatory plan, contract, or arrangement if the registrant is a wholly owned subsidiary of a company that has a class of securities registered pursuant to section 12 or files reports pursuant to section 15(d) of the Exchange Act and is filing a report on Form 10-K or registering debt instruments or preferred stock which are not voting securities on Form S-2.

Instruction: With the exception of management contracts, in order to comply with paragraph (iii) above, registrants need only file copies of the various remunerative plans and need not file each individual director's or executive officer's personal agreement under the plans unless there are particular provisions in such personal agreements whose disclosure in an exhibit is necessary to an investor's understanding of that individual's compensation under the plan.

(11) *Statement re computation of per share earnings.* A statement setting forth in reasonable detail the computation of per share earnings, unless the computation can be clearly determined from the material contained in the registration statement or report. The information with respect to the computation of per share earnings on both primary and fully diluted bases, presented by exhibit or otherwise, must be furnished even though the amounts of per share earnings on the fully diluted basis are not required to be presented in the income statement under the provisions of Accounting Principles Board Opinion No. 15. That Opinion provides that any reduction of less than 3 % need not be considered as dilution (see footnote to paragraph 14 of the Opinion) and that a computation on the fully diluted basis which results in improvement of earnings per share not be taken into account (see paragraph 40 of the Opinion).

(12) *Statements re computation of ratios* — A statement setting forth in reasonable detail the computation of any ratio of earnings to fixed charges, any ratio of earnings to combined fixed charges and preferred stock dividends or any other ratios which appear in the registration statement or report. See Item 503(d) of Regulation S-K (§229.503(d)).

(13) *Annual report to security holders, Form 10-Q or quarterly report to security holders* — The registrant's annual report to security holders for its last fiscal year, its Form 10-Q (if specifically incorporated by reference in the prospectus) or its quarterly report to security holders, if all or a portion thereof is incorporated by reference in the filing. Such report, except for those portions thereof which are expressly incorporated by reference in the filing, is to be furnished for the information of the Commission and is not to be deemed "filed" as part of the filing. If the financial statements in the report have been incorporated by reference in the filing, the accountant's certificate shall be manually signed in one copy. See Rule 411(b) (§230.411(b) of this chapter).

(14) *Material foreign patents* — Each material foreign patent for an invention not covered by a United States patent. If the filing is a registration statement and if a substantial part of the securities to be offered or if the proceeds therefrom have been or are to be used for the particular purposes of acquiring, developing or exploiting one or more material foreign patents or patent rights, furnish a list showing the number and a brief identification of each such patent or patent right.

(15) *Letter re unaudited interim financial information* — A letter, where applicable, from the independent accountant which acknowledges awareness of the use in a registration statement of a report on unaudited interim financial information which pursuant to Rule 436(c) under the Securities Act (§230.436(c) of this chapter) is not considered a part of a registration statement prepared or certified by an accountant or a report prepared or certified by an accountant within the meaning of sections 7 and 11 of that Act. Such letter may be filed with the registration statement, an amendment thereto, or a report on Form 10-Q which is incorporated by reference into the registration statement.

(16) *Letter re change in certifying accountant* — A letter from the registrant's former independent accountant regarding its concurrence or disagreement with the statements made by the registrant in the current report concerning the resignation or dismissal as the registrant's principal accountant.

(17) *Letter re director resignation* — Any letter from a former director which sets forth a description of a disagreement with the registrant that led to the director's resignation or refusal to stand for re-election and which requests that the matter be disclosed.

(18) *Letter re change in accounting principles* — Unless previously filed, a letter from the registrant's independent accountant indicating whether any change in accounting principles or practices followed by the registrant, or any change in the method

of applying any such accounting principles or practices, which affected the financial statements being filed with the Commission in the report or which is reasonably certain to affect the financial statements of future fiscal years is to an alternative principal which in his judgment is preferable under the circumstances. No such letter need be filed when such change is made in response to a standard adopted by the Financial Accounting Standards Board that creates a new accounting principle, that expresses a preference for an accounting principle, or that rejects a specific accounting principle.

(19) *Previously unfiled documents —*

    (i) Any unfiled document, which was executed or in effect during the reporting period, shall be filed if such document would have been required to be filed as an exhibit to a registration statement on Form 10.

    (ii) Any amendment or modification to a document which was previously filed with the Commission as an exhibit to Forms 10, 10-K or 10-Q. Such amendment or modification need not be filed where such previously filed exhibit would not be currently required.

(20) *Report furnished to security holders —* If the registrant makes available to its stockholders or otherwise publishes, within the period prescribed for filing the report, a document or statement containing information meeting some or all of the requirements of Part I of Form 10-Q, the information called for may be incorporated by reference to such published document or statement provided copies thereof are included as an exhibit to the registration statement or to Part I of the Form 10-Q report.

(21) *Other documents or statements to security holders —* If the registrant makes available to its stockholders or otherwise publishes, within the period prescribed for filing the report, a document or statement containing information meeting some or all of the requirements of this form the information called for may be incorporated by reference to such published document or statement provided copies thereof are filed as an exhibit to the report on this form.

(22) *Subsidiaries of the registrant —*

    (i) List all subsidiaries of the registrant, the state or other jurisdiction of incorporation or organization of each, and the names under which such subsidiaries do business. This list may be incorporated by reference from a document which includes a complete and accurate list.

    (ii) The names of particular subsidiaries may be omitted if the unnamed subsidiaries, considered in the aggregate as a single subsidiary, would not constitute a significant subsidiary as of the end of the year covered by this report. (See the definition of "significant subsidiary" in Rule 1-02(v) (17 CFR 210.1-02(v)) of Regulation S-X.) The names of consolidated wholly-owned multiple subsidiaries carrying on the same line of business, such as chain stores or small loan companies, may be omitted, provided the name of the immediate parent, the line of business, the number of omitted subsidiaries operating in the United States and the number operating in foreign countries are given. This instruction shall not apply, however, to banks, insurance companies, savings and loan associations or to any subsidiary subject to regulation by another Federal agency.

(23) *Published report regarding matters submitted to vote of security holders —* Published reports containing all of the information called for by Item 4 of Part II of Form 10-Q or Item 4 of Part I of Form 10-K which is referred to therein in lieu of providing disclosure in Form 10-Q or 10-K, which are required to be filed as exhibits by Rule 12b-23(a)(3) under the Exchange Act (§240.12b-23(a)(3) of this chapter).

(24) *Consents of experts and counsel —*

    (i) Securities Act filings — All written consents required to be filed shall be dated and manually signed. Where the consent of an expert or counsel is contained in his report or opinion or elsewhere in the registration statement or document filed therewith, a reference shall be made in the index to the report, the part of the registration statement or document or opinion, containing the consent.

    (ii) Exchange Act reports — where the filing of a written consent is required with respect to material incorporated by reference in a previously filed registration statement under the Securities Act, such consent may be filed as an exhibit to the material incorporated by reference. Such consents shall be dated and manually signed.

(25) *Power of attorney —* If any name is signed to the registration statement or report pursuant to power of attorney, manually signed copies of such power of attorney shall be filed. Where the power of attorney is contained elsewhere in the registration statement or documents filed therewith a reference shall be made in the index to the part of the registration statement or document containing such power of attorney. In addition, if the name of any officer signing on behalf of the registrant is signed pursuant to a power of attorney, certified copies of a resolution of the registrant's board of directors authorizing such signature shall also be filed.

(26) *Statement of eligibility of trustee* — A statement of eligibility and qualification of each person designated to act as trustee under an indenture to be qualified under the Trust Indenture Act of 1939. Such statement of eligibility shall be bound separately from the other exhibits.

(27) *Invitations for competitive bids* — If the registration statement covers securities to be offered at competitive bidding, any form of communication which is an invitation for competitive bid which will be sent or given to any person shall be filed.

(28) *Additional exhibits* —

    (i) Any additional exhibits which the registrant may wish to file shall be so marked as to indicate clearly the subject matters to which they refer.

    (ii) Any document (except for an exhibit) or part thereof which is incorporated by reference in the filing and is not otherwise required to be filed by this Item or is not a Commission filed document incorporated by reference in a Securities Act registration statement.

(29) *Information from reports furnished to state insurance regulatory authorities.*

    (i) If reserves for unpaid property-casualty ("P/C") claims and claim adjustment expenses of the registrant and its consolidated subsidiaries, its unconsolidated subsidiaries and the proportionate share of the registrant and its other subsidiaries in the unpaid P/C claims and claim adjustment expenses of its 50 % -or-less-owned equity investees, taken in the aggregate after intercompany eliminations, exceed one-half of the common stockholders' equity of the registrant and its consolidated subsidiaries as of the beginning of the latest fiscal year the following information should be supplied.

    (ii) The information included in Schedules O and P of Annual Statements provided to state regulatory authorities by the registrant and/or its P/C insurance company affiliates for the last year should be presented in the same format and on the same statutory basis, on a combined or consolidated basis as appropriate, separately for each of the following:

        (A) the registrant and its consolidated subsidiaries and

        (B) the registrant's unconsolidated subsidiaries and

        (C) fifty-percent-or-less-owned equity investees of the registrant and its subsidiaries

    (iii) The combined or consolidated Schedules O and P of 50 % -or-less-owned equity investees may be omitted if they file the same information with the Commission as registrants in their own right, if that fact and the name and ownership percentage of such registrants is stated.

    (iv) If ending reserves in category (A), (B), or the proportionate share of the registrant and its other subsidiaries in (C) above are less than 5 % of the total ending reserves in (A), (B), and the proportionate share of (C), that category may be omitted and that fact so noted. If the amount of the reserves attributable to 50 % -or-less-owned equity investees that file this information as registrants in their own right exceeds 95 % of the total category (C) reserves, information for the other 50 % -or-less-owned equity investees need not be provided.

    (v) Schedule O and P information need not be included for entities that are not required to file Schedules O and P with insurance regulatory authorities. However, the nature and extent of any such exclusions should be clearly noted in the Exhibit.

    (vi) Registrants whose fiscal year differs from the calendar year should present Schedules O and P as of the end of the calendar year that falls within their fiscal year.

    (vii) The nature and amount of the difference between reserves for claims and claim adjustment expenses reflected on Schedules O and P and the aggregate P/C statutory reserves for claims and claim adjustment expenses as of the latest calendar year end should be disclosed in a note to those Schedules.

Subpart 229.700 — Miscellaneous

Recent Sales of Unregistered Securities

Reg. §229.701. Item 701. Furnish the following information as to all securities of the registrant sold by the registrant within the past three years which were not registered under the Securities Act. Include sales of reacquired securities, as well as new issues, securities issued in exchange for property, services, or other securities, and new securities resulting from the modification of outstanding securities.

(a) *Securities sold.* Give the date of sale and the title and amount of securities sold.

(b) *Underwriters and other purchasers.* Give the names of the principal underwriters, if any. As to any such securities not publicly offered, name the persons or identify the class of persons to whom the securities were sold.

(c) *Consideration.* As to securities sold for cash, state the aggregate offering price and the aggregate underwriting discounts or commissions. As to any securities sold otherwise than for cash, state the nature of the transaction and the nature and aggregate amount of consideration received by the registrant.

(d) *Exemption from registration claimed.* Indicate the section of the Securities Act or the rule of the Commission under which exemption from registration was claimed and state briefly the facts relied upon to make the exemption available.

Instructions.

1. Information required by this Item 701 need not be set forth as to notes, drafts, bills of exchange, or bankers' acceptances which mature not later than one year from the date of issuance.

2. If the sales were made in a series of transactions, the information may be given by such totals and periods as will reasonably convey the information required.

Indemnification of Directors and Officers

Reg. §229.702. Item 702. State the general effect of any statute, charter provisions, by-laws, contract or other arrangements under which any controlling persons, director or officer of the registrant is insured or indemnified in any manner against liability which he may incur in his capacity as such.

Subpart 229.800 — List of Industry Guides

Securities Act Industry Guides

Reg. §229.801.

(a) Guide 1. Disclosure of principal sources of electric and gas revenues.

(b) Guide 2. Disclosure of oil and gas operations.

(c) Guide 3. Statistical disclosure by bank holding companies.

(d) Guide 4. Prospectuses relating to interests in oil and gas programs.

(e) Guide 5. Preparation of registration statements relating to interests in real estate limited partnerships.

(f) Guide 6. Disclosures concerning unpaid claims and claim adjustment expenses of property-casualty underwriters.

Exchange Act Industry Guides

Reg. §229.802.

(a) Guide 1. Disclosure of principal sources of electric and gas revenues.

(b) Guide 2. Disclosure of oil and gas operations.

(c) Guide 3. Statistical disclosure by bank holding companies.

(d) Guide 4. Disclosures concerning unpaid claims and claim adjustment expenses of property-casualty underwriters.

APPENDIX B

REGULATION S-B

UNITED STATES
SECURITIES AND EXCHANGE COMMISSION
Washington, D.C. 20549

OMB APPROVAL	
OMB Number:	3235-0417
Expires:	October 31, 1995
Estimated average burden hours per response	...... 1.0

Regulation S-B

PART 228 -INTEGRATED DISCLOSURE SYSTEM FOR SMALL BUSINESS ISSUERS

Subpart A - Regulation S-B

§228.10 (Item 10)   General.
§228.101 (Item 101)   Description of Business.
§228.102 (Item 102)   Description of Property.
§228.103 (Item 103)   Legal Proceedings.
§228.201 (Item 201)   Market for Common Stock and Related Stockholder Matters.
§228.202 (Item 202)   Description of Securities.
§228.303 (Item 303)   Management's Discussion and Analysis or Plan of Operation.
§228.304 (Item 304)   Changes In and Disagreements With Accountants on Accounting and Financial Disclosure.
§228.310 (Item 310)   Financial Statements.
§228.401 (Item 401)   Directors, Executive Officers, Promoters and Control Persons.
§228.402 (Item 402)   Executive Compensation.
§228.403 (Item 403)   Security Ownership of Certain Beneficial Owners and Management.
§228.404 (Item 404)   Certain Relationships and Related Transactions.
§228.405 (Item 405)   Compliance With Section 16(a) of the Exchange Act.
§228.501 (Item 501)   Front of Registration Statement and Outside Front Cover of Prospectus.
§228.502 (Item 502)   Inside Front and Outside Back Cover Pages of Prospectus.
§228.503 (Item 503)   Summary Information and Risk Factors.
§228.504 (Item 504)   Use of Proceeds.
§228.505 (Item 505)   Determination of Offering Price.
§228.506 (Item 506)   Dilution.
§228.507 (Item 507)   Selling Security Holders.
§228.508 (Item 508)   Plan of Distribution.
§228.509 (Item 509)   Interest of Named Experts and Counsel.
§228.510 (Item 510)   Disclosure of Commission Position on Indemnification for Securities Act Liabilities.
§228.511 (Item 511)   Other Expenses of Issuance and Distribution.
§228.512 (Item 512)   Undertakings.
§228.601 (Item 601)   Exhibits.
§228.701 (Item 701)   Recent Sales of Unregistered Securities.
§228.702 (Item 702)   Indemnification of Directors and Officers.

§§228.10 (Item 10) General.

(a) *Application of Regulation S-B*. Regulation S-B is the source of disclosure requirements for "small business issuer" filings under the Securities Act of 1933 (the "Securities Act") and the Securities Exchange Act of 1934 (the "Exchange Act").

   (1) *Definition of small business issuer*. A small business issuer is defined as a company that meets all of the following criteria:

      (i)   has revenues of less than $25,000,000;

      (ii)   is a U.S. or Canadian issuer;

      (iii)   is not an investment company; and

      (iv)   if a majority owned subsidiary, the parent corporation is also a small business issuer.

   Provided however, that an entity is not a small business issuer if it has a public float (the aggregate market value of the issuer's outstanding securities held by non-affiliates) of $25,000,000 or more.

   NOTE: The public float of a reporting company shall be computed by use of the price at which the stock was last sold, or the average of the bid and asked prices of such stock, on a date within 60 days prior to the end of its most recent fiscal year. The public float of a company filing an initial registration statement under the Exchange Act shall be determined as of a date within 60 days of the date the registration statement is filed. In the case of an initial public offering of securities, public float shall be computed on the basis of the number of shares outstanding prior to the offering and the estimated public offering price of the securities.

(2) *Entering and Exiting the Small Business Disclosure System.*

    (i) A company that meets the definition of small business issuer may use Form SB-2 for registration of its securities under the Securities Act; Form 10-SB for registration of its securities under the Exchange Act; and Forms 10-KSB and 10-QSB for its annual and quarterly reports.

    (ii) For a non-reporting company entering the disclosure system for the first time either by filing a registration statement under the Securities Act on Form SB-2 or a registration statement under the Exchange Act on Form 10-SB, the determination as to whether a company is a small business issuer is made with reference to its revenues during its last fiscal year and public float as of a date within 60 days of the date the registration statement is filed. *See* Note to paragraph (a) of this Item.

    (iii) Once a small business issuer becomes a reporting company it will remain a small business issuer until it exceeds the revenue limit or the public float limit at the end of two consecutive years. For example, if a company exceeds the revenue limit for two consecutive years, it will no longer be considered a small business. However, if it exceeds the revenue limit in one year and the next year exceeds the public float limit, but not the revenue limit, it will still be considered a small business. *See* Note to paragraph (a) of this Item.

    (iv) A reporting company that is not a small business company must meet the definition of a small business issuer at the end of two consecutive fiscal years before it will be considered a small business issuer for purposes of using Form SB-2, Form 10-SB, Form 10-KSB and Form 10-QSB. *See* Note to paragraph (a) of this Item.

    (v) The determination as to the reporting category (small business issuer or other issuer) made for a non-reporting company at the time it enters the disclosure system governs all reports relating to the remainder of the fiscal year. The determination made for a reporting company at the end of its fiscal year governs all reports relating to the next fiscal year. An issuer may not change from one category to another with respect to its reports under the Exchange Act for a single fiscal year. A company may, however, choose not to use a Form SB-2 for a registration under the Securities Act.

(b) *Definitions of terms.*

    (1) *Common Equity* - means the small business issuer's common stock. If the small business issuer is a limited partnership, the term refers to the equity interests in the partnership.

    (2) *Public market* - no public market shall be deemed to exist unless, within the past 60 business days, both bid and asked quotations at fixed prices (excluding "bid wanted" or "offer wanted" quotations) have appeared regularly in any established quotation system on at least half of such business days. Transactions arranged without the participation of a broker or dealer functioning as such are not indicative of a "public market."

    (3) *Reporting company* - means a company that is obligated to file periodic reports with the Securities and Exchange Commission under section 15(d) or 13(a) of the Exchange Act.

    (4) *Small business issuer* - refers to the issuer and all of its consolidated subsidiaries.

(c) *Preparing the disclosure document.*

    (1) The purpose of a disclosure document is to inform investors. Hence, information should be presented in a clear, concise and understandable fashion. Avoid unnecessary details, repetition or the use of technical language. The responses to the items of this Regulation should be brief and to the point.

    (2) Small business issuers should consult the General Rules and Regulations under the Securities Act and Exchange Act for requirements concerning the preparation and filing of documents. Small business issuers should be aware that there are special rules concerning such matters as the kind and size of paper that is allowed and how filings should be bound. These special rules are located in Regulation C of the Securities Act (17 CFR 230.400 *et seq.*) and in Regulation 12B of the Exchange Act (17 CFR 240.12b-1 *et seq.*).

(d) *Commission policy on projections.* The Commission encourages the use of management's projections of future economic performance that have a reasonable basis and are presented in an appropriate format. The guidelines below set forth the Commission's views on important factors to be considered in preparing and disclosing such projections. (*See also* 17 CFR 230.175 and 240.3b-6).

(1) *Basis for projections.* Management has the option to present in Commission filings its good faith assessment of a small business issuer's future performance. Management, however, must have a reasonable basis for such an assessment. An outside review of management's projections may furnish additional support in this regard. If management decides to include a report of such a review in a Commission filing, it should also disclose the qualifications of the reviewer, the extent of the review, the relationship between the reviewer and the registrant, and other material factors concerning the process by which any outside review was sought or obtained. Moreover, in the case of a registration statement under the Securities Act, the reviewer would be deemed an expert and an appropriate consent must be filed with the registration statement.

(2) *Format for projections.* Traditionally, projections have been given for three financial items generally considered to be of primary importance to investors (revenues, net income (loss) and earnings (loss) per share), projection information need not necessarily be limited to these three items. However, management should take care to assure that the choice of items projected is not susceptible to misleading inferences through selective projection of only favorable items. It generally would be misleading to present sales or revenue projections without one of the foregoing measures of income. The period that appropriately may be covered by a projection depends to a large extent on the particular circumstances of the company involved. For certain companies in certain industries, a projection covering a two or three year period may be entirely reasonable. Other companies may not have a reasonable basis for projections beyond the current year.

(3) *Investor understanding.* Disclosures accompanying the projections should facilitate investor understanding of the basis for and limitations of projections. The Commission believes that investor understanding would be enhanced by disclosure of the assumptions which in management's opinion are most significant to the projections or are the key factors upon which the financial results of the enterprise depend and encourages disclosure of assumptions in a manner that will provide a frame-work for analysis of the projection. Management also should consider whether disclosure of the accuracy or inaccuracy of previous projections would provide investors with important insights into the limitations of projections.

(e) *Commission policy on security ratings.* In view of the importance of security ratings ("ratings") to investors and the marketplace, the Commission permits small business issuers to disclose ratings assigned by rating organizations to classes of debt securities, convertible debt securities and preferred stock in registration statements and periodic reports. In addition, the Commission permits, disclosure of ratings assigned by any nationally recognized statistical rating organizations ("NRSROs") in certain communications deemed not to be a prospectus ("tombstone advertisements"). Below are the Commission's views on important matters to be considered in disclosing security ratings.

(1) (i) If a small business issuer includes in a filing any rating(s) assigned to a class of securities, it should consider including any other rating assigned by a different NRSRO that is materially different. A statement that a security rating is not a recommendation to buy, sell or hold securities and that it may be subject to revision or withdrawal at any time by the assigning rating organization should also be included.

(ii) (A) If the rating is included in a filing under the Securities Act, the written consent of any rating organization that is not a NRSRO whose rating is included should be filed. The consent of any NRSRO is not required. (*See* Rule 436(g) under the Securities Act (§ 230.436(g) of this chapter.)

(B) If a change in a rating already included is available before effectiveness of the registration statement, the small business issuer should consider including such rating change in the prospectus. If the rating change is material, consideration should be given to recirculating the preliminary prospectus.

(C) If a materially different additional NRSRO rating or a material change in a rating already included becomes available during any period in which offers or sales are being made, the small business issuer should consider disclosing this information in a sticker to the prospectus.

(iii) If there is a material change in the rating(s) assigned by any NRSRO(s) to any outstanding class(es) of securities of a reporting company, the registrant should consider filing a report on Form 8-K (§ 249.308 of this chapter) or other appropriate report under the Exchange Act disclosing such rating change.

§228.101 (Item 101) Description of Business.

(a) *Business Development.* Describe the development of the small business issuer during the last three years. If the small business issuer has not been in business for three years, give the same information for predecessor(s) of the small business issuer if there are any. This business development description should include:

(1) Form and year of organization;

(2) Any bankruptcy, receivership or similar proceeding; and

(3) Any material reclassification, merger, consolidation, or purchase or sale of a significant amount of assets not in the ordinary course of business.

3

(b) *Business of Issuer*. Briefly describe the business and include, to the extent material to an understanding of the issuer:

    (1) Principal products or services and their markets;

    (2) Distribution methods of the products or services;

    (3) Status of any publicly announced new product or service;

    (4) Competitive business conditions and the small business issuer's competitive position in the industry and methods of competition;

    (5) Sources and availability of raw materials and the names of principal suppliers;

    (6) Dependence on one or a few major customers;

    (7) Patents, trademarks, licenses, franchises, concessions, royalty agreements or labor contracts, including duration;

    (8) Need for any government approval of principal products or services. If government approval is necessary and the small business issuer has not yet received that approval, discuss the status of the approval within the government approval process;

    (9) Effect of existing or probable governmental regulations on the business;

    (10) Estimate of the amount spent during each of the last two fiscal years on research and development activities, and if applicable the extent to which the cost of such activities are borne directly by customers;

    (11) Costs and effects of compliance with environmental laws (federal, state and local); and

    (12) Number of total employees and number of full time employees.

§228.102 (Item 102) Description of Property.

(a) Give the location of the principal plants and other property of the small business issuer and describe the condition of the property. If the small business issuer does not have complete ownership of the property, for example, others also own the property or there is a mortgage or lien on the property, describe the limitations on the ownership.

Instructions to Item 102(a).

    1. Small business issuers engaged in significant mining operations also should provide the information in Guide 7 (§229.801(g) and §229.802(g) of this chapter).

    2. Small business issuers engaged in oil and gas producing activities also should provide the information in Guide 2 (§229.801(b) and §229.802(b) of this chapter).

    3. Small business issuers engaged in real estate activities should, in addition to Guide 5 (§229.801(e) of this chapter) provide responses to the following Items:

(b) *Investment Policies*

Describe the policy of the small business issuer with respect to each of the following types of investments. State whether there are any limitations on the percentage of assets which may be invested in any one investment, or type of investment, and indicate whether such policy may be changed without a vote of security holders. State whether it is the small business issuer's policy to acquire assets primarily for possible capital gain or primarily for income.

    (1) *Investments in real estate or interests in real estate.*

        Indicate the types of real estate in which the small business issuer may invest, for example, office or apartment buildings, shopping centers, industrial or commercial properties, special purpose buildings and undeveloped acreage, and the geographic area(s) of these properties. Briefly describe the method, or proposed method, of operating and financing these properties. Indicate any limitations on the number or amount of mortgages which may be placed on any one piece of property.

    (2) *Investments in real estate mortgages.*

        Indicate the types of mortgages, for example, first or second mortgages, and the types of properties subject to mortgages in which the small business issuer intends to invest, for example, single family dwellings, apartment buildings, office buildings, unimproved land, and the nature of any guarantees or insurance. Describe each type of mortgage activity in which the small business issuer intends to engage such as originating, servicing and warehousing, and the portfolio turnover policy.

(3) *Securities of or interests in persons primarily engaged in real estate activities.*

Indicate the types of securities in which the small business issuer may invest, for example, common stock, interest in real estate investment trusts, partnership interests. Indicate the primary activities of persons in which the small business issuer will invest, such as mortgage sales, investments in developed or undeveloped properties and state the investment policies of such persons.

(c) *Description of Real Estate and Operating Data.*

This information shall be furnished separately for each property the book value of which amounts to ten percent or more of the total assets of the small business issuer and its consolidated subsidiaries for the last fiscal year. With respect to other properties, the information shall be given by such classes or groups and in such detail as will reasonably convey the information required.

(1) Describe the general character and location of all materially important properties held or intended to be acquired by or leased to the small business issuer and describe the present or proposed use of such properties and their suitability and adequacy for such use. Properties not yet acquired shall be identified as such.

(2) State the nature of the small business issuer's title to, or other interest in such properties and the nature and amount of all material mortgages, liens or encumbrances against such properties. Disclose the current principal amount of each material encumbrance, interest and amortization provisions, prepayment provisions, maturity date and the balance due at maturity assuming no prepayments.

(3) Outline briefly the principal terms of any lease of any of such properties or any option or contract to purchase or sell any of such properties.

(4) Outline briefly any proposed program for the renovation, improvement or development of such properties, including the estimated cost thereof and the method of financing to be used. If there are no present plans for the improvement or development of any unimproved or undeveloped property, so state and indicate the purpose for which the property is to be held or acquired.

(5) Describe the general competitive conditions to which the properties are or may be subject.

(6) Include a statement as to whether, in the opinion of the management of the small business issuer, the properties are adequately covered by insurance.

(7) With respect to each improved property which is separately described, provide the following in addition to the above:

(i) Occupancy rate;

(ii) Number of tenants occupying ten percent or more of the rentable square footage and principal nature of business of each such tenant and the principal provisions of each of their leases;

(iii) Principal business, occupations and professions carried on in, or from the building;

(iv) The average effective annual rental per square foot or unit;

(v) Schedule of the lease expirations for each of the ten years starting with the year in which the registration statement is filed, stating:

(A) the number of tenants whose leases will expire,

(B) the total area in square feet covered by such leases,

(C) the annual rental represented by such leases, and

(D) the percentage of gross annual rental represented by such leases;

(vi) Each of the properties and components thereof upon which depreciation is taken, setting forth the:

(A) federal tax basis,

(B) rate,

(C) method, and

(D) life claimed with respect to such property or component thereof for purposes of depreciation;

(vii)The realty tax rate, annual realty taxes and estimated taxes on any proposed improvements.

5

Instruction

If the small business issuer has a number of properties, the information may be given in tabular form.

§228.103 (Item 103) Legal Proceedings.

(a) If a small business issuer is a party to any pending legal proceeding (or its property is the subject of a pending legal proceeding), give the following information (no information is necessary as to routine litigation that is incidental to the business):

    (1) name of court or agency where proceeding is pending;

    (2) date proceeding began;

    (3) principal parties;

    (4) description of facts underlying the proceedings; and

    (5) relief sought.

(b) Include the information called for by paragraphs (a)(1) through (5) of this Item for any proceeding that a governmental authority is contemplating (if the small business issuer is aware of the proceeding).

Instructions to Item 103.

1. A proceeding that primarily involves a claim for damages does not need to be described if the amount involved, exclusive of interest and costs, does not exceed 10% of the current assets of the small business issuer. If any proceeding presents the same legal and factual issues as other proceedings pending or known to be contemplated, the amount involved in such other proceedings shall be included in computing such percentage.

2. The following types of proceedings with respect to the registrant are not "routine litigation incidental to the business" and, notwithstanding instruction 1 of this Item, must be described: bankruptcy, receivership, or similar proceeding.

3. Any proceeding that involves federal, state or local environmental laws must be described if it is material; involves a damages claim for more than 10% of the current assets of the issuer; or potentially involves more than $100,000 in sanctions and a governmental authority is a party.

4. Disclose any material proceeding to which any director, officer or affiliate of the issuer, any owner of record or beneficially of more than 5% of any class of voting securities of the small business issuer, or security holder is a party adverse to the small business issuer or has a material interest adverse to the small business issuer.

§228.201 (Item 201) Market for Common Equity and Related Stockholder Matters.

(a) *Market information.*

    (1) Identify the principal market or markets where the small business issuer's common equity is traded. If there is no public trading market, so state.

        (i) If the principal market for the small business issuer's common equity is an exchange, give the high and low sales prices for each quarter within the last two fiscal years and any subsequent interim period for which financial statements are required by Item 310(b).

        (ii) If the principal market is not an exchange, give the range of high and low bid information for the small business issuer's common equity for each quarter within the last two fiscal years and any subsequent interim period for which financial statements are required by Item 310(b). Show the source of the high and low bid information. If over-the-counter market quotations are provided, also state that the quotations reflect inter-dealer prices, without retail mark-up, mark-down or commission and may not represent actual transactions.

    (2) If the information called for by paragraph (a) of this Item is being presented in a registration statement relating to a class of common equity for which at the time of filing there is no established public trading market, indicate the amount(s) of common equity:

        (i) that is subject to outstanding options or warrants to purchase, or securities convertible into, common equity of the registrant;

        (ii) that could be sold pursuant to Rule 144 under the Securities Act or that the registrant has agreed to register under the Securities Act for sale by security holders; or

        (iii) that is being or has been proposed to be, publicly offered by the registrant unless such common equity is being offered pursuant to an employee benefit plan or dividend reinvestment plan), the offering of which could have a material effect on the market price of the registrant's common equity.

(b) *Holders.* Give the approximate number of holders of record of each class of common equity.

(c) *Dividends.*

    (1) Discuss any cash dividends declared on each class of common equity for the last two fiscal years and in any subsequent period for which financial information is required.

    (2) Describe any restrictions that limit the ability to pay dividends on common equity or that are likely to do so in the future.

Instruction

Canadian issuers should, in addition to the information called for by this Item, provide the information in Item 201(a)(1)(iv) of Regulation S-K and Instruction 4 thereto.

§228.202 (Item 202) Description of Securities.

(a) *Common or Preferred Stock.*

    (1) If the small business issuer is offering common equity, describe any dividend, voting and preemption rights.

    (2) If the small business issuer is offering preferred stock, describe the dividend, voting, conversion and liquidation rights as well as redemption or sinking fund provisions.

    (3) Describe any other material rights of common or preferred stockholders.

    (4) Describe any provision in the charter or by-laws that would delay, defer or prevent a change in control of the small business issuer.

(b) *Debt Securities.*

    (1) If the small business issuer is offering debt securities, describe the maturity date, interest rate, conversion or redemption features and sinking fund requirements.

    (2) Describe all other material provisions giving or limiting the rights of debtholders. For example, describe subordination provisions, limitations on the declaration of dividends, restrictions on the issuance of additional debt, maintenance of asset ratios, etc.

    (3) Give the name of any trustee(s) designated by the indenture and describe the circumstances under which the trustee must act on behalf of the debtholders.

    (4) Discuss the tax effects of any securities offered at an "original issue discount."

(c) *Other Securities To Be Registered.* If the small business issuer is registering other securities, provide similar information concerning the material provisions of those securities.

§228.303 (Item 303) Management's Discussion and Analysis or Plan of Operation.

Small business issuers that have not had revenues from operations in each of the last two fiscal years, or the last fiscal year and any interim period in the current fiscal year for which financial statements are furnished in the disclosure document, shall provide the information in paragraph (a) of this Item. All other issuers shall provide the information in paragraph (b) of this Item.

(a) *Plan of operation.*

    (1) Describe the small business issuer's plan of operation for the next twelve months. This description should include such matters as:

        (i) a discussion of how long the small business issuer can satisfy its cash requirements and whether it will have to raise additional funds in the next twelve months;

        (ii) a summary of any product research and development that the small business issuer will perform for the term of the plan;

        (iii) any expected purchase or sale of plant and significant equipment; and

        (iv) any expected significant changes in the number of employees.

(b) *Management's Discussion and Analysis of Financial Condition and Results of Operations.*

    (1) *Full fiscal years.* Discuss the small business issuer's financial condition, changes in financial condition and results of operations for each of the last two fiscal years. This discussion should address the past and future financial condition and results of operation of the small business issuer, with particular emphasis on the prospects for the future. The discussion

should also address those key variable and other qualitative and quantitative factors which are necessary to an understanding and evaluation of the small business issuer. If material, the small business issuer should disclose the following:

    (i) Any known trends, events or uncertainties that have or are reasonably likely to have a material impact on the small business issuer's short-term or long-term liquidity;

    (ii) Internal and external sources of liquidity;

    (iii) Any material commitments for capital expenditures and the expected sources of funds for such expenditures;

    (iv) Any known trends, events or uncertainties that have had or that are reasonably expected to have a material impact on the net sales or revenues or income from continuing operations;

    (v) Any significant elements of income or loss that do not arise from the small business issuer's continuing operations;

    (vi) The causes for any material changes from period to period in one or more line items of the small business issuer's financial statements; and

    (vii) Any seasonal aspects that had a material effect on the financial condition or results of operation.

  (2) *Interim Periods.* If the small business issuer must include interim financial statements in the registration statement or report, provide a comparable discussion that will enable the reader to assess material changes in financial condition and results of operations since the end of the last fiscal year and for the comparable interim period in the preceding year.

Instructions to Item 303

  1. The discussion and analysis shall focus specifically on material events and uncertainties known to management that would cause reported financial information not to be necessarily indicative of future operating results or of future financial condition.

  2. Small business issuers are encouraged, but not required, to supply forward looking information. This is distinguished from presently known data which will impact upon future operating results, such as known future increases in costs of labor or materials. This latter data may be required to be disclosed.

§228.304 (Item 304) Changes In and Disagreements With Accountants on Accounting and Financial Disclosure.

(a) (1) If, during the small business issuer's two most recent fiscal years or any later interim period, the principal independent accountant or a significant subsidiary's independent accountant on whom the principal accountant expressed reliance in its report, resigned (or declined to stand for re-election) or was dismissed, then the small business issuer shall state:

    (i) Whether the former accountant resigned, declined to stand for re-election or was dismissed and the date;

    (ii) Whether the principal accountant's report on the financial statements for either of the past two years contained an adverse opinion or disclaimer of opinion, or was modified as to uncertainty, audit scope, or accounting principles, and also describe the nature of each such adverse opinion, disclaimer of opinion or modification;

    (iii) Whether the decision to change accountants was recommended or approved by the board of directors or an audit or similar committee of the board of directors; and

    (iv) (A) Whether there were any disagreements with the former accountant, whether or not resolved, on any matter of accounting principles or practices, financial statement disclosure, or auditing scope or procedure, which, if not resolved to the former accountant's satisfaction, would have caused it to make reference to the subject matter of the disagreement(s) in connection with its report; or

        (B) The following information only if applicable. Indicate whether the former accountant advised the small business issuer that:

            (1) internal controls necessary to develop reliable financial statements did not exist; or

            (2) information has come to the attention of the former accountant which made the accountant unwilling to rely on management's representations, or unwilling to be associated with the financial statements prepared by management; or

            (3) the scope of the audit should be expanded significantly, or information has come to the accountant's attention that the accountant has concluded will, or if further investigated might, materially impact the fairness or reliability of a previously issued audit report or the underlying financial statements, or the financial statements issued or to be issued covering the fiscal period(s) subsequent to the date of the most recent audited financial statements (including information that might preclude the issuance of an unqualified audit report), and the issue was not resolved to the accountant's satisfaction prior to its resignation or dismissal; and

        (C) The subject matter of each such disagreement or event identified in response to paragraph (a)(1)(iv) of this Item;

(D) Whether any committee of the board of directors, or the board of directors, discussed the subject matter of the disagreement with the former accountant; and

(E) Whether the small business issuer has authorized the former accountant to respond fully to the inquiries of the successor accountant concerning the subject matter of each of such disagreements or events and, if not, describe the nature of and reason for any limitation.

(2) If during the period specified in paragraph (a)(1) of this Item, a new accountant has been engaged as either the principal accountant to audit the issuer's financial statements or as the auditor of a significant subsidiary and on whom the principal accountant is expected to express reliance in its report, identify the new accountant and the engagement date. Additionally, if the issuer (or someone on its behalf) consulted the new accountant regarding:

(i) The application of accounting principles to a specific completed or contemplated transaction, or the type of audit opinion that might be rendered on the small business issuer's financial statements and either written or oral advice was provided that was an important factor considered by the small business issuer in reaching a decision as to the accounting, auditing or financial reporting issue; or

(ii) Any matter that was the subject of a disagreement or event identified in response to paragraph (a)(1)(iv) of this Item, then the small business issuer shall:

(A) Identify the issues that were the subjects of those consultations;

(B) Briefly describe the views of the new accountant given to the small business issuer and, if written views were received by the small business issuer, file them as an exhibit to the report or registration statement;

(C) State whether the former accountant was consulted by the small business issuer regarding any such issues, and if so, describe the former accountant's views; and

(D) Request the new accountant to review the disclosure required by this Item before it is filed with the Commission and provide the new accountant the opportunity to furnish the small business issuer with a letter addressed to the Commission containing any new information, clarification of the small business issuer's expression of its views, or the respects in which it does not agree with the statements made in response to this Item. Any such letter shall be filed as an exhibit to the report or registration statement containing the disclosure required by this Item.

(3) The small business issuer shall provide the former accountant with a copy of the disclosures it is making in response to this Item no later than the day that the disclosures are filed with the Commission. The small business issuer shall request the former accountant to furnish a letter addressed to the Commission stating whether it agrees with the statements made by the issuer and, if not, stating the respects in which it does not agree. The small business issuer shall file the letter as an exhibit to the report or registration statement containing this disclosure. If the letter is unavailable at the time of filing, the small business issuer shall request the former accountant to provide the letter so that it can be filed with the Commission within ten business days after the filing of the report or registration statement. Notwithstanding the ten business day period, the letter shall be filed within two business days of receipt. The former accountant may provide an interim letter highlighting specific areas of concern and indicating that a more detailed letter will be forthcoming within the ten business day period noted above. The interim letter, if any, shall be filed with the report or registration statement or by amendment within two business days of receipt.

(b) If the conditions in paragraphs (b)(1) through (b)(3) of this Item exist, the small business issuer shall describe the nature of the disagreement or event and the effect on the financial statements if the method had been followed which the former accountants apparently would have concluded was required (unless that method ceases to be generally accepted because of authoritative standards or interpretations issued after the disagreement or event):

(1) In connection with a change in accountants subject to paragraph (a) of this Item, there was any disagreement or event as described in paragraph (a)(1)(iv) of this Item;

(2) During the fiscal year in which the change in accountants took place or during the later fiscal year, there have been any transactions or events similar to those involved in such disagreement or event; and

(3) Such transactions or events were material and were accounted for or disclosed in a manner different from that which the former accountants apparently would have concluded was required.

Instructions to Item 304.

1. The disclosure called for by paragraph (a) of this Item need not be provided if it has been previously reported as that term is defined in Rule 12b-2 under the Exchange Act (§240.12b-2); the disclosure called for by paragraph (a) of this Item must be provided, however, notwithstanding prior disclosure, if required pursuant to Item 9 of Schedule 14A (§249.14a-101 *et seq.*). The disclosure called for by paragraph (b) of this Item must be furnished, where required, notwithstanding any prior disclosure about accountant changes or disagreements.

2. When disclosure is required by paragraph (a) of this Item in an annual report to security holders pursuant to Rule 14a-3 or Rule 14c-3 (§240.14a-3 or 240.14c-3 of this chapter), or in a proxy or information statement filed pursuant to the requirements of Schedule 14A (§240.14a-101 *et seq.*) or 14C (§240.14c-101 *et seq.*), in lieu of a letter pursuant to paragraph (a)(2)(ii)(D) or (a)(3) of this Item, before filing such materials with or furnishing such materials to the Commission, the small business issuer shall furnish the disclosure required by paragraph (a) of this Item to each accountant who was engaged during the period set forth in paragraph (a) of this Item. If any such accountant believes that the statements made in response to paragraph (a) of this Item are incorrect or incomplete, it may present its views in a brief statement, ordinarily expected not to exceed 200 words, to be included in the annual report or proxy or information statement. This statement shall be submitted to the small business issuer within ten business days of the date the accountant receives the small business issuer's disclosure. Further, unless the written views of the newly engaged accountant required to be filed as an exhibit by paragraph (a)(2)(ii)(D) of this Item have been previously filed with the Commission, the small business issuer shall file a Form 8-K (17 CFR 249.308 of this chapter) along with the annual report or proxy or information statement for the purpose of filing the written views as exhibits.

3. The information required by this Item need not be provided for a company being acquired by the small business issuer if such acquiree has not been subject to the filing requirements of either section 13(a) or 15(d) of the Exchange Act, or, because of section 12(i) of the Exchange Act, has not furnished an annual report to security holders pursuant to Rule 14a-3 or Rule 14c-3 (§240.14a-3 or 240.14c-3 of this chapter) for its latest fiscal year.

4. In determining whether any disagreement or reportable event has occurred, an oral communication from the engagement partner or another person responsible for rendering the accounting firm's opinion (or their designee) will generally suffice as the accountant advising the small business issuer of a reportable event or as a statement of a disagreement at the "decision-making level" within the accounting firm and require disclosure under this Item.

§228.310 (Item 310) Financial Statements.

NOTES-

1. Financial statements of a small business issuer, its predecessors or any businesses to which the small business issuer is a successor shall be prepared in accordance with generally accepted accounting principles in the United States.

2. Regulation S-X [17 CFR 210.1 - 210.12] Form and Content of and Requirements for Financial Statements shall not apply to the preparation of such financial statements, except that the report and qualifications of the independent accountant shall comply with the requirements of Article 2 of Regulation S-X [17 CFR 210.2], Articles 3-19 and 3-20 shall apply to financial statements of foreign private issuers and small business issuers engaged in oil and gas producing activities shall follow the financial accounting and reporting standards specified in Article 4-10 of Regulation S-X [17 CFR 210.4-10] with respect to such activities. To the extent that Article 11-01 [17 CFR 210.11-01] (Pro Forma Presentation Requirements) offers enhanced guidelines for the preparation, presentation and disclosure of pro forma financial information, small business issuers may wish to consider these items. Financial statements of foreign private issuers shall be prepared and presented in accordance with the requirements of Item 18 of Form 20-F except that Item 17 may be followed for financial statements included in filings other than registration statements for offerings of securities unless the only securities being offered are: (a) upon the exercise of outstanding rights granted by the issuer of the securities to be offered, if such rights are granted by the issuer of the securities to be offered, if such rights are granted on a pro rata basis to all existing securities holders of the class of securities to which the rights attach and there is no standby underwriting in the United States or similar arrangement; or (b) pursuant to a dividend or interest reinvestment plan; or (c) upon the conversion of outstanding convertible securities or upon the exercise of outstanding transferrable warrants issued by the issuer of the securities being offered, or by an affiliate of such issuer.

3. The Commission, where consistent with the protection of investors, may permit the omission of one or more of the financial statements or the substitution of appropriate statements of comparable character. The Commission by informal written notice may require the filing of other financial statements where necessary or appropriate.

   (a) *Annual Financial Statements.* Small business issuers shall file an audited balance sheet as of the end of the most recent fiscal year, or as of a date within 135 days if the issuers existed for a period less than one fiscal year, and audited statements of income, cash flows and changes in stockholders' equity for each of the two fiscal years preceding the date of such audited balance sheet (or such shorter period as the registrant has been in business).

   (b) *Interim Financial Statements.* Interim financial statements, which may be unaudited, shall include a balance sheet as of the end of the issuer's most recent fiscal quarter and income statements and statements of cash flows for the interim period up to the date of such balance sheet and the comparable period of the preceding fiscal year.

Instructions to Item 310(b)

1. Where Item 310 is applicable to a Form 10-QSB (§249.308b) and the interim period is more than one quarter, income statements must also be provided for the most recent interim quarter and the comparable quarter of the preceding fiscal year.

2. Interim financial statements must include all adjustments which in the opinion of management are necessary in order to make the financial statements not misleading. An affirmative statement that the financial statements have been so adjusted must be included with the interim financial statements.

    (1) *Condensed Format.* Interim financial statements may be condensed as follows:

        (i) Balance sheets should include separate captions for each balance sheet component presented in the annual financial statements which represents 10% or more of total assets. Cash and retained earnings should be presented regardless of relative significance to total assets. Registrants which present a classified balance sheet in their annual financial statements should present totals for current assets and current liabilities.

        (ii) Income statements should include net sales or gross revenue, each cost and expense category presented in the annual financial statements which exceeds 20% of sales or gross revenues, provision for income taxes, discontinued operations, extraordinary items and cumulative effects of changes in accounting principles or practices. (Financial institutions should substitute net interest income for sales for purposes of determining items to be disclosed.) Dividends per share should be presented.

        (iii) Cash flow statements should include cash flows from operating, investing and financing activities as well as cash at the beginning and end of each period and the increase or decrease in such balance.

        (iv) Additional line items may be presented to facilitate the usefulness of the interim financial statements including their comparability with annual financial statements.

    (2) *Disclosure required and additional instructions as to Content.*

        (i) *Footnotes.* Footnote and other disclosures should be provided as needed for fair presentation and to ensure that the financial statements are not misleading.

        (ii) *Material Subsequent Events and Contingencies.* Disclosure must be provided of material subsequent events and material contingencies notwithstanding disclosure in the annual financial statements.

        (iii) *Significant Equity Investees.* Sales, gross profit, net income (loss) from continuing operations and net income must be disclosed for equity investees which constitute 20% or more of a registrant's consolidated assets, equity or income from continuing operations.

        (iv) *Significant Dispositions and Purchase Business Combinations.* If a significant disposition or purchase business combination has occurred during the most recent interim period and the transaction required the filing of a Form 8-K (§249.308 of this chapter), pro forma data must be presented which reflects revenue, income from continuing operations, net income and income per share for the current interim period and the corresponding interim period of the preceding fiscal year as though the transaction occurred at the beginning of the periods.

        (v) *Material Accounting Changes.* Disclosure must be provided of the date and reasons for any material accounting change. The registrant's independent accountant must provide a letter in the first Form 10-QSB (§249.308b of this chapter) filed subsequent to the change indicating whether or not the change is to a preferable method. Disclosure must be provided of any retroactive change to prior period financial statements, including the effect of any such change on income and income per share.

        (vi) *Development Stage Companies.* A registrant in the development stage must provide cumulative from inception financial information.

(c) *Financial Statements of Businesses Acquired or to be Acquired.*

    (1) Financial statements for the periods specified in paragraph (c)(3) of this Item should be furnished if any of the following conditions exist:

        (i) Consummation of a significant business combination accounted for as a purchase has occurred or is probable (the term "purchase" encompasses the purchase of an interest in a business accounted for by the equity method); or

        (ii) Consummation of a significant business combination to be accounted for as a pooling is probable.

    (2) A business combination is considered significant if a comparison of the most recent annual financial statements of the business acquired or to be acquired and the small business issuer's most recent annual financial statements filed at or prior to the date of acquisition indicates that the business acquired or to be acquired meets any of the following conditions:

        (i) The small business issuer's and its other subsidiaries' investments in and advances to the acquiree exceeds 10 percent of the total assets of the small business issuer and its subsidiaries consolidated as of the end of the most recently completed fiscal year (for a proposed business combination to be accounted for as a pooling of interests, this condition is also met when the number of common shares exchanged or to be exchanged by the small business issuer exceeds 10 percent of its total common shares outstanding at the date the combination is initiated) or

(ii) The small business issuer's and its other subsidiaries' proportionate share of the total assets (after intercompany eliminations) of the acquiree exceeds 10 percent of the total assets of the registrants and its subsidiaries consolidated as of the end of the most recently completed fiscal year, or

(iii) The small business issuer's equity in the income from continuing operations before income taxes, extraordinary items and cumulative effect of a change in accounting principles of the acquiree exceeds 10 percent of such income of the small business issuer and its subsidiaries consolidated for the most recently completed fiscal year.

Computational note: For purposes of making the prescribed income test the following guidance should be applied: If income of the small business issuer and its subsidiaries consolidated for the most recent fiscal year is at least 10 percent lower than the average of the income for the last five fiscal years, such average income should be substituted for purposes of the computation. Any loss years should be omitted for purposes of computing average income.

(3) (i) Financial statements shall be furnished for the periods prior to the date of acquisition, for those periods for which the small business issuer is required to furnish financial statements.

(ii) The financial statements covering fiscal years shall be audited.

(iii) The separate audited balance sheet of the acquired business is not required when the small business issuer's most recent audited balance sheet filed is for a date after the acquisition was consummated.

(iv) If none of the conditions in the definitions of significant subsidiary in paragraph (c)(2) of this Item exceeds 20%, income statements of the acquired business for only the most recent fiscal year and any interim period need be filed.

(4) If consummation of more than one transaction has occurred or is probable, the significance tests shall be made using the aggregate impact of the businesses and the financial statements may be presented on a combined basis, if appropriate.

(5) If the small business issuer made a significant business acquisition subsequent to the latest fiscal year end and filed a report on Form 8-K which included audited financial statements of such acquired business for the periods required by paragraph (c)(3) and the pro forma financial information required by paragraph (d) of this Item, the determination of significance may be made by using the pro forma amounts for the latest fiscal year in the report on Form 8-K rather than by using the historical amounts for the latest fiscal year of the registrant. The tests may not be made by "annualizing" data.

(d) *Pro Forma Financial Information:*

(1) Pro forma information shall be furnished if any of the following conditions exist (for purposes of this Item, the term "purchase" encompasses the purchase of an interest in a business accounted for by the equity method):

(i) During the most recent fiscal year or subsequent interim period for which a balance sheet is required by paragraph (b) of this Item, a significant business combination accounted for as a purchase has occurred;

(ii) After the date of the most recent balance sheet filed pursuant to paragraph (a) or (b) of this Item, consummation of a significant business combination accounted for as a purchase or a pooling has occurred or is probable.

(2) The provisions of paragraphs (c)(2) and (4) of this Item apply to paragraph (d) of this Item.

(3) Pro forma statements should be condensed, in columnar form showing pro forma adjustments and results and should include the following:

(i) If the transaction was consummated during the most recent fiscal year or subsequent interim period, pro forma statements of income reflecting the combined operations of the entities for the latest fiscal year and interim period, if any, or;

(ii) If consummation of the transaction has occurred or is probable after the date of the most recent balance sheet required by paragraph (a) or (b) of this Item, a pro forma balance sheet giving effect to the combination as of the date of the most recent balance sheet. For a purchase, pro forma statements of income reflecting the combined operations of the entities for the latest fiscal year and interim period, if any, and for a pooling of interests, pro forma statements of income for all periods for which income statements of the small business issuer are required.

(e) *Real Estate Operations Acquired or to be Acquired.* If, during the period for which income statements are required, the small business issuer has acquired one or more properties which in the aggregate are significant, or since the date of the latest balance sheet required by paragraph (a) or (b) of this Item, has acquired or proposes to acquire one or more properties which in the aggregate are significant, the following shall be furnished with respect to such properties:

(1) Audited income statements (not including earnings per unit) for the two most recent years, which shall exclude items not comparable to the proposed future operations of the property such as mortgage interest, leasehold rental, depreciation, corporate expenses and federal and state income taxes; *Provided, however,* That such audited statements need be presented for only the most recent fiscal year if:

(i) the property is not acquired from a related party;

12

(ii) material factors considered by the small business issuer in assessing the property are described with specificity in the registration statement with regard to the property, including source of revenue (including, but not limited to, competition in the rental market, comparative rents, occupancy rates) and expenses (including but not limited to, utilities, *ad valorem* tax rates, maintenance expenses, capital improvements anticipated); and

(iii) the small business issuer indicates that, after reasonable inquiry, it is not aware of any material factors relating to the specific property other than those discussed in response to paragraph (e)(1)(ii) of this Item that would cause the reported financial information not to be necessarily indicative of future operating results.

(2) If the property will be operated by the small business issuer, a statement shall be furnished showing the estimated taxable operating results of the small business issuer based on the most recent twelve month period including such adjustments as can be factually supported. If the property will be acquired subject to a net lease, the estimated taxable operating results shall be based on the rent to be paid for the first year of the lease. In either case, the estimated amount of cash to be made available by operations shall be shown. Disclosure must be provided of the principal assumptions which have been made in preparing the statements of estimated taxable operating results and cash to be made available by operations.

(3) If appropriate under the circumstances, a table should be provided which shows, for a limited number of years, the estimated cash distribution per unit indicating the portion reportable as taxable income and the portion representing a return of capital with an explanation of annual variations, if any. If taxable net income per unit will be greater than the cash available for distribution per unit, that fact and approximate year of occurrence shall be stated, if significant.

(f) *Limited Partnerships.*

(1) Small business issuers which are limited partnerships must provide the balance sheets of the general partners as described in paragraphs (f)(2) through (f)(4) of this Item.

(2) Where a general partner is a corporation, the audited balance sheet of the corporation as of the end of its most recently completed fiscal year must be filed. Receivables, other than trade receivables, from affiliates of the general partner should be deducted from shareholders' equity of the general partner. Where an affiliate has committed itself to increase or maintain the general partner's capital, the audited balance sheet of such affiliate must also be presented.

(3) Where a general partner is a partnership, there shall be filed an audited balance sheet of such partnership as of the end of its most recently completed fiscal year.

(4) Where the general partner is a natural person, there shall be filed, as supplemental information, a balance sheet of such natural person as of a recent date. Such balance sheet need not be audited. The assets and liabilities should be carried at estimated fair market value, with provisions for estimated income taxes on unrealized gains. The net worth of such general partner(s), based on such balance sheet(s), singly or in the aggregate, shall be disclosed in the registration statement.

(g) *Age of Financial Statements.* At the date of filing, financial statements included in filings other than filings on Form 10-KSB must be not less current than financial statements which would be required in Forms 10-KSB and 10-QSB if such reports were required to be filed. If required financial statements are as of a date 135 days or more prior to the date a registration statement becomes effective or proxy material is expected to be mailed, the financial statements shall be updated to include financial statements for an interim period ending within 135 days of the effective or expected mailing date. Interim financial statements should be prepared and presented in accordance with paragraph (b) of this Item:

(1) When the anticipated effective or mailing date falls within 45 days after the end of the fiscal year, the filing may include financial statements only as current as the end of the third fiscal quarter; *Provided, however,* That if the audited financial statements for the recently completed fiscal year are available or become available prior to effectiveness or mailing, they must be included in the filing;

(2) If the effective date or anticipated mailing date falls after 45 days but within 90 days of the end of the small business issuer's fiscal year, the small business issuer is not required to provide the audited financial statements for such year end provided that the following conditions are met:

(i) The small business issuer is a reporting company and all reports due have been filed;

(ii) For the most recent fiscal year for which audited financial statements are not yet available, the small business issuer reasonably and in good faith expects to report income from continuing operations before taxes; and

(iii) For at least one of the two fiscal years immediately preceding the most recent fiscal year the small business issuer reported income from continuing operations before taxes.

§228.401 (Item 401) Directors, Executive Officers, Promoters and Control Persons.

(a) *Identify directors and executive officers.*

    (1) List the names and ages of all directors and executive officers and all persons nominated or chosen to become such;

    (2) List the positions and offices that each such person held with the small business issuer;

    (3) Give the person's term of office as a director and the period during which the person has served;

    (4) Briefly describe the person's business experience during the past five years; and

    (5) If a director, identify other directorships held in reporting companies naming each company.

(b) *Identify Significant Employees.* Give the information specified in paragraph (a) of this Item for each person who is not an executive officer but who is expected by the small business issuer to make a significant contribution to the business.

(c) *Family relationships.* Describe any family relationships among directors, executive officers, or persons nominated or chosen by the small business issuer to become directors or executive officers.

(d) *Involvement in certain legal proceedings.* Describe any of the following events that occurred during the past five years that are material to an evaluation of the ability or integrity of any director, person nominated to become a director, executive officer, promoter or control person of the small business issuer:

    (1) Any bankruptcy petition filed by or against any business of which such person was a general partner or executive officer either at the time of the bankruptcy or within two years prior to that time;

    (2) Any conviction in a criminal proceeding or being subject to a pending criminal proceeding (excluding traffic violations and other minor offenses);

    (3) Being subject to any order, judgment, or decree, not subsequently reversed, suspended or vacated, of any court of competent jurisdiction, permanently or temporarily enjoining, barring, suspending or otherwise limiting his involvement in any type of business, securities or banking activities; and

    (4) Being found by a court of competent jurisdiction (in a civil action), the Commission or the Commodity Futures Trading Commission to have violated a federal or state securities or commodities law, and the judgment has not been reversed, suspended, or vacated.

§228.402 (Item 402) Executive compensation.

(a) *General.*

    (1) *All Compensation Covered.* This item requires clear, concise and understandable disclosure of all plan and non-plan compensation awarded to, earned by, or paid to the named executive officers designated under paragraph (a)(2) of this item, and directors covered by paragraph (f) of this item by any person for all services rendered in all capacities to the registrant and its subsidiaries, unless otherwise specified in this item. Except as provided by paragraph (a)(4) of this item, all such compensation shall be reported pursuant to this item even if also called for by another requirement, including transactions between the registrant and a third party where the primary purpose of the transaction is to furnish compensation to any such named executive officer or director. No item reported as compensation for one fiscal year need be reported as compensation for a subsequent fiscal year.

    (2) *Persons Covered.* Disclosure shall be provided pursuant to this item for each of the following (the "named executive officers"):

        (i) the registrant's Chief Executive Officer or any individual acting in a similar capacity ("CEO") at the end of the last completed fiscal year, regardless of compensation level; and

        (ii) the registrant's four most highly compensated executive officers other than the CEO who served as executive officers at the end of the last completed fiscal year.

        Instructions to Item 402(a)(2).

        1. *Determination of Most Highly Compensated Executive Officers.* The determination as to which executive officers are most highly compensated shall be made by reference to total annual salary and bonus for the last completed fiscal year (as required to be disclosed pursuant to paragraph (b)(2)(iii)(A) and (B) of this item), but including the dollar value of salary or bonus amounts forgone pursuant to Instruction 3 to paragraph (b)(2)(iii)(A) and (B) of this item, *provided, however,* that no disclosure need be provided for any executive officer, other than the CEO, whose total annual salary and bonus, as so determined, does not exceed $100,000.

2. *Inclusion of Executive Officer of Subsidiary.* It may be appropriate in certain circumstances for a registrant to include an executive officer of a subsidiary in the disclosure required by this item. *See* Rule 3b-7 under the Exchange Act [17 CFR 240.3b-7].

3. *Exclusion of Executive Officer due to Unusual or Overseas Compensation.* It may be appropriate in limited circumstances for a registrant not to include in the disclosure required by this item an individual, other than its CEO, who is one of the registrant's most highly compensated executive officers. Among the factors that should be considered in determining not to name an individual are: (a) the distribution or accrual of an unusually large amount of cash compensation (such as a bonus or commission) that is not part of a recurring arrangement and is unlikely to continue; and (b) the payment of amounts of cash compensation relating to overseas assignments that may be attributed predominantly to such assignments.

(3) *Information for Full Fiscal Year.* If the CEO served in that capacity during any part of a fiscal year with respect to which information is required, information should be provided as to all of his or her compensation for the full fiscal year. If a named executive officer (other than the CEO) served as an executive officer of the registrant (whether or not in the same, position) during any part of a fiscal year with respect to which information is required, information shall be provided as to all compensation of that individual for the full fiscal year.

(4) *Transactions With Third Parties Reported under Item 404.* This item includes transactions between the registrant and a third party where the primary purpose of the transaction is to furnish compensation to a named executive officer. No information need be given in response to any paragraph of this item as to any such third-party transaction if the transaction has been reported in response to Item 404 of Regulation S-B (§ 228.404).

(5) *Omission of Table or Column.* A table or column may be omitted, if there has been no compensation awarded to, earned by or paid to any of the named executives required to be reported in that table or column in any fiscal year covered by that table.

(6) *Definitions.* For purposes of this item:

 (i) The term "stock appreciation rights" ("SARs") refers to SARs payable in cash or stock, including SARs payable in cash or stock at the election of the registrant or a named executive officer.

 (ii) The term "plan" includes, but is not limited to, the following: any plan, contract, authorization or arrangement, whether or not set forth in any formal documents, pursuant to which the following may be received: cash, stock, restricted stock or restricted stock units, phantom stock, stock options, SARs, stock options in tandem with SARs, warrants, convertible securities, performance units and performance shares, and similar instruments. A plan may be applicable to one person. Registrants may omit information regarding group life, health, hospitalization, medical reimbursement or relocation plans that do not discriminate in scope, terms or operation, in favor of executive officers or directors of the registrant and that are available generally to all salaried employees.

 (iii) The term "long-term incentive plan" means any plan providing compensation intended to serve as incentive for performance to occur over a period longer than one fiscal year, whether such performance is measured by reference to financial performance of the registrant or an affiliate, the registrant's stock price, or any other measure, but excluding restricted stock, stock option and SAR plans.

(7) *Location of Specified Information.* The information required by paragraph (h) of this item need not be provided in any filings other than a registrant proxy or information statement relating to an annual meeting of security holders at which directors are to be elected (or special meeting or written consents in lieu of such meeting). Such information will not be deemed to be incorporated by reference into any filing under the Securities Act or the Exchange Act, except to the extent that the registrant specifically incorporates it by reference.

(b) *Summary Compensation Table.*

    (1) *General.* The information specified in paragraph (b)(2) of this item, concerning the compensation of the named executive officers for each of the registrant's last three completed fiscal years, shall be provided in a Summary Compensation Table, in the tabular format specified below.

SUMMARY COMPENSATION TABLE

		Annual Compensation			Long Term Compensation			
					Awards		Payouts	
(a)	(b)	(c)	(d)	(e)	(f)	(g)	(h)	(i)
Name and Principal Position	Year	Salary ($)	Bonus ($)	Other Annual Compensation ($)	Restricted Stock Award(s) ($)	Options/ SARs (#)	LTIP Payouts ($)	All Other Compensation ($)
CEO	—— —— ——							
A	—— —— ——							
B	—— —— ——							
C	—— —— ——							
D	—— —— ——							

    (2) The Table shall include:

        (i) The name and principal position of the executive officer (column (a));

        (ii) Fiscal year covered (column (b));

        (iii) Annual compensation (columns (c), (d) and (e)), including:

            (A) The dollar value of base salary (cash and non-cash) earned by the named executive officer during the fiscal year covered (column (c));

            (B) The dollar value of bonus (cash and non-cash) earned by the named executive officer during the fiscal year covered (column (d)); and

        Instructions to Item 402(b)(2)(iii)(A) and (B).

          1. Amounts deferred at the election of a named executive officer, whether pursuant to a plan established under Section 401(k) of the Internal Revenue Code [26 U.S.C. 401(k)], or otherwise, shall be included in the salary column (column (c)) or bonus column (column (d)), as appropriate, for the fiscal year in which earned. If the amount of salary or bonus earned in a given fiscal year is not calculable through the latest practicable date, that fact must be disclosed in a footnote and such amount must be disclosed in the subsequent fiscal year in the appropriate column for the fiscal year in which earned.

          2. For stock or any other form of non-cash compensation, disclose the fair market value at the time the compensation is awarded, earned or paid.

16

3. Registrants need not include in the salary column (column (c)) or bonus column (column (d)) any amount of salary or bonus forgone at the election of a named executive officer pursuant to a registrant program under which stock, stock-based or other forms of non-cash compensation may be received by a named executive in lieu of a portion of annual compensation earned in a covered fiscal year. However, the receipt of any such form of non-cash compensation in lieu of salary or bonus earned for a covered fiscal year must be disclosed in the appropriate column of the Table corresponding to that fiscal year (i.e., restricted stock awards (column (f)); options or SARs (column (g)); all other compensation (column (i)), or, if made pursuant to a long-term incentive plan and therefore not reportable at grant in the Summary Compensation Table, a footnote must be added to the salary or bonus column so disclosing and referring to the Long-Term Incentive Plan Table (required by paragraph (e) of this item) where the award is reported.

(C) The dollar value of other annual compensation not properly categorized as salary or bonus, as follows (column (e)):

(1) Perquisites and other personal benefits, securities or property, unless the aggregate amount of such compensation is the lesser of either $50,000 or 10% of the total of annual salary and bonus reported for the named executive officer in columns (c) and (d);

(2) Above-market or preferential earnings on restricted stock, options, SARs or deferred compensation paid during the fiscal year or payable during that period but deferred at the election of the named executive officer;

(3) Earnings on long-term incentive plan compensation paid during the fiscal year or payable during that period but deferred at the election of the named executive officer;

(4) Amounts reimbursed during the fiscal year for the payment of taxes; and

(5) The dollar value of the difference between the price paid by a named executive officer for any security of the registrant or its subsidiaries purchased from the registrant or its subsidiaries (through deferral of salary or bonus, or otherwise), and the fair market value of such security at the date of purchase, unless that discount is available generally, either to all security holders or to all salaried employees of the registrant.

Instructions to Item 402(b)(2)(iii)(C).

1. Each perquisite or other personal benefit exceeding 25% of the total perquisites and other personal benefits reported for a named executive officer must be identified by type and amount in a footnote or accompanying narrative discussion to column (e).

2. Perquisites and other personal benefits shall be valued on the basis of the aggregate incremental cost to the registrant and its subsidiaries.

3. Interest on deferred or long-term compensation is above-market only if the rate of interest exceeds 120% of the applicable federal long-term rate, with compounding (as prescribed under Section 1274(d) of the Internal Revenue Code, [26 U.S.C. 1274(d)]) at the rate that corresponds most closely to the rate under the registrant's plan at the time the interest rate or formula is set. In the event of a discretionary reset of the interest rate, the requisite calculation must be made on the basis of the interest rate at the time of such reset, rather than when originally established. Only the above-market portion of the interest must be included. If the applicable interest rates vary depending upon conditions such as a minimum period of continued service, the reported amount should be calculated assuming satisfaction of all conditions to receiving interest at the highest rate.

4. Dividends (and dividend equivalents) on restricted stock, options, SARs or deferred compensation denominated in stock ("deferred stock") are preferential only if earned at a rate higher than dividends on the registrant's common stock. Only the preferential portion of the dividends or equivalents must be included.

(iv) Long-term compensation (columns (f), (g) and (h)), including:

(A) The dollar value (net of any consideration paid by the named executive officer) of any award of restricted stock, including share units (calculated by multiplying the closing market price of the registrant's unrestricted stock on the date of grant by the number of shares awarded) (column (f));

(B) The sum of the number of stock options granted, with or without tandem SARs, and the number of freestanding SARs (column (g)); and

(C) The dollar value of all payouts pursuant to long-term incentive plans ("LTIPs") as defined in paragraph (a)(6)(iii) of this item (column (h)).

Instructions to Item 402(b)(2)(iv).

1. Awards of restricted stock that are subject to performance-based conditions to vesting, in addition to lapse of time and/or continued service with the registrant or a subsidiary, may be reported as LTIP awards pursuant to

17

paragraph (e) of this item instead of in column (f). If this approach is selected, once the restricted stock vests, it must be reported as an LTIP payout in column (h).

2. The registrant shall, in a footnote to column (f), disclose:

   a. the number and value of the aggregate restricted stock holdings at the end of the last completed fiscal year. Value shall be calculated as specified in paragraph (b)(2)(iv)(A) of this item;

   b. for any restricted stock award that will vest, in whole or in part, in under three years from the date of grant, the total number of shares awarded and the vesting schedule; and

   c. whether dividends will be paid on the restricted stock reported in the column.

3. If at any time during the last completed fiscal year, the registrant has adjusted or amended the exercise price of stock options or freestanding SARs previously awarded to a named executive officer, whether through amendment, cancellation or replacement grants, or any other means ("repriced"), the registrant shall include the number of options or freestanding SARs so repriced as Stock Options/SARs granted and required to be reported in column (g).

4. If any specified performance target, goal or condition to payout was waived with respect to any amount included in LTIP payouts reported in column (h), the registrant shall so state in a footnote to column (h).

(v) All other compensation for the covered fiscal year that the registrant could not properly report in any other column of the Summary Compensation Table (column (i)). Any compensation reported in this column for the last completed fiscal year shall be identified and quantified in a footnote. Such compensation shall include, but not be limited to:

(A) The amount paid, payable or accrued to any named executive officer pursuant to a plan or arrangement in connection with:

   (1) the resignation, retirement or any other termination of such executive officer's employment with the registrant and its subsidiaries; or

   (2) a change in control of the registrant or a change in the executive officer's responsibilities following such a change in control.

(B) The dollar value of above-market or preferential amounts earned on restricted stock, options, SARs or deferred compensation during the fiscal year, or calculated with respect to that period, except that if such amounts are paid during the period, or payable during the period but deferred at the election of a named executive officer, this information shall be reported as Other Annual Compensation in column (e). See Instructions 3 and 4 to paragraph 402(b)(2)(iii)(C) of this item;

(C) The dollar value of amounts earned on long-term incentive plan compensation during the fiscal year, or calculated with respect to that period, except that if such amounts are paid during that period, or payable during that period at the election of the named executive officer, this information shall be reported as Other Annual Compensation in column (e);

(D) Annual registrant contributions or other allocations to vested and unvested defined contribution plans; and

(E) The dollar value of any insurance premiums paid by, or on behalf of, the registrant during the covered fiscal year with respect to term life insurance for the benefit of a named executive officer, and, if there is any arrangement or understanding, whether formal or informal, that such executive officer has or will receive or be allocated an interest in any cash surrender value under the insurance policy, either:

   (1) The full dollar value of the remainder of the premiums paid by, or on behalf of, the registrant; or

   (2) If the premiums will be refunded to the registrant on termination of the policy, the dollar value of the benefit to the executive officer of the remainder of the premium paid by, or on behalf of, the registrant during the fiscal year. The benefit shall be determined for the period, projected on an actuarial basis, between payment of the premium and the refund.

Instructions to Item 402(b)(2)(v).

1. LTIP awards and amounts received on exercise of options and SARs need not be reported as All Other Compensation in column (i).

2. Information relating to defined benefit and actuarial plans need not be reported.

3. Where alternative methods of reporting are available under paragraph (b)(2)(v)(E) of this item, the same method should be used for each of the named executive officers. If the registrant chooses to change methods from one year to the next, that fact, and the reason therefor, should be disclosed in a footnote to column (i).

18

Information with respect to fiscal years prior to the last completed fiscal year will not be required if the registrant was not a reporting company pursuant to Section 13(a) or 15(d) of the Exchange Act at any time during that year, except that the registrant will be required to provide information for any such year if that information previously was required to be provided in response to a Commission filing requirement.

(c) *Option/SAR Grants Table.*

    (1) The information specified in paragraph (c)(2) of this item, concerning individual grants of stock options (whether or not in tandem with SARs), and freestanding SARs made during the last completed fiscal year to each of the named executive officers shall be provided in the tabular format specified below:

Option/SAR Grants in Last Fiscal Year

Individual Grants

(a) Name	(b) Options/ SARs Granted (#)	(c) % of Total Options/SARs Granted to Employees in Fiscal Year	(d) Exercise or Base Price ($/Sh)	(e) Expiration Date
CEO				
A				
B				
C				
D				

    (2) The Table shall include, with respect to each grant:

        (i) The name of the executive officer (column (a));

        (ii) The number of options and SARs granted (column (b));

        (iii) The percent the grant represents of total options and SARs granted to employees during the fiscal year (column (c));

        (iv) The per-share exercise or base price of the options or SARs granted (column (d)). If such exercise or base price is less than the market price of the underlying security on the date of grant, a separate, adjoining column shall be added showing market price on the date of grant; and

        (v) The expiration date of the options or SARs (column (e)).

Instructions to Item 402(c).

1. If more than one grant of options and/or freestanding SARs was made to a named executive officer during the last completed fiscal year, a separate line should be used to provide disclosure of each such grant. However, multiple grants during a single fiscal year may be aggregated where each grant was made at the same exercise and/or base price and has the same expiration date, and the same performance vesting thresholds, if any. A single grant consisting of options and/or freestanding SARs shall be reported as separate grants with respect to each tranche with a different exercise and/or base price, performance vesting threshold, or expiration date.

2. Options or freestanding SARs granted in connection with an option repricing transaction shall be reported in this table. *See* Instruction 3 to paragraph (b)(2)(iv) of this item.

3. Any material term of the grant, including but not limited to the date of exercisability, the number of SARs, performance units or other instruments granted in tandem with options, a performance-based condition to exercisability, a reload feature, or a tax- reimbursement feature, shall be footnoted.

4. If the exercise or base price is adjustable over the term of any option or freestanding SAR in accordance with any prescribed standard or formula, including but not limited to an index or premium price provision, describe the following, either by footnote to

column (c) or in narrative accompanying the Table: (a) the standard or formula; and (b) any constant assumption made by the registrant regarding any adjustment to the exercise price in calculating the potential option or SAR value.

5. If any provision of a grant (other than an antidilution provision) could cause the exercise price to be lowered, registrants must clearly and fully disclose these provisions and their potential consequences either by a footnote or accompanying textual narrative.

6. In determining the grant-date market or base price of the security underlying options or freestanding SARs, the registrant may use either the closing market price per share of the security, or any other formula prescribed for the security.

(d) *Aggregated Option/SAR Exercises and Fiscal Year-End Option/SAR Value Table.*

(1) The information specified in paragraph (d)(2) of this item, concerning each exercise of stock options (or tandem SARs) and freestanding SARs during the last completed fiscal year by each of the named executive officers and the fiscal year-end value of unexercised options and SARs, shall be provided on an aggregated basis in the tabular format specified below:

**Aggregated Option/SAR Exercises in Last Fiscal Year
and FY-End Option/SAR Values**

(a)	(b)	(c)	(d)	(e)
			Number of Unexercised Options/SARs at FY-End (#)	Value of Unexercised In-the-Money Options/SARs at FY-End ($)
Name	Shares Acquired on Exercise (#)	Value Realized ($)	Exercisable/ Unexercisable	Exercisable/ Unexercisable
CEO				
A				
B				
C				
D				

(2) The table shall include:

(i) The name of the executive officer (column (a));

(ii) The number of shares received upon exercise, or, if no shares were received, the number of securities with respect to which the options or SARs were exercised (column (b));

(iii) The aggregate dollar value realized upon exercise (column (c));

(iv) The total number of unexercised options and SARs held at the end of the last completed fiscal year, separately identifying the exercisable and unexercisable options and SARs (column (d)); and

(v) The aggregate dollar value of in-the-money, unexercised options and SARs held at the end of the fiscal year, separately identifying the exercisable and unexercisable options and SARs (column (e)).

Instructions to Item 402(d)(2).

1. Options or freestanding SARs are in-the-money if the fair market value of the underlying securities exceeds the exercise or base price of the option or SAR. The dollar values in columns (c) and (e) are calculated by determining the difference between the fair market value of the securities underlying the options or SARs and the exercise or base price of the options or SARs at exercise or fiscal year-end, respectively.

2. In calculating the dollar value realized upon exercise (column (c)), the value of any related payment or other consideration provided (or to be provided) by the registrant to or on behalf of a named executive officer, whether in payment of the exercise price or related taxes, shall not be included. Payments by the registrant in reimbursement of tax obligations incurred by a named executive officer are required to be disclosed in accordance with paragraph (b)(2)(iii)(C)(*4*) of this item.

(e) *Long-Term Incentive Plan ("LTIP") Awards Table.*

(1) The information specified in paragraph (e)(2) of this item, regarding each award made to a named executive officer in the last completed fiscal year under any LTIP, shall be provided in the tabular format specified below:

Long-Term Incentive Plans - Awards in Last Fiscal Year

(a)	(b)	(c)	Estimated Future Payouts under Non-Stock Price-Based Plans		
			(d)	(e)	(f)
	Number of Shares, Units or Other	Performance or Other Period Until Maturation or	Threshold	Target	Maximum
Name	Rights (#)	Payout	($ or #)	($ or #)	($ or #)
CEO					
A					
B					
C					
D					

(2) The Table shall include:

(i) The name of the executive officer (column (a));

(ii) The number of shares, units or other rights awarded under any LTIP, and, if applicable, the number of shares underlying any such unit or right (column (b));

(iii) The performance or other time period until payout or maturation of the award (column (c)); and

(iv) For plans not based on stock price, the dollar value of the estimated payout or range of estimated payouts under the award (threshold, target and maximum amount), whether such award is denominated in stock or cash (columns (d) through (f)).

Instructions to Item 402(e).

1. For purposes of this paragraph, the term "long-term incentive plan" or "LTIP" shall be defined in accordance with paragraph (a)(6)(iii) of this item.

2. Describe in a footnote or in narrative text accompanying this table the material terms of any award, including a general description of the formula or criteria to be applied in determining the amounts payable. Registrants are not required to disclose any factor, criterion or performance-related or other condition to payout or maturation of a particular award that involves confidential commercial or business information, disclosure of which would adversely affect the registrant's competitive position.

3. Separate disclosure shall be provided in the Table for each award made to a named executive officer, accompanied by the information specified in Instruction 2 to this paragraph. If awards are made to a named executive officer during the fiscal year under more than one plan, identify the particular plan under which each such award was made.

4. For column (d), "threshold" refers to the minimum amount payable for a certain level of performance under the plan. For column (e), "target" refers to the amount payable if the specified performance target(s) are reached. For column (f), "maximum" refers to the maximum payout possible under the plan.

5. In column (e), registrants must provide a representative amount based on the previous fiscal year's performance if the target award is not determinable.

6. A tandem grant of two instruments, only one of which is pursuant to a LTIP, need be reported only in the table applicable to the other instrument. For example, an option granted in tandem with a performance share would be reported only as an option grant, with the tandem feature noted.

(f) *Compensation of Directors.*

(1) *Standard Arrangements.* Describe any standard arrangements, stating amounts, pursuant to which directors of the registrant are compensated for any services provided as a director, including any additional amounts payable for committee participation or special assignments.

(2) *Other Arrangements.* Describe any other arrangements pursuant to which any director of the registrant was compensated during the registrant's last completed fiscal year for any service provided as a director, stating the amount paid and the name of the director.

Instruction to Item 402(f)(2).

The information required by paragraph (f)(2) of this item shall include any arrangement, including consulting contracts, entered into in consideration of the director's service on the board. The material terms of any such arrangement shall be included.

(g) *Employment Contracts and Termination of Employment and Change-in-Control Arrangements.* Describe the terms and conditions of each of the following contracts or arrangements:

(1) Any employment contract between the registrant and a named executive officer; and

(2) Any compensatory plan or arrangement, including payments to be received from the registrant, with respect to a named executive officer, if such plan or arrangement results or will result from the resignation, retirement or any other termination of such executive officer's employment with the registrant and its subsidiaries or from a change-in-control of the registrant or a change in the named executive officer's responsibilities following a change-in-control and the amount involved, including all periodic payments or installments, exceeds $100,000.

(h) *Report on Repricing of Options/SARs.*

(1) If at any time during the last completed fiscal year, the registrant, while a reporting company pursuant to Section 13(a) or 15(d) of the Exchange Act [15 U.S.C. 78m(a), 78o(d)], has adjusted or amended the exercise price of stock options or SARs previously awarded to any of the named executive officers, whether through amendment, cancellation or replacement grants, or any other means ("repriced"), the registrant shall provide the information specified in paragraph (h)(2) of this item.

(2) The compensation committee (or other board committee performing equivalent functions or, in the absence of any such committee, the entire board of directors) shall explain in reasonable detail any such repricing of options and or SARs held by a named executive officer in the last completed fiscal year, as well as the basis for each such repricing.

Instructions to Item 402(h).

1. A replacement grant is any grant of options or SARs reasonably related to any prior or potential option or SAR cancellation, whether by an exchange of existing options or SARs for options or SARs with new terms; the grant of new options or SARs in tandem with previously granted options or SARs that will operate to cancel the previously granted options or SARs upon exercise; repricing of previously granted options or SARs; or otherwise. If a corresponding original grant was canceled in a prior year, information about such grant nevertheless must be disclosed pursuant to this paragraph.

2. If the replacement grant is not made at the current market price, describe the terms of the grant in a footnote or accompanying textual narrative.

3. This paragraph shall not apply to any repricing occurring through the operation of:

   a. a plan formula or mechanism that results in the periodic adjustment of the option or SAR exercise or base price;

   b. a plan antidilution provision; or

   c. a recapitalization or similar transaction equally affecting all holders of the class of securities underlying the options or SARs.

§228.403 (Item 403) Security Ownership of Certain Beneficial Owners and Management.

(a) *Security ownership of certain beneficial owners.* Complete the table below for any person (including any "group") who is known to the small business issuer to be the beneficial owner of more than five percent of any class of the small business issuer's voting securities.

(1)	(2)	(3)	(4)
	Name and	Amount and	
	Address of	Nature of	
	Beneficial	Beneficial	
Title of Class	Owner	Owner	Percent of Class

(b) *Security ownership of management.* Furnish the following information, as of the most recent practicable date, in substantially the tabular form indicated, as to each class of equity securities of the registrant or any of its parents or subsidiaries other than directors' qualifying shares, beneficially owned by all directors and nominees, naming them, each of the named executive officers as defined in Item 402(a)(2) (§ 228.402(a)(2)), and directors and executive officers of the registrant as a group, without naming them. Show in column (3) the total number of shares beneficially owned and in column (4) the percent of class so owned. Of the number of shares shown in column (3), indicate, by footnote or otherwise, the amount of shares with respect to which such persons have the right to acquire beneficial ownership as specified in § 240.13d-3(d)(1) of this chapter.

(1)	(2)	(3)	(4)
	Name and	Amount and	
	Address of	Nature of	
	Beneficial	Beneficial	
Title of Class	Owner	Owner	Percent of Class

(c) *Changes in control.* Describe any arrangements which may result in a change in control of the small business issuer.

Instructions to Item 403.

1. Of the number of shares shown in column (3) of paragraphs (a) and (b) of this Item, state in a footnote the amount which the listed beneficial owner has the right to acquire within sixty days, from options, warrants, rights, conversion privilege or similar obligations.

2. Where persons hold more than 5% of a class under a voting trust or similar agreement, provide the following:

   (a) the title of such securities;

   (b) the amount that they hold under the trust or agreement (if not clear from the table);

   (c) the duration of the agreement;

   (d) the names and addresses of the voting trustees; and

   (e) a brief outline of the voting rights and other powers of the voting trustees under the trust or agreement.

3. Calculate the percentages on the basis of the amount of outstanding securities plus, for each person or group, any securities that person or group has the right to acquire within 60 days pursuant to options, warrants, conversion privileges or other rights.

4. In this Item, a *beneficial owner* of a security means:

   (a) Any person who, directly or indirectly, through any contract, arrangement, understanding, relationship or otherwise has or shares:

      (1) Voting power, which includes the power to vote, or to direct the voting of, such security; or

      (2) Investment power, which includes the power to dispose, or to direct the disposition of, such security.

   (b) Any person who, directly or indirectly, creates or uses a trust, proxy, power of attorney, pooling arrangement or any other contract, arrangement or device with the purpose or effect of divesting such person of beneficial ownership of a security or preventing the vesting of such beneficial ownership.

5. All securities of the same class beneficially owned by a person, regardless of the form that such beneficial ownership takes, shall be totaled in calculating the number of shares beneficially owned by such person.

6. The small business issuer is responsible for knowing the contents of any statements filed with the Commission under section 13(d) or 13(g) of the Exchange Act concerning the beneficial ownership of securities and may rely upon the information in such statements unless it knows or has reason to believe that the information is not complete or accurate.

7. The term "group" means two or more persons acting as a partnership, syndicate, or other group for the purpose of acquiring, holding or disposing of securities of an issuer.

8. Where the small business issuer lists more than one beneficial owner for the same securities, adequate disclosure should be included to avoid confusion.

§228.404 (Item 404) Certain Relationships and Related Transactions.

(a) Describe any transaction during the last two years, or proposed transactions, to which the small business issuer was or is to be a party, in which any of the following persons had or is to have a direct or indirect material interest. Give the name of the person, the relationship to the issuer, nature of the person's interest in the transaction and, the amount of such interest:

    (1) Any director or executive officer of the small business issuer;

    (2) Any nominee for election as a director;

    (3) Any security holder named in response to Item 403 (§228.403); and

    (4) Any member of the immediate family (including spouse, parents, children, siblings, and in-laws) of any of the persons in paragraphs (a)(1), (2) or (3) of this Item.

(b) No information need be included for any transaction where:

    (1) Competitive bids determine the rates or charges involved in the transaction;

    (2) The transaction involves services at rates or charges fixed by law or governmental authority;

    (3) The transaction involves services as a bank depositary of funds, transfer agent, registrar, trustee under a trust indenture, or similar services;

    (4) The amount involved in the transaction or a series of similar transactions does not exceed $60,000; or

    (5) The interest of the person arises solely from the ownership of securities of the small business issuer and the person receives no extra or special benefit that was not shared equally (pro rata) by all holders of securities of the class.

(c) List all parents of the small business issuer showing the basis of control and as to each parent, the percentage of voting securities owned or other basis of control by its immediate parent if any.

(d) *Transactions with promoters.* Issuers organized within the past five years shall:

    (1) State the names of the promoters, the nature and amount of anything of value (including money, property, contracts, options or rights of any kind) received or to be received by each promoter, directly or indirectly, from the issuer and the nature and amount of any assets, services or other consideration therefore received or to be received by the registrant; and

    (2) As to any assets acquired or to be acquired from a promoter, state the amount at which the assets were acquired or are to be acquired and the principle followed or to be followed in determining such amount and identify the persons making the determination and their relationship, if any, with the registrant or any promoter. If the assets were acquired by the promoter within two years prior to their transfer to the issuer, also state the cost thereof to the promoter.

Instructions to Item 404.

1. A person does not have a material indirect interest in a transaction within the meaning of this Item where:

    (a) The interest arises only:

        (1) from such person's position as a director of another corporation or organization (other than a partnership) which is a party to the transaction and/or

        (2) from the total ownership (direct or indirect) by all specified persons of less than a 10% equity interest in another person (other than a partnership) which is a party to the transaction;

    (b) The interest arises only from such person's position as a limited partner in a partnership in which he and all other specified persons had an interest of less than 10 percent; or

    (c) The interest of such person arises solely from holding an equity interest (but not a general partnership interest) or a creditor interest in another person that is a party to the transaction and the transaction is not material to such other person.

2. Include information for any material underwriting discounts and commissions upon the sale of securities by the small business issuer where any of the specified persons was or is to be a principal underwriter or is a controlling person or member of a firm that was or is to be a principle underwriter.

3. As to any transaction involving the purchase or sale of assets by or to the small business issuer otherwise than in the ordinary course of business, state the cost of the assets to the purchase and if acquired by the seller within two years before the transaction, the cost thereof to the seller.

§228.405 (Item 405) Compliance With Section 16(a) of the Exchange Act.

Every small business issuer that has a class of equity securities registered pursuant to Section 12 of the Exchange Act (15 U.S.C. 78l) shall:

(a) Based solely upon a review of Forms 3 and 4 (17 CFR 249.103 and 249.104 of this chapter) and amendments thereto furnished to the registrant under Rule 16a-3(d) (17 CFR 240.16a-3(e) of this chapter) during its most recent fiscal year and Forms 5 and amendments thereto (§249.105 of this chapter) furnished to the registrant with respect to its most recent fiscal year, and any written representation referred to in paragraph (b)(2)(i) of this Item:

  (1) Identify each person who, at any time during the fiscal year, was a director, officer, beneficial owner of more than ten percent of any class of equity securities of the registrant registered pursuant to Section 12 ("reporting person") that failed to file on a timely basis, as disclosed in the above Forms, reports required by Section 16(a) during the most recent fiscal year or prior years.

  (2) For each such person, set forth the number of late reports, the number of transactions that were not reported on a timely basis, and any known failure to file a required Form.

NOTE: The disclosure requirement is based on a review of the forms submitted to the registrant during and with respect to its most recent fiscal year, as specified above. Accordingly, a failure to file timely need only be disclosed once. For example, if in the most recently concluded fiscal year a reporting person filed a Form 4 disclosing a transaction that took place in the prior fiscal year, and should have been reported in that year, the registrant should disclose that late filing and transaction pursuant to this Item for the most recent fiscal year, but not in material filed with respect to subsequent years.

(b) With respect to the disclosure required by paragraph (a) of this Item:

  (1) A form received by the registrant within three calendar days of the required filing date may be presumed to have been filed with the Commission by the required filing date.

  (2) If the registrant:

    (i) receives a written representation from the reporting person that no Form 5 is required; and

    (ii) maintains the representation for two years, making a copy available to the Commission or its staff upon request, the registrant need not identify such reporting person pursuant to paragraph (a) of this Item as having failed to file a Form 5 with respect to that fiscal year.

§228.501 (Item 501) Front of Registration Statement and Outside Front Cover of Prospectus.

On the outside front cover page of the prospectus, give the following information:

  (1) Name of the small business issuer;

  (2) Title, amount and description of securities offered;

  (3) If there are selling security holders, a statement to that effect;

  (4) Cross reference to the risk factors section of the prospectus;

  (5) The following statement in capital letters:

THESE SECURITIES HAVE NOT BEEN APPROVED OR DISAPPROVED BY THE SECURITIES AND EXCHANGE COMMISSION NOR HAS THE COMMISSION PASSED UPON THE ACCURACY OR ADEQUACY OF THIS PROSPECTUS. ANY REPRESENTATION TO THE CONTRARY IS A CRIMINAL OFFENSE.

  (6) If the small business issuer is not a reporting company and a preliminary prospectus will be circulated, a bona fide estimate of the range of the maximum offering price and maximum number of shares or other units of securities to be offered, or a bona fide estimate of the principal amount of debt securities to be offered;

  (7) The following table as to all securities to be registered (estimated, if necessary):

25

	Price to public	Underwriting discounts and commissions	Proceeds to issuer or other persons
Per unit			
Total			
Total minimum			
Total maximum			

The "total minimum" and "total maximum" items are required (in lieu of the "Total" item) only if the offering is made on a best efforts basis. If so, disclose in the summary section (or on the cover page if material): the date the offering will end; any minimum purchase requirement and any arrangements to place funds in an escrow, trust, or similar account. If there is an over-allotment option, the maximum-minimum information must be based on the purchase of all or none of the shares subject to that option in addition to any other minimum/maximum information;

(8) If a prospectus will be used before the effective date of the registration statement (or, prior to the determination of the initial public offering price in the case of a prospectus that omits information as permitted by Rule 430A under the Securities Act [§230.430A of this chapter]), include the caption "Subject to Completion," the date of its issuance, and the following statement printed in type as large as that generally used in the body of the prospectus:

Information contained herein is subject to completion or amendment. A registration statement relating to these securities has been filed with the Securities and Exchange Commission. These securities may not be sold nor may offers to buy be accepted prior to the time the registration statement becomes effective. This prospectus shall not constitute an offer to sell or the solicitation of an offer to buy nor shall there be any sale of these securities in any State in which such offer, solicitation or sale would be unlawful prior to registration or qualification under the securities laws of any such State.

(9) Any legend or information required by the law of any State in which the securities are to be offered;

(10) The date of the prospectus; and

(11) In a footnote to the table, disclose the other expenses of the offering specified in Item 511 of this Regulation S-B.

§228.502 (Item 502) Inside Front and Outside Back Cover Pages of Prospectus.

On the inside front cover page of the prospectus (or on the outside back cover page for paragraphs (e) and (f) of this Item) disclose the following:

(a) (1) *Available information.* State whether or not the small business issuer is a reporting company.

(2) If the small business issuer is a reporting company, state that the reports and other information filed by the small business issuer may be inspected and copied at the public reference facilities of the Commission in Washington, D.C., and at some of its Regional Offices, (include addresses), and that copies of such material can be obtained from the Public Reference Section of the Commission, Washington, D.C. 20549 at prescribed rates; and

(3) Name any national securities exchange on which the small business issuer's securities are listed and state that reports and other information concerning the small business issuer can be inspected at such exchanges.

(b) *Reports to security holders.* Where a small business issuer is not required to deliver an annual report to security holders, indicate whether voluntary reports will be sent and, if so, the frequency of such reports and whether they will include audited financial statements.

(c) *Incorporation by reference.* State that small business issuer will provide without charge to each person who receives a prospectus, upon written or oral request of such person, a copy of any of the information that was incorporated by reference in the prospectus (not including exhibits to the information that is incorporated by reference unless the exhibits are themselves specifically incorporated by reference) and the address (including title or department) and telephone number to which such a request is to be directed.

(d) *Stabilization.*

(1) Include the following statement, if true:

IN CONNECTION WITH THIS OFFERING, THE UNDERWRITERS MAY OVER-ALLOT OR EFFECT TRANSAC-
TIONS WHICH STABILIZE OR MAINTAIN THE MARKET PRICE OF (IDENTIFY EACH CLASS OF
SECURITIES IN WHICH SUCH TRANSACTIONS MAY BE EFFECTED) AT A LEVEL ABOVE THAT WHICH
MIGHT OTHERWISE PREVAIL IN THE OPEN MARKET. SUCH TRANSACTIONS MAY BE EFFECTED ON
(IDENTIFY EACH EXCHANGE ON WHICH STABILIZING TRANSACTIONS MAY BE EFFECTED; IF NONE,
OMIT THIS SENTENCE.) SUCH STABILIZING, IF COMMENCED, MAY BE DISCONTINUED AT ANY TIME.

(2) If the stabilizing began before the effective date of the registration statement, state the amount of securities bought, the
prices at which they were bought and the period within which they were bought. In the event that Rule 430A under the
Securities Act [§230.430A of this chapter] is used, the final prospectus must include information as to stabilizing transactions before the public offering price was set.

(3) If the securities are to be offered to existing security holders pursuant to warrants or rights and any securities not taken by
security holders are to be reoffered to the public after the expiration of the rights offering period, state in the prospectus
used to reoffer the securities:

    (i) the amount of securities bought in stabilization activities during the rights offering period and the price or range of
prices at which such securities were bought;

    (ii) the amount of the offered securities subscribed for during such period;

    (iii) the amount of the offered securities subscribed for by the underwriters during such period;

    (iv) the amount of the offered securities sold during such period by the underwriters and the price, or range of prices, at
which such securities were sold; and

    (v) the amount of the offered securities to be reoffered to the public and the public offering price.

(e) *Delivery of prospectuses by dealers.* The following legend shall be printed in bold-face or italic type:

Until (insert date) all dealers effecting transactions in the registered securities, whether or not participating in this distribution,
may be required to deliver a prospectus. This is in addition to the obligation of dealers to deliver a prospectus when acting as
underwriters and with respect to their unsold allotments or subscriptions.

The date to be inserted should be determined by reference to Section 4(3) of the Securities Act and Rule 174 (§230.174 of this
chapter).

(f) *Table of contents.* Include a detailed table of contents showing the various sections or subdivisions of the prospectus and the
page number on which each such section or subdivision begins.

Introduction

Canadian issuers should, in addition to the disclosure required by this Item, provide the information required by Item 502(f) of
Regulation S-K.

§228.503 (Item 503) Summary Information and Risk Factors.

(a) *Summary.* A summary of the information contained in the prospectus where the length and complexity of the prospectus make
a summary useful.

(b) *Address and telephone number.* In the beginning of the prospectus the complete mailing address and the telephone number of
their principal executive offices.

(c) *Risk factors.* Immediately following the cover page of the prospectus or the summary section, discuss any factors that make
the offering speculative or risky. These factors may include no operating history, no recent profit from operations, poor financial position, the kind of business in which the small business issuer is engaged or proposes to engage, or no market for the
small business issuer's securities.

§228.504 (Item 504) Use of Proceeds.

State how the net proceeds of the offering will be used, indicating the amount to be used for each purpose and the priority of each
purpose, if all of the securities are not sold. If all or a substantial part of the proceeds are not allocated for a specific purpose, so state
and discuss the principal reasons for the offering.

Instructions to Item 504.

1. If a material amount of proceeds will discharge debt, state the interest rate and maturity. If that debt was incurred within one year,
describe the use of the proceeds of that debt other than short-term borrowings used for working capital.

2. If any material amount of the proceeds is to be used to acquire assets or finance the acquisitions of other businesses, describe the assets or businesses and identify the persons from whom they will be bought. State the cost of the assets and, where such assets are to be acquired from affiliates of the small business issuer or their associates, give the names of the persons from whom they are to be acquired and set forth the principle followed in determining the cost to the small business issuer.

§228.505 (Item 505) Determination of Offering Price.

(a) If there is no established public market for the common equity being registered or if there is a significant difference between the offering price and the market price of the stock, give the factors that were considered in determining the offering price.

(b) If warrants, rights and convertible securities are being registered and there is no public market for the underlying securities, describe the factors considered in determining the exercise or conversion price.

§228.506 (Item 506) Dilution.

(a) If the small business issuer is not a reporting company and is selling common equity at a price significantly more than the price paid by officers, directors, promoters and affiliated persons for common equity purchased by them during the past five years (or which they have rights to purchase), compare these prices.

(b) If paragraph (a) of this Item applies and the issuer had losses in each of its last three fiscal years, or since its inception, whichever period is shorter, and there is a material dilution of the purchasers' equity interest, disclose the following:

(1) The net tangible book value per share before and after the distribution;

(2) The amount of the increase in such net tangible book value per share attributable to the cash payments made by purchasers of the shares being offered; and

(3) The amount of the immediate dilution from the public offering price which will be absorbed by such purchasers.

§228.507 (Item 507) Selling Security Holders.

If security holders of a small business issuer is offering securities, name each selling security holder, state any position, office, or other material relationship which the selling security holder has had within the past three years with the small business issuer or any of its predecessors or affiliates, and state the amount of securities of the class owned by such security holder before the offering, the amount to be offered for the security holder's account, the amount and (if one percent or more) the percentage of the class to be owned by such security holder after the offering is complete.

Instruction

Responses to this item may be combined with disclosure in response to Item 403.

§228.508 (Item 508) Plan of Distribution.

(a) *Underwriters and underwriting obligation.* If the securities are to be offered through underwriters, name the principal underwriters, and state the respective amounts underwritten. Identify each such underwriter having a material relationship with the small business issuer and state the nature of the relationship. State the nature of the obligation of the underwriter(s) to take the securities, *i.e.*, firm commitment, best efforts.

(b) *New underwriters.* Describe the business experience of managing or principal underwriters that have been in business less than three years, state their principal business function and identify any material relationships between the promoters of the issuer and the underwriter(s). This information need not be given if:

(1) the issuer is a reporting company; and

(2) an offering has no material risks.

(c) *Other distributions.* Outline briefly the plan of distribution of any securities to be registered that are to be offered otherwise than through underwriters.

(d) *Underwriter's representative on the board of directors.* Describe any arrangement whereby the underwriter has the right to designate or nominate a member or members of the board of directors of the small business issuer. Identify any director so designated or nominated and indicate any relationship with the small business issuer.

(e) *Indemnification of underwriters.* If the underwriting agreement provides for indemnification by the small business issuer of the underwriters or their controlling persons against any liability arising under the Securities Act, furnish a brief description of such indemnification provisions.

(f) *Dealers' compensation*. State briefly the discounts and commissions to be allowed or paid to dealers, including all cash, securities, contracts or other considerations to be received by any dealer in connection with the sale of the securities.

(g) *Finders*. Identify any finder and describe the nature of any material relationship between such finder and the small business issuer or associates or affiliates of the small business issuer.

(h) *Discretionary accounts*. If the small business issuer is not a reporting company, identify any principal underwriter that intends to sell to any discretionary accounts and include an estimate of the amount of securities so intended to be sold. The response to this paragraph shall be contained in a pre-effective amendment which shall be circulated if the information is not available when the registration statement is filed.

§228.509 (Item 509) Interest of Named Experts and Counsel.

If an "expert" or "counsel" was hired on a contingent basis, will receive a direct or indirect interest in the small business issuer or was a promoter, underwriter, voting trustee, director, officer, or employee, of the small business issuer, describe the contingent basis, interest, or connection.

(a) *Expert* - is a person who is named as preparing or certifying all or part of the small business issuer's registration statement or a report or valuation for use in connection with the registration statement.

(b) *Counsel* - is counsel named in the prospectus as having given an opinion on the validity of the securities being registered or upon other legal matters concerning the registration or offering of the securities.

Instruction to Item 509.

1. The small business issuer does not need to disclose the interest of an expert (other than an accountant) or counsel if their interest (including the fair market value of all securities of the small business issuer received and to be received, or subject to options, warrants or rights received or to be received) does not exceed $50,000.

§228.510 (Item 510) Disclosure of Commission Position on Indemnification for Securities Act Liabilities.

Describe the indemnification provisions for directors, officers and controlling persons of the small business issuer against liability under the Securities Act. This includes any provision in the underwriting agreement which indemnifies the underwriter or its controlling persons against such liabilities where a director, officer or controlling person of the small business issuer is such an underwriter or controlling person or a member of any firm which is such an underwriter. In addition, provide the undertaking in the first sentence of Item 512(e).

§228.511 (Item 511) Other Expenses of Issuance and Distribution.

(a) Give an itemized statement of all expenses of the offering, other than underwriting discounts and commissions. If any of the securities are registered for sale by security holders, state how much of the expenses the security holders will pay.

(1) The itemized list should generally include registration fees, federal taxes, state taxes and fees, trustees' and transfer agents' fees, costs of printing and engraving, legal, accounting, and engineering fees and any listing fees.

(2) Include as a separate item any premium paid by the small business issuer or any selling security holder on any policy to insure or indemnify directors or officers against any liabilities they may incur in the registration, offering, or sale of these securities.

Instruction to Item 511.

1. If the amounts of any items are not known, give estimates but identify them as such.

§228.512 (Item 512) Undertakings.

Include each of the following undertakings that apply to the offering.

(a) *Rule 415 Offering*. If the small business issuer is registering securities under Rule 415 of the Securities Act (§230.415 of this chapter), that the small business issuer will:

(1) File, during any period in which it offers or sells securities, a post-effective amendment to this registration statement to:

(i) Include any prospectus required by section 10(a)(3) of the Securities Act;

(ii) Reflect in the prospectus any facts or events which, individually or together, represent a fundamental change in the information in the registration statement; and

(iii) Include any additional or changed material information on the plan of distribution.

NOTE: Small business issuers do not need to give the statements in paragraphs (a)(1)(i) and (a)(1)(ii) of this Item if the registration statement is on Form S-3 or S-8 (§§239.13 or 239.16b of this chapter), and the information required in a post-effective amendment is incorporated by reference from periodic reports filed by the small business issuer under the Exchange Act.

(2) For determining liability under the Securities Act, treat each post-effective amendment as a new registration statement of the securities offered, and the offering of the securities at that time to be the initial bona fide offering.

(3) File a post-effective amendment to remove from registration any of the securities that remain unsold at the end of the offering.

(b) *Warrants and rights offerings.* If the small business issuer will offer the securities to existing security holders under warrants or rights and the small business issuer will reoffer to the public any securities not taken by security holders, with any modifications that suit the particular case — The small business issuer will supplement the prospectus, after the end of the subscription period, to include the results of the subscription offer, the transactions by the underwriters during the subscription period, the amount of unsubscribed securities that the underwriters will purchase and the terms of any later reoffering. If the underwriters make any public offering of the securities on terms different from those on the cover page of the prospectus, the small business issuer will file a post-effective amendment to state the terms of such offering.

(c) *Competitive bids.* If the small business issuer is offering securities at competitive bidding, with modifications to suit the particular case, the small business issuer will:

(1) use its best efforts to distribute before the opening of bids, to prospective bidders, underwriters, and dealers, a reasonable number of copies of a prospectus that meet the requirements of section 10(a) of the Securities Act, and relating to the securities offered at competitive bidding, as contained in the registration statement, together with any supplements; and

(2) file an amendment to the registration statement reflecting the results of bidding, the terms of the reoffering and related matters where required by the applicable form, not later than the first use, authorized by the issuer after the opening of bids, of a prospectus relating to the securities offered at competitive bidding, unless the issuer proposes no further public offering of such securities by the issuer or by the purchasers.

(d) *Equity offerings of nonreporting small business issuers.* If a small business issuer that before the offering had no duty to file reports with the Commission under section 13(a) or 15(d) of the Exchange Act is registering equity securities for sale in an underwritten offering — The small business issuer will provide to the underwriter at the closing specified in the underwriting agreement certificates in such denominations and registered in such names as required by the underwriter to permit prompt delivery to each purchaser.

(e) *Request for acceleration of effective date.* If the small business issuer will request acceleration of the effective date of the registration statement under Rule 461 under the Securities Act, include the following:

Insofar as indemnification for liabilities arising under the Securities Act of 1933 (the "Act") may be permitted to directors, officers and controlling persons of the small business issuer pursuant to the foregoing provisions, or otherwise, the small business issuer has been advised that in the opinion of the Securities and Exchange Commission such indemnification is against public policy as expressed in the Act and is, therefore, unenforceable.

In the event that a claim for indemnification against such liabilities (other than the payment by the small business issuer of expenses incurred or paid by a director, officer or controlling person of the small business issuer in the successful defense of any action, suit or proceeding) is asserted by such director, officer or controlling person in connection with the securities being registered, the small business issuer will, unless in the opinion of its counsel the matter has been settled by controlling precedent, submit to a court of appropriate jurisdiction the question whether such indemnification by it is against public policy as expressed in the Securities Act and will be governed by the final adjudication of such issue.

(f) If the issuer relies on Rule 430A under the Securities Act [§230.430A of this chapter], that the small business issuer will:

(1) For determining any liability under the Securities Act, treat the information omitted from the form of prospectus filed as part of this registration statement in reliance upon Rule 430A and contained in a form of prospectus filed by the small business issuer under Rule 424(b)(1), or (4) or 497(h) under the Securities Act (§§230.424(b)(1), (4) or 230.497(h)) as part of this registration statement as of the time the Commission declared it effective.

(2) For determining any liability under the Securities Act, treat each post-effective amendment that contains a form of prospectus as a new registration statement for the securities offered in the registration statement, and that offering of the securities at that time as the initial bona fide offering of those securities.

30

§228.601 (Item 601) Exhibits.

(a) *Exhibits and index of exhibits.*

    (1) The exhibits required by the exhibit table must be filed or incorporated by reference.

    (2) Each filing must have an index of exhibits. The exhibit index must list exhibits in the same order as the exhibit table. If the exhibits are incorporated by reference, this fact should be noted in the exhibit index. In the manually signed registration statement or report, the exhibit index should give the page number of each exhibit.

Instructions to Item 601(a).

1. If an exhibit (other than an opinion or consent) is filed in preliminary form and is later changed to include only interest, dividend or conversion rates, redemption or conversion prices, purchase or offering prices, underwriters' or dealers' commissions, names, addresses or participation of underwriters or similar matters and the information appears elsewhere in the registration statement or a prospectus, no amendment need be filed.

2. Small business issuers may file copies of each exhibit, rather than originals, except as otherwise specifically noted.

Exhibit Table

	Securities Act forms				Exchange Act forms				
	SB-2	S-2	S-3	S-4***	S-8	10SB	8-K	10-QSB	10-KSB
(1) Underwriting agreement	X	X	X	X			X		
(2) Plan of Acquisition, reorg., arrgmnt, liquid, or succession	X	X	X	X		X	X	X	
(3) Articles of Incorporation and by-laws	X			X		X			X
(4) Instruments defining the rights of holders, incl. indenture	X	X	X	X	X	X	X	X	X
(5) Opinion re: legality	X	X	X	X	X				
(6) No exhibit required	N/A	N/A	N/A	N/A	N/A	N/A	N/A	N/A	N/A
(7) Opinion re: liquidation preference	X	X		X		X			
(8) Opinion re: tax matters	X	X	X	X					
(9) Voting Trust agreement	X			X		X			X
(10) Material contracts	X	X		X		X			
(11) Statement re: computation of per share earnings	X	X		X		X		X	X
(12) No exhibit required	N/A	N/A	N/A	N/A	N/A	N/A	N/A	N/A	N/A
(13) Annual or quarterly reports, Form 10-Q*	X	X		X					X
(14) Material foreign patents	X			X		X			
(15) Letter on unaudited interim financial information	X	X	X	X	X			X	
(16) Letter on change in certifying accountant****	X	X		X		X	X		X
(17) Letter on director resignation							X		
(18) Letter on change in accounting principles								X	X
(19) Previously unfiled documents								X	X
(20) Reports furnished to security holders							X		
(21) Other documents or statements to security holders							X		
(22) Subsidiaries of the registrants	X			X		X			X
(23) Published report regarding matters submitted to vote								X	X
(24) Consent of experts and counsel	X	X	X	X	X		X**	X**	X**
(25) Power of attorney	X	X	X	X	X	X	X	X	X
(26) Statement of eligibility of trustee	X	X	X	X					
(27) Invitations for competitive bids	X	X	X	X					
(28) Additional exhibits	X	X	X	X	X	X	X	X	X
(29) Info. from reports furnished to State Insurance authorities	X	X	X	X	X	X			X

* Only if incorporated by reference into a prospectus and delivered to holders along with the prospectus as permitted by the registration statement; or in the case of a Form 10-KSB, where the annual report is incorporated by reference into the text of the Form 10-KSB.

** Where the opinion of the expert or counsel has been incorporated by reference into a previously filed securities Act registration statement.

*** An issuer need not provide exhibit if: (1) an election was made under Form S-4 to provide S-2 or S-3 disclosure; and (2) the form selected (S-2 or S-3) would not require the company to provide exhibit.

**** If required under Item 304 of Regulation S-B.

(b) *Description of exhibits.* Below is a description of each document listed in the exhibit table.

  (1) *Underwriting agreement.* Each agreement with a principal underwriter for the distribution of the securities. If the terms have been determined and the securities are to be registered on Form S-3 (§239.13), the agreement may be filed on Form 8-K (§249.308) after the effectiveness of the registration statement.

  (2) *Plan of purchase, sale, reorganization, arrangement, liquidation or succession.* Any such plan described in the filing. Schedules or attachments may be omitted if they are listed in the index and provided to the Commission upon request.

  (3) *Articles of incorporation and by-laws.* The complete copies of articles of incorporation and by-laws or comparable instruments, as amended.

  (4) *Instruments defining the rights of security holders, including indentures.*

    (i) All instruments that define the rights of holders of the equity or debt securities that the issuer is registering, including the pages from the articles of incorporation or by-laws that define those rights.

    (ii) All instruments defining the rights of holders of long term debt unless the total amount of debt covered by the instrument does not exceed 10% of the total assets of the small business issuer.

    (iii) Copies of indentures to be qualified under the Trust Indenture Act of 1939 shall include an itemized table of contents and a cross reference sheet showing the location of the provisions inserted in accordance with Sections 310 through 318(a) of that Act.

  (5) *Opinion on legality.*

    (i) An opinion of counsel on the legality of the securities being registered stating whether they will, when sold, be legally issued, fully paid and non-assessable, and, if debt securities, whether they will be binding obligations of the small business issuer.

    (ii) If the securities being registered are issued under a plan that is subject to the requirements of ERISA furnish either:

      (A) An opinion of counsel which confirms compliance with ERISA; or

      (B) A copy of the Internal Revenue Service determination letter that the plan is qualified under section 401 of the Internal Revenue Code.

If the plan is later amended, the small business issuer must have the opinion of counsel and the IRS determination letter updated to confirm compliance and qualification.

  (6) No Exhibit Required.

  (7) *Opinion on liquidation preference.* If the liquidation preference of shares exceeds their par or stated value, an opinion of counsel as to whether there are any resulting restrictions on surplus. The opinion should also state any remedies available to security holders before or after payment of any dividend that would reduce surplus to an amount less than the amount of such excess. The opinion shall cite to applicable constitutional and statutory provisions and controlling case law.

  (8) *Opinion on tax matters.* If tax consequences of the transaction are material to an investor, an opinion of counsel, an independent public or certified public accountant or, a revenue ruling from the Internal Revenue Service, supporting the tax matters and consequences to the shareholders. The exhibit is required for filings to which Securities Act Industry Guide 5 applies.

  (9) *Voting trust agreement and amendments.*

  (10) *Material contracts.*

    (i) Every material contract, not made in the ordinary course of business, that will be performed after the filing of the registration statement or report or was entered into not more than two years before such filing. Also include the following contracts:

      (A) Any contract to which directors, officers, promoters, voting trustees, security holders named in the registration statement or report, or underwriters are parties other than contracts involving only the purchase or sale of current assets having a determinable market price, at such market price;

      (B) Any contract upon which the small business issuer's business is substantially dependent, such as contracts with principal customers, principal suppliers, franchise agreements, etc.;

      (C) Any contract for the purchase or sale of any property, plant or equipment for a consideration exceeding 15 percent of such assets of the small business issuer; or

      (D) Any material lease under which a part of the property described in the registration statement or report is held by the small business issuer.

(ii) (A) Any management contract or any compensatory plan, contract or arrangement, including but not limited to plans relating to options, warrants or rights, pension, retirement or deferred compensation or bonus, incentive or profit sharing (or if not set forth in any formal document, a written description thereof) in which any director or any of the named executive officers of the registrant as defined by Item 402(a)(2) (§ 228.402(a)(2)) participates shall be deemed material and shall be filed; and any other management contract or any other compensatory plan, contract, or arrangement in which any other executive officer of the registrant participates shall be filed unless immaterial in amount or significance.

   (B) The following management contracts or compensatory plans need not be filed:

      (1) Ordinary purchase and sales agency agreements;

      (2) Agreements with managers of stores in a chain organization or similar organization;

      (3) Contracts providing for labor or salesmen's bonuses or payments to a class of security holders, as such;

      (4) Any compensatory plan which is available to employees, officers or directors generally and provides for the same method of allocation of benefits between management and nonmanagement participants; and

      (5) Any compensatory plan if the issuer is a wholly owned subsidiary of a reporting company and is filing a report on Form 10-KSB (§249.310b), or registering debt or non-voting preferred stock on Form S-2 (§239.12).

Instruction to Item 601(b)(10)

1. **Only** copies of the various remunerative plans need be filed. Each individual director's or executive officer's personal agreement **under** the plans need not be filed, unless they contain material provisions.

   (11)*Statement re computation of per share earnings.* An explanation of the computation of per share earnings on both a primary and fully diluted basis unless the computation can be clearly determined from the registration statement or report.

   (12)No exhibit required.

   (13)Annual report to security holders for the last fiscal year, Form 10-Q or 10-QSB or quarterly report to security holders, if incorporated by reference in the filing. Such reports, except for the parts which are expressly incorporated by reference in the filing are not deemed "filed" as part of the filing. If the financial statements in the report have been incorporated by reference in the filing, the accountant's certificate shall be manually signed in one copy. See Rule 411(b) (§230.411(b) of this chapter).

   (14)*Material foreign patents.* Each material foreign patent for an invention not covered by a United States patent.

   (15)*Letter on unaudited interim financial information.* A letter, where applicable, from the independent accountant which acknowledges awareness of the use in a registration statement of a report on unaudited interim financial information. The letter is not considered a part of a registration statement prepared or certified by an accountant or a report prepared or certified by an accountant within the meaning of sections 7 and 11 of the Securities Act. Such letter may be filed with the registration statement, an amendment thereto, or a report on Form 10-QSB (§249.308b) which is incorporated by reference into the registration statement.

   (16)*Letter on change in certifying accountant.* File the letter required by Item 304(a)(3).

   (17)*Letter on director resignation.* Any letter from a former director which describes a disagreement with the small business issuer that led to the director's resignation or refusal to stand for re-election and which requests that the matter be disclosed.

   (18)*Letter on change in accounting principles.* Unless previously filed, a letter from the issuer's accountant stating whether any change in accounting principles or practices followed by the issuer, or any change in the method of applying any such accounting principles or practices, which affected the financial statements being filed with the Commission in the report or which is expected to affect the financial statements of future fiscal years is to an alternative principle which in his judgment is preferable under the circumstances. No such letter need be filed when such change is made in response to a standard adopted by the Financial Accounting Standards Board that creates a new accounting principle, that expresses a preference for an accounting principle, or that rejects a specific accounting principle.

   (19)*Previously unfiled documents.*

      (i) Any unfiled document, which was executed or in effect during the reporting period, if such document would have been required to be filed as an exhibit to a registration statement on Form 10-SB (§249.210b).

      (ii) Any amendment or change to a document which was previously filed.

(20) *Report furnished to security holders.* If the issuer makes available to its stockholders or otherwise publishes, within the period prescribed for filing the report, a document or statement containing information meeting some or all of the requirements of Part I of Form 10-Q or 10-QSB, the information called for may be incorporated by reference to such published document or statement provided copies thereof are included as an exhibit to the registration statement or to Part I of the Form 10-Q or 10-QSB report.

(21) Other documents or statements to security holders or any document incorporated by reference.

(22) *Subsidiaries of the small business issuer.* A list of all subsidiaries, the state or other jurisdiction of incorporation or organization of each, and the names under which such subsidiaries do business.

(23) *Published report regarding matters submitted to vote of security holders.* Published reports containing all of the information called for by Item 4 of Part II of Form 10-Q (or 10-QSB) or Item 4 of Part I of Form 10-K or 10-KSB which is referred to therein in lieu of providing disclosure in Form 10-Q (10-QSB) or 10-K (10-KSB), which are required to be filed as exhibits by Rule 12b-23(a)(3) under the Exchange Act.

(24) *Consents of experts and counsel.*

    (i)   Securities Act filings — Dated and manually signed written consents or a reference in the index to the location of the consent.

    (ii) Exchange Act reports. If required to file a consent for material incorporated by reference in a previously filed registration statement under the Securities Act, the dated and manually signed consent to the material incorporated by reference. The consents shall be dated and manually signed.

(25) *Power of attorney.* If a person signs a registration statement or report under a power of attorney, a manually signed copy of such power of attorney or if located elsewhere in the registration statement, a reference in the index to where it is located. In addition, if an officer signs a registration statement for the small business issuer by a power of attorney, a certified copy of a resolution of the board of directors authorizing such signature.

(26) *Statement of eligibility of trustee.* Form T-1 (§269.1 of this chapter) if an indenture is being qualified under the Trust Indenture Act, bound separately from the other exhibits.

(27) *Invitations for competitive bids.* If the registration statement covers securities that the small business issuer is offering at competitive bidding, any invitation for competitive bid that the small business issuer will send or give to any person shall be filed.

(28) *Additional exhibits.* Any additional exhibits if listed and described in the exhibit index.

(29) *Information from reports furnished to state insurance regulatory authorities.*

    (i)   If reserves for unpaid property-casualty ("P/C") claims and claim adjustment expenses of the small business issuer, its unconsolidated subsidiaries and the proportionate share of the small business issuer and the other subsidiaries in the unpaid P/C claims and claim adjustment expenses of its 50%-or-less-owned equity investees, taken in the aggregate after small business issuer eliminations, exceed one-half of the common stockholders' equity of the small business issuer as of the beginning of the latest fiscal year the following information should be supplied.

    (ii) the information included in Schedules O and P of Annual Statements provided to state regulatory authorities by the small business issuer or its P/C insurance small business issuer affiliates for the latest year on a combined or consolidated basis as appropriate, separately for each of the following:

        (A) the small business issuer;

        (B) its unconsolidated subsidiaries; and

        (C) fifty percent-or-less-owned equity investees of the small business issuer and its subsidiaries.

    (iii) Small business issuers may omit the combined or consolidated Schedules O and P of fifty percent-or-less-owned equity investees, if they file the same information with the Commission as companies in their own right, and if they state that fact and the name and ownership percentage of such companies.

    (iv) If ending reserves in paragraphs (b)(29)(ii)(A) and (b)(29)(ii)(B) of this Item or the proportionate share of the small business issuer and its other subsidiaries in paragraph (b)(29)(ii)(C) of this Item are less than 5% of the total ending reserves in paragraphs (b)(29)(ii)(A) and (b)(29)(ii)(B) of this Item, and the proportionate share of (b)(29)(ii)(C) of this Item, small business issuers may omit that category and note that fact. If the amount of the reserves attributable to fifty percent-or-less-owned equity investees that file this information as companies in their own right exceeds 95% of the total paragraph (b)(29)(ii)(C) of this Item small business issuers do not need to provide reserves, information for the other fifty percent-or-less-owned equity investees.

(v) Small business issuers do not need to include Schedules O and P information if they are not required to file Schedules O and P with insurance regulatory authorities. However, clearly note the nature and extent of any such exclusions in the Exhibit.

(vi) Companies whose fiscal year differs from the calendar year should present Schedules O and P as of the end of the calendar year that falls within their fiscal year.

(vii) The nature and amount of the difference between reserves for claims and claim adjustment expenses reflected on Schedules O and P and the total P/C statutory reserves for claims and disclose claim adjustment expenses as of the latest calendar year in a note to those Schedules.

§228.701 (Item 701) Recent Sales of Unregistered Securities.

Give the following information for all securities that the small business issuer sold within the past three years without registering the securities under the Securities Act.

(a) The date, title and amount of securities sold.

(b) Give the names of the principal underwriters, if any. If the small business issuer did not publicly offer any securities, identify the persons or class of persons to whom the small business issuer sold the securities.

(c) For securities sold for cash, the total offering price and the total underwriting discounts or commissions. For securities sold other than for cash, describe the transaction and the type and amount of consideration received by the small business issuer.

(d) The section of the Securities Act or the rule of the Commission under which the small business issuer claimed exemption from registration and the facts relied upon to make the exemption available.

§228.702 (Item 702) Indemnification of Directors and Officers.

State whether any statute, charter provisions, by-laws, contract or other arrangements that insures or indemnifies a controlling person, director or officer of the small business issuer affects his or her liability in that capacity.

ENDNOTES

1. *See Hanson Trust PLC v. ML SCM Acquisition, Inc.*, 781 F.2d 264 (2d Cir. 1986); *Grobow v. Perot*, 539 A.2d 180 (Del. 1988); *Smith v. Van Gorkom*, 488 A.2d 858 (Del. 1985).

2. Many states have enacted statutes designed to protect the senior manager by limiting liability, requiring greater proof of misfeasance than mere negligence (e.g., gross negligence, recklessness, or intent), or allowing for favorable insurance or indemnity policies. Courts have proposed varying standards of care depending on whether the senior manager is considered an insider of the corporation or an outsider, such as an outside director. Although such statutes and case law may prove valuable to the senior manager's efforts at limiting or avoiding liability, detailed discussion of such matters is not within the scope of this guide. However, for general information purposes, liability under a claim of gross negligence generally requires a showing of intentional or reckless misconduct, whereas liability under a claim of negligence requires a showing that the defendant breached the standard of care in accordance with which an ordinary prudent and reasonable person would have acted under similar circumstances.

3. Exchange Act Release No. 18,694, [1982 Transfer Binder] Fed. Sec. L. Rep. (CCH) ¶ 83,209 (Apr. 29, 1982); *see also* Exchange Act Release No. 17,059, [1980 Transfer Binder] Fed. Sec. L. Rep. (CCH) ¶ 82,635 (Aug. 13, 1980) (relating to personal benefits received).

4. Investment Advisors Act Release No. 814, [1982 Transfer Binder] Fed. Sec. L. Rep. (CCH) ¶ 83,240 (July 21, 1982).

5. *See* 401 F.2d 833 (2d Cir. 1968), *cert. denied sub nom.*, 394 U.S. 976 (1969); 832 F.2d 726 (2d Cir. 1987); 930 F.2d 826 (10th Cir. 1991); 531 F.2d 39 (2d Cir. 1976); 494 F.2d 1301 (2d Cir. 1974); Exchange Act Section 16(b) prohibiting insider short-swing profits.

6. Exchange Act Release No. 34-30532, Fed. Sec. L. Rep. (CCH) ¶ 73,830 (Mar. 31, 1992).

7. Accounting and Auditing Enforcement Release No. 416, Exchange Act Release No. 31934, Fed. Sec. L. Rep. (CCH) ¶ 73,902 (Mar. 1, 1993).

8. *See* Sec. Reg. & L. Rep. (BNA) 1548 (Oct. 2, 1992); Sec. Reg. & L. Rep. (BNA) 1637–38 (Oct. 23, 1992).

9. 628 F.2d 1214 (9th Cir. 1980); 646 F.2d 271 (7th Cir. 1981), *cert. denied,* 454 U.S. 1092 (1981).

10. *See, e.g.,* 485 U.S. 224 (1988) (also holding that disclosure alone does not make information material); 426 U.S. 438 (1976).

11. *See, e.g.,* 485 U.S. 224 (1988); 401 F.2d 833, 849 (2d Cir. 1968), *cert. denied sub nom.,* 394 U.S. 976 (1969).

12. *See* William F. Bavinger & John T. Sant, *Disclosure of Unasserted Claims under GAAP and the Securities Laws: Inviting Liability, INSIGHTS, Sept. 1992, at 14, 15 n.10.*

13. 388 F. Supp. 812 (D. Del. 1974).

14. 483 F.2d 247 (2d Cir. 1973).

15. 387 F. Supp. 1310 (S.D.N.Y. 1974), rev'd on other grounds, 543 F.2d 421 (2d Cir. 1976), *cert. denied,* 429 U.S. 1062 (1977).

16. 473 F.2d 777 (2d Cir. 1972).

17. Litigation Release No. 10093, [1983–1984 Transfer Binder] Fed. Sec. L. Rep. (CCH) ¶ 99,464 (Aug. 15, 1983).

18. Accounting and Auditing Enforcement Release No. 50, Exchange Act Release No. 21872, [1982-1987 Transfer Binder] Fed. Sec. L. Rep. (CCH) ¶ 73,450 (Mar. 20, 1985).

19. Exchange Act Release No. 22,792, [1985–1986 Transfer Binder] Fed. Sec. L. Rep. (CCH) ¶ 83,958 (Jan. 15, 1986).

20. Speech by John M. Fedders, Failure to Disclose Illegal Conduct, *in* 14 Sec. Reg. & L. Rep. (BNA) 2057, 2058 (Nov. 26, 1982).

21. 890 F.2d 628, 640 (3d Cir. 1989); 733 F. Supp. 668, 674–75, 677–78 (S.D.N.Y. 1990).

22. 814 F.2d 22, 25 (1st Cir. 1987).

23. 645 F.2d 761, 776–79 (9th Cir. 1981), *cert. denied,* 454 U.S. 1145 (1981).

24. *See* 645 F.2d 761 (9th Cir. 1981), *cert. denied,* 454 U.S. 1145 (1981).

25. 890 F.2d 628 (3d Cir. 1989).

26. 744 F.2d 978 (3d Cir. 1984).

27. If the report of an outside reviewer is included in an SEC filing, the company should also consider disclosure of the qualifications of the reviewer, the extent of the review, the relationship between the reviewer and the business, and

any other material factors concerning the process by which the outside review was sought or obtained.

28. Such a caution probably should at least state that projections are based on assumptions and estimates that are inherently subject to uncertainty and that the company does not represent the forecasts as results that will actually occur or be achieved. In many situations (e.g., where the company or product does not have sufficient operating history), a more extreme warning may be warranted, possibly including a statement that the investment is speculative and/or is limited to or suitable only for wealthy investors or persons in a position to lose a substantial portion or all of their investment.

29. 374 F. Supp. 341 (S.D.N.Y. 1974).

30. 358 F. Supp. 413 (D. Or. 1973).

31. 984 F.2d 1050 (9th Cir. 1993).

32. 307 F. Supp. 910 (S.D.N.Y. 1969), *aff'd,* 425 F.2d 842 (2d Cir. 1970).

33. 465 F. Supp. 904 (S.D.N.Y. 1979), *rev'd on other grounds,* 607 F.2d 545 (2d Cir. 1979). *See also* the following cases relating to forecasts, prospectuses, and other financial information: 910 F.2d 10 (1st Cir. 1990); 881 F.2d 1236 (3d Cir. 1989); 847 F.2d 186 (5th Cir. 1988), *cert. denied,* 488 U.S. 926 (1988); 742 F.2d 751 (3d Cir. 1984).

34. 890 F.2d 628 (3d Cir. 1989).

35. Interpretative Release Relating to Proxy Rules, Release No. 34-16833, Fed. Sec. L. Rep. (CCH) ¶ 24,117 (May 23, 1980) (holding that in those circumstances, the inclusion of an appraisal or valuation may be appropriate, but only if it is made in good faith, on a reasonable basis, and where accompanied by appropriate related disclosures).

36. Schedule 13E-3, Item 9 (relating to Rule 13e-3 transactions in which an issuer purchases its own securities) requires the disclosure of, and certain summary information relating to, any appraisal from an outside party, and that the appraisal be made available for inspection.

37. 744 F.2d 978, 988 (3d Cir. 1984); *see also* 890 F.2d 628, 643 (3d Cir. 1989).

38. 737 F.2d 1227, 1233 (1st Cir. 1984).

39. *See* 735 F. Supp. 1105, 1118–19 (D.R.I. 1990).

40. 772 F.2d 231, 241 (6th Cir. 1985).

41. 772 F.2d at 243.

42. 478 F.2d 1281 (2d Cir. 1970).

43. 700 F. Supp. 1265, 1272 (S.D.N.Y. 1988).

44. 930 F.2d 826 (10th Cir. 1991).

45. 847 F.2d 186 (5th Cir. 1988), *cert. denied,* 488 U.S. 926 (1988).

46. 628 F.2d 1214 (9th Cir. 1980).

47. 669 F.2d 1265 (9th Cir. 1982).

48. *See* 685 F.2d 1116, 1121 (9th Cir. 1982); 790 F.2d 742, 752 (9th Cir. 1986); 797 F.2d 713, 723 (9th Cir. 1986); 823 F.2d 1361, 1365 (9th Cir. 1987).

49. 772 F.2d 231 (6th Cir. 1985), *cert. denied,* 475 U.S. 1015 (1986); 814 F.2d 22 (1st Cir. 1987).

50. *See, e.g.,* NYSE Listed Company Manual at § 202.05; AMEX Company Guide at § 401.

51. 654 F.2d 843 (2d Cir. 1981).

52. 445 U.S. 222 (1980); 814 F.2d 22 (1st Cir. 1977); 553 F.2d 1033 (7th Cir. 1977), *cert. denied,* 434 U.S. 875 (1977); 507 F.2d 485 (9th Cir. 1974).

53. *See, e.g.,* 745 F. Supp. 1511 (N.D. Cal. 1990).

54. 401 F.2d 833 (2d Cir. 1968), *cert. denied sub nom.,* 394 U.S. 976 (1969).

55. 711 F.2d 11 (2d Cir. 1983).

56. 628 F.2d 1214 (9th Cir. 1980); 646 F.2d 271 (7th Cir. 1981), *cert. denied,* 454 U.S. 1092 (1981). However, when a disclosure is made, liability is not limited to statements of material fact, but in that circumstance extend to all information actually disclosed (e.g., including opinions, forecasts and projections). 766 F.2d 770 (3d Cir. 1985), *cert. denied sub nom.,* 474 U.S. 946 (1985); 745 F. Supp. 1511 (N.D. Cal. 1990).

57. 485 U.S. 224 (1988).

58. 742 F.2d 751 (3d Cir. 1984), *cert. denied,* 469 U.S. 1215 (1985); 772 F.2d 231 (6th Cir. 1985), *cert. denied,* 475 U.S. 1015 (1986); 672 F.2d 1196 (3d Cir. 1982).

59. *See, e.g.,* 768 F. Supp. 54, 58 (W.D.N.Y. 1991), *aff'd,* 952 F.2d 394 (2d Cir. 1991).

60. 742 F.2d 751 (3d Cir. 1984), *cert. denied,* 469 U.S. 1215 (1985); *see also* 401 F.2d 833, 850 (2d Cir. 1968) (holding that the delayed disclosure of a mineral discovery may be justified pending the acquisition of surrounding leases), *cert. denied sub nom.,* 394 U.S. 976 (1969); 474 F.2d 514, 519 (10th Cir. 1973) (holding that in appropriate circumstances the release of adverse information may be delayed until the information is verifiable), *cert. denied,* 414 U.S. 874 (1973).

61. 485 U.S. 224 (1988) (holding that materiality in the context of a merger is not limited only to those circumstances where price and structure have been agreed to); 401 F.2d 833 (2d Cir. 1968), *cert. denied,* 394 U.S. 976 (1969); 531 F.2d 39 (2d Cir. 1976); 494 F.2d 1301 (2d Cir. 1974); 767 F.2d 1185 (7th Cir. 1985), *cert. denied,* 474 U.S. 1057 (1986); 723 F. Supp. 976 (S.D.N.Y. 1989), *aff'd,* 873 F.2d 411 (1st Cir. 1989).

62. 654 F.2d 843 (2d Cir. 1981); 409 F.2d 937 (2d Cir. 1969); 635 F.2d 156 (2d Cir. 1980).

63. 358 F. Supp. 413 (D. Or. 1973) (holding that a special relationship existed such that statements issued in a report by the company's underwriter were attributed to the company); 417 F.2d 147 (7th Cir. 1969), *cert. denied,* 397 U.S. 989 (1970); 522 F.2d 84 (5th Cir. 1975); *but see* 635 F.2d 156 (2d Cir. 1980).

64. Exchange Act Release No. 22214, [1984–85 Transfer Binder] Fed. Sec. L. Rep. (CCH ¶ 83,801 (July 8, 1985); 772 F.2d 231 (6th Cir. 1985), *cert. denied,* 475 U.S. 1015 (1986); 814 F.2d 22 (1st Cir. 1987).

65. *See, e.g.,* NYSE Listed Company Manual at § 202.03; AMEX Company Guide at § 401.

66. *See, e.g.,* 742 F.2d 751 (3d Cir. 1984), *cert. denied,* 469 U.S. 1215 (1985).

67. Exchange Act Release No. 22214, [1984–85 Transfer Binder] Fed. Sec. L. Rep. (CCH) ¶ 83,801 (July 8, 1985).

68. 485 U.S. 224 (1988).

69. *See* NYSE Listed Company Manual at § 202.05.

70. *See* AMEX Company Guide at § 401.

71. *See* NASD Manual at Schedule D.

72. The Federal Deposit Insurance Corporation Improvement Act of 1991 requires in relevant part:

1. That most depository institutions have independent audit committees, solely composed of outside directors, for years beginning after December 31, 1992.

2. That, in addition to audited financial statements, each institution regulated by the act prepare statements (1) of management's *responsibilities* for the preparation of the financial statements, the establishment and maintenance of adequate internal control, and compliance with certain laws and regulations; and (2) of management's *assessment* of the effectiveness of the internal controls and of the institution's compliance with certain laws and regulations relating to safety and fiscal soundness.

3. That with respect to management's reports or statements described above relating to internal control and safety and soundness laws and regulations, the institution's independent public accountant attest to—that is, conduct an audit of—the assertions of management contained therein. However, AICPA AU Section 642.12 and *Statement on Standards for Attestation Engagements* No. 2 provide that an auditor's opinion on management's compliance with laws, rules, regulations, contracts, or grants does not provide a legal determination regarding the business's compliance.

The act also imposes further restrictions on audit committees of "large" institutions, requiring that those audit committees (1) include members with banking or related financial management expertise, (2) have access to outside legal counsel that is independent of the institution, and (3) not include members who are also large customers of the institution.

The rules adopted by the Federal Deposit Insurance Corporation relating to the accounting provisions of the act, effective July 2, 1993, provide that management's assessments of internal control and compliance with safety and soundness laws and regulations encompass all significant items. The rules do not define the term *significant*. The institution's independent accountants are required to provide a specific opinion regarding the adequacy of the institution's overall internal control system and a limited engagement special opinion on the safety and soundness areas specified by the Federal Deposit Insurance Corporation. The safety and soundness areas include affiliated transactions, legal lending limits, loans to insiders, dividend restrictions, and Call and Thrift Financial Reports.

73. Accounting and Auditing Enforcement Release No. 416, Exchange Act Release No. 31934, Fed. Sec. L. Rep. (CCH) ¶ 73,902 (Mar. 1, 1993).

GLOSSARY

AICPA   American Institute of Certified Public Accountants.

CPA   Certified Public Accountant.

FASB   Financial Accounting Standards Board.

FCPA   Foreign Corrupt Practices Act.

FIFO   First-in, first-out.

GAAP   Generally Accepted Accounting Principles.

GAAS   Generally Accepted Accounting Standards.

LIFO   Last-in, first-out.

MD&A   Management's Discussion and Analysis of Financial Condition and Results of Operations.

SAS   Statements on Auditing Standards.

SEC   Securities and Exchange Commission.

Securities Act   Securities Act of 1933.

Securities Exchange Act   Securities Exchange Act of 1934.

SFAS   Statement of Financial Accounting Standards.

INDEX